Governing the Locals

Governing the Locals

Local Self-Government and Ethnic Mobilization in Russia

TOMILA LANKINA

ROWMAN & LITTLEFIELD PUBLISHERS, INC.
Lanham • Boulder • New York • Toronto • Oxford

ROWMAN & LITTLEFIELD PUBLISHERS, INC.

Published in the United States of America
by Rowman & Littlefield Publishers, Inc.
A wholly owned subsidiary of The Rowman & Littlefield Publishing Group, Inc.
4501 Forbes Boulevard, Suite 200, Lanham, MD 20706
www.rowmanlittlefield.com

P.O. Box 317, Oxford OX2 9RU, UK

British Library Cataloguing in Publication Information Available

Library of Congress Cataloging-in-Publication Data

Lankina, Tomila.
    Governing the locals : local self-government and ethnic mobilization in Russia /
Tomila Lankina.
        p. cm.
    Includes bibliographical references and index.
    ISBN 0-7425-3021-3 (cloth : alk. paper)
    1. Local government—Russia (Federation). 2. Russia (Federation)—Ethnic
relations. I. Title.
JS6117.3.A2L36 2004
320.8 0947—dc22

                                                                            2004006820

Printed in the United States of America

♾™ The paper used in this publication meets the minimum requirements of American
National Standard for Information Sciences—Permanence of Paper for Printed Library
Materials, ANSI/NISO Z39.48-1992.

To my sister Rada
and to the memory of my mother, Sofya Aleksandrovna Chernikova

Contents

Figures and Tables

Figures

Tables

Preface

Without properly constituted local self government, there can be no stable or prosperous life, and the very concept of civic freedom loses all meaning.

It [local self-government] represents a level that is most certain to take root because it will involve the vital concerns of each locality: ensuring unpolluted water and air, over-seeing housing, hospitals, nurseries, schools, shops, and the local distribution of goods, while also giving vigorous support to the growth of untrammeled local economic initiatives.

—Solzhenitsyn, *Rebuilding Russia*

In terms of their [the local administrations'] power, it is more absolute than in the communist times, one can call it semifeudal.

Heads of local administrations gather people before the elections—I happened to be at a preelection meeting—and say: If you don't vote [a certain way] you won't get your pensions, will lose your jobs, etc.

—Interview with local observer, Bashkortostan, 9 June 1999

This study originated as an interest in nationalist movements in late Soviet and post-Soviet Russia's provinces in the 1990s. The collapse of the Soviet system served as a catalyst for the enabling of an autonomous society, which the Soviet regime attempted to crush, control, or cajole. The result was the mushrooming of independent groups of civic, democratic, and nationalist orientation. One such group of actors was comprised of the minority movements in Russia's ethnically diverse republics. As the republics attained greater sovereignty from Moscow, their minorities resisted ethnic exclusion by the newly empowered "titular" groups. To the extent that these "nontitular" nationalist movements represented a segment of the "awakening society," independent from the state, they made for a fascinating subject of inquiry. By 1992, however, these movements had petered away or turned into classical "sofa" organizations, sometimes limited to the lunatic fringe. The fact of the *nonmovements* of the over twelve million disenfranchised nontitulars, however, was puzzling, much like the overall social passivity that ensued throughout post-Soviet Russia.

I therefore set out to investigate the ideas, goals, strategies, and resources of these failed provincial groups—factors that the Western social movement literature deems crucial to movement outcomes. Yet, as the research progressed, I was struck by the presence of the local state organs—the municipalities—as actors in almost every instance of social or ethnic protest. The state has of course been present in the social movement literature, much of which has even considered it a crucial variable. Yet, none of the studies suggested the centrality of the local state bodies of the kind that was evident in Russia.

In the early 1990s, it was usually the local soviet which housed opposition groups, provided them with meeting space, and served as the source of movement leadership. Subsequently, it was the local administrations that were blamed for the groups' failures, and became associated with effective "countermovement" measures: they dispersed protest gatherings, curtailed public transportation to locations of proposed mass meetings, cut off electricity in places where groups were to meet, or denied them office space. As if that was not enough, they mobilized police squads and harassed the few private printing houses that ventured to help the opposition. They also ordered private and state enterprises to dismiss individual employees who were reputed to have engaged in opposition activism. That failing, they withdrew the licenses and tax privileges of the private businesses, leaving them bankrupt.

These instances did not simply represent rich anecdotal material on local politics, of interest more to a provincial columnist than to a scholar. Instead, the seeming localness of these apparently isolated anecdotal phenomena suggested fascinating conceptual ideas about the relationship between society and state in late Soviet and post-Soviet Russia. Indeed, they rendered inaccurate the notion that social agencies were becoming autonomous in the post-Soviet period. It is the local bodies that ensured this fusion of society and state, or at least a high degree of control over it. This situation, normally associated with the Soviet times, withstood numerous efforts of reform, and has continued well into the present.

When Gorbachev came to power in 1986, he made the reform of the soviets a centerpiece of his program of political liberalization. The slogan of "All Power to the Soviets!" had quickly become the hallmark of the time, chanted at numerous popular demonstrations and gatherings of the liberal-minded public. The corrupted system of the soviets was perceived as the root of the malaise of the system, of the enslavement of the masses, while their reform was associated with democracy and freedom. The soviets did not simply fail to represent the grassroots and enable local self-government; they were there to control, to stifle, and to subordinate the social agencies to the state.

In 1990, the first contested elections to the local soviets allowed for a brief period of local freedom. For the first time in Soviet history, the local soviets appeared to articulate the desires of the local communities, and often conflicted with the superior bodies. Big cities in particular produced liberal assemblies, which challenged regional regimes and politicians in Moscow along democratic, ethnic, or other lines. By 1992, the euphoria had dissipated. The local soviets were disbanded or scaled down, and their formerly elected heads appointed by regional executives. The names of these agencies changed to "prefectures," "municipalities," "*dumy*," "assemblies," and other fancy titles with a democratic ring to them. Yet, they were quick to resume their Soviet-style social control functions, and they did so with a vengeance.

This book identifies local government as central to explaining ethnopolitical or other social movements and the generally peaceful nature of post-Soviet transformations at the expense of an active and free society. This broad finding is based on an examination of the relationship between the local governing bodies and one group of social agencies—the nontitular nationalist groups. However, the book's arguments are applicable to all prima facie "social" and political agencies—civic, cultural, and nationalist groups, political parties, and even the private sector. This is because these ostensibly autonomous agencies continue to depend on the state, which ensures such dependence through its municipal outreach agencies in the grassroots.

Acknowledgments

This book would not have been possible without the intellectual and emotional support and encouragement from a great number of colleagues, peers, and friends. I am particularly indebted to Professor Archie Brown, who steered me away from the originally chosen narrow D.Phil. dissertation topic to the broader subject of aspects of Russian federalism. I would also like to thank the Brown family as a whole—Pat, Archie, Doug, and Susan—whose hospitality and warmth added to the wonderful experience of being at Oxford.

I am also greatly indebted to Professor Alfred Stepan, and Drs. Alex Pravda and Stephen Whitefield, who provided suggestions and comments on the project, as well as many opportunities for intellectual exchange while I was at Oxford. Many of my fellow D.Phil. students at Oxford were always eager to comment on the manuscript in progress. I would like to thank particularly Petra Schleiter and Ed Morgan-Jones. I am also thankful for comments by Ian Bayley, Jeff Kahn, Brian Morgan, Sheppley Orr, Beata Razumilovich, Mike Thornhill, and Shamil Valiullin.

Other academic colleagues gave useful comments on my work at its various stages. I am very grateful to Hannes Adomeit, Yitzhak Brudny, Lynn Eden, Nisha Fazal, Vladimir Gel'man, Elise Giuliano, Andreas Heinemann-Grüder, Anneke Hudalla, Jim Hughes, Jacques Hymans, Mike Kenney, Paul Kolstoe, David Laitin, Gail Lapidus, Neil Melvin, Marie Mendras, Bob Orttung, Darrell Slider, Jeremi Suri, Edward Walker, and Hellmut Wollmann for their comments on the manuscript or manuscript-based conference and seminar papers.

The book involved much travel in hardship and even dangerous places in Russia's regions, where I had no friends, relatives, or prior contacts. It is only thanks to the amazing hospitality of people whom I met on these trips that I was able to conduct research in a safe way and open the doors of Russian bureaucracy, which seemed to become less and less accessible the deeper I descended into the provinces. I am grateful to Alexander Dzadziev and his wife Nina in North Ossetiya, Farida Suyunova in Karachay-Cherkessiya, Svetlana Akkieva in Kabardino-Balkariya, Asya Shkhacheva and Oleg Tsvetkov in Adygeya, and Roza Valiullina and Sergey Fufaev in Bashkortostan.

In conducting research for the book, hours and months were spent in libraries. Jackie Willcox was a great asset to have for research in the St. Antony's

Russian library. I am also grateful to the librarians whose help made the potentially hellish experience of sifting through dusty Russian regional newspapers in Khimki—an outpost of the Lenin library in the middle of nowhere—both possible and enjoyable. The staffs of the Ingush mission in Moscow, and of the human rights group Memorial, were very helpful with providing materials on the Ingush movement. I would also like to thank my research assistant in Berlin, Jacqueline Kühn, who provided excellent help during the final preparation of the manuscript, and Matthias Gumz, who helped me format the text.

None of the research, of course, would have been possible without the generous financial support I received from various colleges, foundations, and institutions. I am particularly grateful to the Open Society Institute in New York for providing funding for the doctorate. St. Antony's college funded many of my field trips to Russia. The Jowett Scholarship that I received from Balliol College helped fund my final two years at Oxford and provided a splendid academic atmosphere in Holywell Manor and many new friends. The European Union-funded summer school on federalism in Portugal offered an opportunity to increase my knowledge of the topic, and a pleasant break by the sea from travels in Adygeya and Bashkortostan. I would also like to acknowledge the Center for International Security and Cooperation at Stanford. Not only did the Center offer a Hamburg fellowship for the final year of my doctoral thesis writing, but it also provided an incredibly stimulating intellectual environment, access to superb academic resources, and the quiet of a private workstation. I would also like to thank the benefactors of the Scatcherd European Fund, the Dulverton fellowship and the Overseas Research Scheme funds, as well as the Oxford University travel grant funds for facilitating research at its various stages.

My most special and warm thanks go to Craig Weller, without whose encouragement, support, patience, brainstorming sessions with me, and hours of proofreading and commenting I would not have been able to complete the research.

I would also like to thank my friends and relatives for support and encouragement. I am particularly grateful to Lullit Getachew, Natasha Khan, Anyuta Lankina, Álvaro Morcillo-Laiz, Aziza Nouritova, Yuna Petrovna, and Ricarda Roos. My father, based on his work in Russia's regions, provided a wealth of anecdotes on the local regimes, reinforcing my convictions about the arguments of the book. Finally, I would like to give very special thanks to my caring sister Rada. Any errors or inaccuracies in the book are of course solely my own.

Chapter 1

Movements and the Post-Soviet State: Networks, Resources, and Agenda Setting

The purpose of this book is to account for nontitular nationalist movements as well as nonmovements. The disintegration of the Soviet Union raised the prospect of contentious struggles for power and rights involving the new "nationalizing" states and their ethnic minorities, possibly leading to large-scale violence. Speculations on potential ethnopolitical dynamics in the new states were quick to draw conceptual distinctions between the "titular" and the "nontitular" groups. The symbolic status with which Stalin's nationalities policy imbued the titular ethnies was, it has been argued, under the changed political circumstances, likely to translate their "sense of ethnonational entitlement" into real politics of affirmative action or even exclusion. Observers predicted that the relationship would be one of "domination" and indeed "ownership" of the polity by the titular group, leading to a "potentially explosive" situation.[1] One of the most serious problems was that of ethnic Russians outside of Russia, whose legacy of imperial expansion left the new states with a combined total of over twenty-five million Russian speakers. The conflict between the Russians and Moldovans in Transdniestriya underlined the salience of the Russian question. Not that the other nontitulars posed less of a challenge to the emerging states: ethnic tensions and violence involving the Armenians in Azerbaijan and the Abkhas in Georgia erupted as the empire was crumbling, continuing well into the post-Soviet period as the new states sought to restrict the nontitulars' access to the nationalizing polities or their right to self-determination.

However, the conceptual titular-nontitular distinction and the problematic that it tackled was and is highly pertinent within the former imperial core, Russia itself. Now a federal state, it preserved the "ethnic homeland" entities, which broadly replicate the Soviet Union-level republics in all but status.[2] Here too, the assertive titular ethnies in entities as small and weak as Adygeya and North Ossetiya, or as powerful as Tatarstan and Bashkortostan were quick to embark on the politics of ethnic exclusion. The laws and constitutions of these "states in embryo"[3] enshrined the "inalienable" right of the titular ethnies to self-

determination, institutionalized their overrepresentation in local power structures, and set frameworks for their social and cultural domination locally.[4] Virtually overnight, the over ten million nontitulars found themselves excluded
from influencing local political decision making in any meaningful way.[5]

Nevertheless, the nontitulars did mobilize, if only briefly, to contest the titulars' nationalizing projects. This episode is easy to brush off ex post as insignifi-
cant, but at the time nontitular mobilization showed significant "power in
movement," threatening to do away with Russia's Stalinist federal system, and
to lead to large-scale ethnic violence.[6] The nontitulars proclaimed the establishment of their own Russian and Cossack autonomies. They formed human chains
and chanted "River Ik—Berlin Wall," comparing the divided German nation to
the administrative separation of the Tatars in Bashkortostan from those in Tatarstan. Some, like the Ingush movement, established "national guards" and rallied
people for "mass marches." They also called for plebiscites on their status;
sponsored letter writing campaigns; and held protest demonstrations. Rather
than limiting their acts to "pressure group" and quiet lobbying tactics characteristic of pluralist politics, they often resorted to high visibility, mass protest acts,
and disruptive tactics. In short, they had many of the attributes of social movements.

Why did these movements peter away so quickly despite the progressive deterioration of the nontitulars' situation?[7] And why did they, with the exception
of the Ingush movement, have a generally peaceful outcome? After all, based on
the experience of the Balkans, many scholars have come to share Samuel Huntington's premise that "democratization . . . promotes communalism and ethnic
conflict."[8] The following sections, drawing on Western social movement scholarship, discuss the various approaches to mobilization, critically assess the literature and its application to the post-Soviet settings, and devise an explanatory
framework for the study.

The Dependent Variable: Social Movements

Before I discuss the resources crucial for generating, sustaining, or, alternatively, constraining social activism, it is important to delineate the subject of
investigation. Sydney Tarrow defines "social movements" as "collective challenges by people with common purposes and solidarity in sustained interaction
with elites, opponents and authorities."[9] Another social movement scholar defines "movements" as "those organized efforts, on the part of excluded groups,
to promote or resist changes in the structure of society that involve recourse to
noninstitutional forms of political participation."[10] To the extent that it broadly
deals with "excluded" groups, the definition fits the description of the nontitulars in the republics. However, the subsequent discussion of the role of the state
in post-Soviet settings in affecting social activism will serve to qualify the above
premise of the juxtaposition of the "excluded" social agencies to "elites" or authorities. Here "movements" will refer to organized efforts by excluded or par-

tially excluded groups, both elite and nonelite, polity members and those outside the polity, to resist changes in structures of political access and society through the use of both institutional and noninstitutional means of political influence.

This book assumes that nationalist movement formation and activism is subject to the same dynamics as that of other social movements, a premise, as Valerie Bunce rightly points out, that is all too often forgotten by students of nationalism.[11] In fact, nationalist movements confront the usual social movement issues of leadership, attracting followers, sustaining membership, and generating resources. And they pursue the same objective of organizing for influencing, resisting, or opposing the state and its policies. The following sections, drawing on the social movement literature, identify the resources needed for collective action. I then suggest that because in Russia crucial movement resources remain concentrated in or controlled by the state, and not the social agencies, the local state organs are central to explaining movement dynamics.

Movement Life-Support Systems

If we assume grievances to be constant, all social activism or lack thereof can be explained by reference to three sets of resources: their life-support systems, we might say. Some are more straightforward than others, but all have been subject to extensive theoretical and empirical treatment. It is in the nuances of the interpretation of the role of these resources—whether they are mobilization constraining or fostering, and where these resources come from—that scholars differ.

The first group could be subsumed under the label of "networks," a term which reinforces awareness of the role of formal organizations, or informal social groups which influence collective behavior. This variable has a long and established tradition in social science: from Alexis de Tocqueville and Arthur Bentley's theories of groups, to Emile Durkheim's emphasis on the role of social networks as imposing an "imaginary wall" on the "collective conscience," to Mancur Olson's theory of formal organization as a solution to the "dilemma of collective action."[12] The second group of variables, which has likewise received extensive treatment in the literature on social movements, could be broadly labeled "material resources."[13] The assumption of their importance for action intuitively makes much sense. Movements need resources to support their activities and those of their leaders.[14]

Finally, the nature of "agenda setting" is crucial in affecting the course of the movement and its successes or failures. I use this broad label to refer to movements' efforts to establish an identity for themselves; to ways that they define their goals; and to cultural, cognitive, symbolic, or other material from which they derive meaning.[15] It is the dynamic interplay of these three sets of resources that accounts for variable movement outcomes. I therefore discuss the three sets of variables in greater detail and identify approaches most relevant for the purpose of this study.

Olson's "dilemma of collective action" brought the organizational dimension of mass activism into sharp focus. While echoing classical social theories on groups and networks, his was a different interpretation of their role. When collective action is pursued in order to obtain a public good, or one whose enjoyment cannot be withheld from any member of the group, he argued, collective action becomes unsustainable since individual group members will have a strong incentive to "free ride."[16] Organizations, he maintained, are essential for overcoming the free-rider problem. They provide "selective incentives" to those who participate. They also punish nonparticipants, the free riders, increasing their incentives to join in. Olson was not concerned with social movements, but with agencies like the trade unions. However, goals pursued by mass movements, such as equality, peace, nondiscrimination, and affirmative action, are classical examples of public goods, and movement scholarship has profited greatly from his insights on formal organization.[17] As Herbert Kitschelt aptly put it, organizations are essential for transforming the otherwise "amorphous masses and their demands" into "concerted and purposive movements."[18]

Olson's premises also logically lead to the potential mobilization-reducing role of networks and organizations. This is not to endorse the classical sociological view of established social networks, which arguably constrain the otherwise restive and irrational "mass society."[19] Instead, organizations are important for creating rational actor incentive structures in favor of, or against, action. While social movement organizations create incentives for collective action, organizations or networks in general may either foster or constrain group behavior through systems of sanctions or rewards.[20]

Whichever option is chosen—to constrain or foster group activism—will depend on the incentives of the actors strategically positioned to influence these networks. Anthony Oberschall integrates the now relatively uncontroversial premises about elite influence on mobilization into a comprehensive theoretical framework. Numerous studies of ethnic and other movements have shown that the impetus to mobilize often comes from hitherto well-integrated minority or other nondominant groups, whose political or other opportunities for "vertical" mobility and integration have been thwarted. Oberschall writes that these individuals' control over cohesive ethnic, religious, professional, or other "horizontal" networks facilitates the mobilization of grievances into mass-based movements. A change in network elite incentives, however, will encourage the same elites to constrain or even repress social activism.[21] The following chapters will take this premise as a starting point in discussing the changing nontitular elite incentives to foster or constrain nationalist movements.

It follows from the above discussion that the possession of material resources by those who control networks or organizations is an important precondition for sustaining membership participation because network leaders can administer a system of sanctions and rewards vis-à-vis average network members.[22] In addition to resources needed for influencing the mobilizing group itself, social movement literature also stresses their indispensability for influencing targeted agencies. Charles Tilly defines "resources" as "labor power, goods, weapons, votes, and any number of other things, just so long as they are usable in acting on shared interests."[23] The definition thus includes material resources and those stemming from possession thereof and the items that Tilly lists are interconnected. Thus, possession of material resources translates into power and influence within a group and vis-à-vis agencies external to it. Within a group, power could be exercised through the mere threat of sanctions or the promise of rewards. Material resources are also indispensable for demonstrating "power in movement" or "collective strength" vis-à-vis targeted agencies.[24] Getting large groups of people together for mass acts requires the renting of buses and premises, and the printing and distribution of information, which require financial assets. Well-organized and well-financed movements demonstrate the pertinence of a given issue for large groups of people and can influence decision making through threats of potential disruptive collective action. But the same resources can be used to constrain mobilization and be channeled to reward nonparticipants.

Finally, the definition of issues and agendas is a powerful tool for influencing aggrieved group movement membership, participation, and its potential goal achievement in struggles with opponents. A given issue may resonate with an individual's value orientations, material or other; if not, collective action is less likely. Scholars have referred to this as "micromobilization"[25] or social psychological factors involved in mobilization, and various explanations have been advanced as variables that affect individual cognitive frameworks.[26] The approach I take differs from those that stress "primordial" or cultural values as an action-motivating ideational factor internal to individual movement participants.[27] Instead, based on the work of David Snow and his collaborators, I focus on the role of external agency, such as leadership or expert "framing entrepreneurs," in strategically appealing to, reinforcing, and shaping individual value orientations in an effort to mobilize people for collective action, or, alternatively, to constrain activism.[28]

Resources, networks, and agenda setting have become standard vocabulary for scholars of social activism.[29] My theoretical framework relies on their rich insights. However, while accepting that the above sets of resources are crucial determinants of movement dynamics, I challenge the assumptions about where these resources come from. This study suggests that the premises of classic social movement scholarship on the subject are questionable not only as applied to the Soviet and late Soviet settings, but also with regard to post-Soviet ones. But far from treating Russia as a unique case, here Russia serves to enhance our understanding of movement dynamics in other settings.

A fundamental assumption of much movement scholarship is the self-generating nature of resources by the social agencies and their juxtaposition to the state. Movements, it is implied, are "antiestablishment" and social in nature. Movement scholars stress the difference of their object of investigation from that of pluralists. And yet, they come from the same society-centered tradition. "Movements may largely be born of environmental opportunities," argued one study, "but their fate is heavily shaped by their own actions."[30] Echoing the above premise, the author of another classic study attributed a movement's success or failure to "unwise selection of strategic options, repeated failures . . . excessively broad membership criteria, inadequate socialization and internal social control, ideological evolution within the movement . . . , and . . . , successful implementation of its program."[31]

This is not to trivialize the assumptions of social movement scholarship, which identifies actors external to the movement as important players in affecting the movement's course, such as elites, rich donors, and even state agencies.[32] The state at large with the "political opportunity structures" that it creates has also featured prominently in the social movement literature.[33] An analytical distinction, however, is maintained between the external actors, most notably the state, and the "social" agencies. Doug McAdam's statement illustrates this distinction: "Emerging as they do, among excluded groups, social movements embody an implicit demand for more influence in political decision-making."[34] The state is still regarded as a facilitator or repressor for "excluded groups." It may affect some of the resources we have identified, but not all of them. The following sections discuss and question the above assumptions as applied to the post-Soviet contexts.

Approaches to Soviet, Late Soviet, and Post-Soviet Social Activism

Sovietologists have had little use for social movement, pluralist, and other society-centered theories of organized social activism, due to the high degree of the Soviet state's permeation of society and the prevention of any autonomous activity. They recognized the existence of limited forms of pluralism, but mostly of an "institutional" kind. Decision making, it was argued, was not strictly of a top-bottom nature, but was a product of pressures from competing state agencies. "Islands of separateness," of social autonomy in family, church, or other social settings, were recognized, but mostly in the attitudinal sense, and statements about their role in the "input" side of the political process were highly qualified. Non-regime-led organized mass-based social activism was not a subject of extensive investigation, as it simply did not exist.[35]

This changed with the advent of *perestroyka* and the rise of nationalist and democratic movements. As the Soviet empire crumbled, society appeared to have exploded. It was described as having "spontaneously" "emerged from the shadows," and as representing a veritable "triumph of the powerless."[36] The soul searching that ensued among Sovietologists because of this shift and their failure to predict things to come is well known. They reacted against Kremlinology with its focus on the state, and its parochial distance from mainstream comparative political science, a fact which one scholar described as "ghettoisation."[37] Hitherto little-used methods and approaches were brought into the discipline, and with them frequently came the major Western assumptions about state and society.

The first major assumption was the autonomy of the social agencies vis-à-vis the state. Steven Fish's book, with the telling title *Democracy from Scratch*, is most representative of early post-Soviet scholarship's antistatist reaction.[38] Writing about the late Gorbachev period, Fish hailed the appearance of *"fully autonomous"* (emphasis mine) social agencies, urging a "crucial analytical distinction between state and societal actors."[39] His objects of investigation were "organizations, groups, and individuals standing outside state institutions."[40]

In Gorbachev's Russia, Fish already found "genuinely autonomous nonstate organizations, and many persons, who, though in some sense products of the old system, broke fully with it and undertook the task of building alternative institutions."[41] Although Fish recognized the limitations of these groups in influencing political outcomes, he assumed the self-organizing and autonomous nature of the social and political actors. The failures of these agencies largely stemmed from their own strategies, leadership conflicts, lack of an ability to devise appropriate ideologies, and so forth. Fish did appreciate the role of the state in influencing social activism; he in fact identified the state as a crucial independent variable. Yet, he described it almost exclusively from the point of view of its repressive role. By the end of the 1980s, Fish argued, state power "had been reduced solely to negative power," the power to obstruct, sabotage, and otherwise undermine social activism.[42]

Fish's study stands out in that he specifically focused on civil society and social movements. As Paul Kubicek rightly points out, most studies of post-Soviet transformations have focused on other aspects of democratization, virtually neglecting organized social activism.[43] However, whether they are dealing with nationalism, democratic institution building, or party formation, many scholars, particularly writing in the early post-Soviet period with its antistatist reaction, have largely shared Fish's views on the autonomy of the social agencies.

This assumption of social autonomy and its relative weight in the input side of the political process leads to the related assumptions about the locus of the three sets of variables that I have identified. If the social agencies are autonomous, they can organize freely on their own, relying on their own social networks, generating material resources independently of state inputs; and their actions naturally stem from their more or less clearly defined interests, grievances, identities, culture, or ethnicity.

Some of the post-Soviet literature on nationalism of nontitular groups is vulnerable to criticism because of its implicit dichotomization of the society and the state and the assumption that ethnic groups may mobilize without the input of state actors. Writing about the Russians in the "near abroad," for example, Jeff Chinn and Robert Kaiser stressed the need to find ways of "channeling Russians' interests into democratic political process."[44] Such a statement presupposes that the Russians have clearly defined interests as a coherent group, and also, that these interests or grievances will lead to organized action: "When majority nationalism becomes both overt and exclusionary," they wrote, "a reactive nationalism is stimulated among minorities in the state."[45] The proposition, as applied to the post-Soviet context, leads to the following prediction: "The more exclusionary the policies of the dominant nation . . . the more likely that members of the subordinate nation will reject and oppose the new state and their new status in it."[46] This assumption of preextant, almost Tocquevillian naturally flowing organization for action is reflected in the scholars' definition of a nation as a "modern political interest group whose members share a desire to control their common destiny."[47]

Other studies of nontitular groups have also sometimes tended to rigidify such large categories as a nation or ethnic group without making a clear distinction between the group and its various actors, on the one hand, and mobilizing agents, including those within the state, on the other. Ian Bremmer wrote, for example, with regard to Russians in the Ukraine: "Ethnic groups may attempt to work within existing parliamentary means, lobby political officials, demonstrate and strike or even use violence," apparently making an analytical distinction between "ethnic groups" and "political officials."[48] Scholars of post-Soviet nontitular nationalism have used Albert Hirschman's categories of exit, voice, and loyalty as applied to the level of ethnic groups.[49] Often, however, studies have overlooked Hirschman's more nuanced disaggregation of the above categories into the average mass and the "quality consumer," in our case able leadership, the elite, or some other crucial external or internal actor.[50] I concur here with Dmitry Gorenburg, who makes a similar point based on his research into titular nationalism in Russia's republics. He wrote that many previous studies "share an assumption that ethnic conflict may be explained entirely at the level of the whole ethnic group," while underestimating the role of resources possessed by its select members.[51]

The methodology of the few studies of nontitular nationalism has also sometimes reflected the above assumptions. Because bona fide social networks or organizations, such as families, clans, or ethnic communities are seen as important in predicting social or political outcomes, scholars have looked at patterns of intermarriage, ethnic cohesion, or within-group cleavages.[52] Because, it is assumed, groups have resources to organize, scholars have tended to make predictions about the likelihood of mobilization based on survey data that reveal that they are disaffected, or legislation and political institution building that might affect their grievances.[53] Finally, because mass grievances, beliefs, identities, and ideas about political issues are considered important predictors of mobilization and political behavior in general, some scholars have largely relied on public opinion survey data, electoral records, or studies of established ethnic stereotypes in explaining or making predictions about ethnic processes.[54]

While the above discussed studies have significantly enhanced our understanding of nontitular nationalism—an area that remains underresearched particularly with regard to Russia—they have insufficiently explored the role of the state in constraining or enabling ethnic mobilization. The focus on society and not the institutions of the state in explaining *nontitular* ethnic outcomes is particularly puzzling considering the contribution of studies of *titular* nationalism in former socialist systems to our understanding of the role of political institutions in shaping mobilization.[55]

Recent scholarship has questioned the initial optimism about the rapidly changing nature of state-society relations in the postcommunist contexts. Instead, scholars have pointed out the phenomenon of what Claus Offe describes as an "identical reproduction of institutions,"[56] state and social, which continues to plague efforts to extricate the postcommunist states from their socialist past. Erik Hoffmann, for example, observes that in Russia "state and social institutions become tangled and their functions and roles intermix . . . and state and society become indistinguishable . . . when most government bureaucrats don two hats, public and private."[57] Echoing him, Michael Urban and his collaborators write: "Interest-based politics [in Russia], . . . is less a public phenomenon than an exercise in Byzantine intrigue conducted inside the state."[58] In Paul Kubicek's Ukraine, "unbroken ties" continue to link privileged "social" agencies to the state at the expense of other, truly independent actors.[59] Not only have such Soviet-style peculiarities of state-society interactions not diminished in recent years, but they have been on the rise in President Putin's Russia, with scholars and observers calling attention to the increasing "bureaucratization," and even "sovietization," of the Russian polity.[60]

Nonetheless, for many studies of relations between state and society actors, the objects of investigation have been mostly national, or at best, regional-level state institutions or the "elites," on the one hand, and the economic actors—industrial managers, the "oligarchs," the trade unions—or such institutions as political parties, which are usually distinguished from civil society and social and nationalist movements, on the other.[61] Relations between the state and other organized social agencies have received less attention. Moreover, state-society relations have largely remained at the *macro* level of investigation, with surveys aimed at determining the attitude of the population as a whole to the state and its institutions, and its overall political and voting preferences (again, mostly at the national level), often the preferred methodology.[62]

I argue that an examination of the state's influence on society and its mezzo structures, including on organized ethnic activism, requires that we establish the precise point of contact between the average citizen and the state. The premise of this book is that an understanding of state-society relations at the *micro*, local level, involving local government organs and the local social actors, is crucial to explaining political outcomes in the polity as a whole.

The Importance of Going Local

In both democratic and undemocratic settings, local governments are usually the primary, and for many people the only, point of direct contact with the state. In democratic settings, the locality is the main locus of "bottom-up" public participation in government affairs for the vast majority of the citizenry.[63] In fact, as some have argued, it is the most meaningful instrument for the representation of citizen interests since "by definition, his vote will count far more the smaller the polity in which he votes."[64] In authoritarian or totalitarian settings, by contrast, local government is often the mechanism for "top-down" penetration of the society by the state. In states that are neither authoritarian nor fully democratic, the central state's failure to penetrate the localities and impose a uniform political order on them can result in the phenomenon of "enclaves of authoritarianism." In such settings, the local populations are dependent on and ruled by the local "caciques" at the behest of the central state, a characteristic of some Latin American countries and Russia.[65] This is why democratic theorists from John Stuart Mill to Robert Dahl and Dunkwart Rustow have laid such great stress on local government as indicative of the degree of the health of democracy in the polity as a whole.[66] This is also why the "crafters"[67] of postcommunist democracies in Poland, Hungary, and Czechoslovakia have placed local government reform at the top of their democratizing agenda.[68]

A peculiar feature of local government, then, is its contact with the citizenry irrespective of whether we are dealing with democratic, authoritarian, or semi-authoritarian settings. This contact provides local governments with unique mobilizational opportunities. Local government agents are familiar with, or made up of, notables from within local social networks; they provide highly visible tribunes for the expression or the framing of public opinion; and they often control important material resources, vital for the communities that they represent.

The few scholars who have touched upon the mobilizational aspect of local government have usually understood "mobilization" in a developmental sense, namely that local governments are used to mobilize the public in support of economic development or modernization.[69] What has been largely overlooked is the role local governments have played in mass movements, revolutions, and other instances of contentious mass mobilization, or in the prevention or suppression thereof.

Local agencies of the state can deliberately rally the mass publics throughout the country's territory against rival national elite forces; alternatively, forces rival to the central state can capture the local bodies, or form alliances against the central state with agents within them, and then mobilize the local publics in support of their cause. Stein Rokkan and Derek Urwin list local government agents as important variables affecting the consolidation of the modern European state system. Whether they "act primarily as the extended arm of the central authority, or . . . choose to view themselves as spokesmen for and defenders of the peripheral population" crucially affects the prospects of state stability and consolidation.[70] Local governments played a central role in the French Revolution, as Lynn Hunt demonstrates in her brilliant essay on Troyes and Reims.[71] They also featured strongly in Theda Skocpol's analysis of the origins and course of the revolutions in France, China, and Russia, and in the lack of a successful revolution in countries like Japan, Germany/Prussia, and England.[72] In all of these cases, Skocpol cites the peculiar institutional makeup of local governments and their relation to the central state as crucial to mass mobilization or lack thereof.[73]

Revolutions are notable for their high visibility and that of their leaders and participants. Local governments, however, have played important mobilizational or mobilization-constraining roles even in stable democratic settings. However, because their agenda-setting role in stable democracies and democratizing states is much more subtle, and is frequently hidden from the public eye, it has received scant, if any, scholarly attention, particularly compared with the volumes of studies of central legislatures, party systems, the presidency, and "voter preferences." Sadly, local government has been underresearched by political scientists and has largely remained the province of scholars of public administration.[74]

At this point it is important to define "local government" (LG), or, as it is misleadingly called in Russia, "local self-government" (LSG), our key independent variable, to highlight its relation to and importance for the state as a whole, and to identify other peculiarities of this institution that make it a crucial player in territorially-based mass mobilization. Contrary to the "orthodox" view of local government, which leans heavily towards its representative function, and even sees it somewhat as a sum total of the local populations—a view also propagated by the Soviet ideologues with reference to the soviets—this book considers local government as the government, that is, as an agency of the state.[75] "The state" here refers to a set of political institutions—administrative, executive, and coercive—aimed at maintaining a certain political order in a given territory. According to Skocpol, "executive authority" is central to the definition of the state with "administrative and coercive organizations [being] the basis of state power as such."[76] "Any state," she writes, "first and fundamentally extracts resources from society and deploys these to create and support coercive and administrative organizations."[77] Skocpol also highlights the role of territorial control, one that is the main component of classical international relations theories of the state, but that appears to be neglected by many scholars focusing on national-level politics. "States," she writes, "are actual organizations controlling or (attempting to control) territories and people."[78]

Although local government has been described both as an "administrative unit" and a "political community," its distinct feature across national systems is that the political and the administrative, or executive, sides of government are fused to a degree larger than in central government administration.[79] Local governments, even when they have independent law-making capacities, or, as in the case of present-day Russia, are legally separate from both federal and regional levels of authority, perform many of the central state's administrative and executive functions. The central state agencies and, in federal states, the subnational governments, rely on the local bodies as outreach organs, as it is simply unfeasible to micromanage and administer state programs in the peripheries from the center, as well as to exercise one of the state's key prerogatives—the use of instruments of coercion, such as the police. This "outreach" role has only increased together with the rise of the modern welfare state, with local governments in many countries becoming the main institutions administering welfare programs and services.[80] Most recently, in some countries undergoing profound economic transformation, such as China, local governments were cast in the leading role of developmental processes, which have "determined the outcome of reform."[81]

Local governments therefore perform functions which make a difference to the immediate, often day-to-day, concerns of the average citizen, more so than the central state, with its ring of a remote agency in Moscow, Washington, or London. They deliver services, administer welfare programs and economic reforms, police the streets and neighborhoods, and are often the prime contact between the state and the organized society, that is, intermediate or mezzo structures, such as nongovernmental organizations (NGOs). One reason for this is that in addition to the service and administrative functions, local government is also supposed to conform to the normative expectations of its ostensible participatory and representative role. Local governments, often embracing very small populations,[82] are meant to serve as instruments of the "schooling in civil society," of "making democracy work," and of fostering civic attitudes even where appropriate "social capital" is missing.[83] Another reason for extensive NGO-LG interactions is the frequent dependence of civic, cultural, religious, or other groups on local governments' funds.

Social movements likewise have to deal with local governments even when they target the national state and pursue explicitly political objectives. The English university city of Oxford, where much of this book has been written, is often the scene of protest acts involving animal rights groups, antiglobalization radicals, and other movements, sometimes of a disruptive kind. Shop windows are broken and walls smeared with eggs and graffiti. At such events, the local police on horseback are as much, and sometimes more of, a conspicuous presence than the protestors themselves.[84] This is because despite the contentious and disruptive nature of the events themselves they are preceded by a quite benign contact with the city or county council, which controls local police forces in the United Kingdom, informing it of the proposed event and perhaps negotiating the location of protest activities.[85]

Soviet local government performed many of the typical service functions of local governments elsewhere, and more. Unlike the party, the local soviets did not formulate grand plans and ideology; instead, they administered and they micromanaged. In the context of a state-planned economy, they performed many of the social services that in capitalist settings are transacted by the private sector or the civil society.[86] These ranged from securing bread supplies for the local shops to resolving family and marital disputes.[87] The local resident would thus most probably visit the local *chinovnik* rather than the faceless central ideologue in order to attend to his basic needs. The more mundane were the needs, the greater the soviets' power over the local citizen.[88] Having a leaking toilet repaired or securing a separate flat for the dreaded mother-in-law were issues much closer to his heart than the party's grand utopian doctrines or the ministries' Five-Year plans.

The extent of the local soviets' "representative" function is a subject of well-known ridicule.[89] Handpicked by the party through its *nomenklatura* system, and elected in an uncontested fashion with a "turnout" of close to 100 percent, the deputies were exemplary regime loyalists from state enterprises and such "voluntary" associations as the Komsomol, the trade unions, "comrade courts," and "neighborhood committees." However, the system went far beyond simply legitimizing the regime.

The soviets' high degree of "netness"[90] ensured the state's almost complete saturation of society through its professional and "social" networks. These umbrella institutions projected regime goals, ideologies, and agenda further down the networks, which they ostensibly represented. In exchange, the loyalists enjoyed greater upward mobility or "vertical integration" along the democratic centralist ladder, with the soviets thereby serving as important stepping-stones into the regime.

The proverbial weakness of these giant sleepy assemblies and their executive branches, dominated by the party *apparatchiki*, compared to the party organs proper and the central state ministries, was thus in fact a source of strength.[91] More than the other state organs they saturated the "grassroots," and created a system of administrative and service dependence, thereby facilitating the state's power and control over local citizenry. As one organizational theorist of local government pointed out, "dependence is the obverse of power."[92]

The system of the soviets ostensibly underwent a profound transformation with the demise of the Soviet state, its ideology, economic planning, and institutions, most notably democratic centralism. The findings of this book challenge such a premise, pointing to the similarities with the soviets in the local bodies' interactions with the local social agencies. With the exception of a brief period over 1990-1992, when the local soviets actively fostered mass mobilization, not only do the local bodies fail to create facilitating "political opportunity structures" for social actors or to enhance their "social capital," but they actively stifle independent social activism. They do so through their control over resources, over local social networks and organizations, and over public agenda setting.

Method

The findings are based on a comparative study of nationalist movements in three republics: Adygeya, Bashkortostan, and North Ossetiya. An examination of the Ingush movement in North Ossetiya and the violent Ossetiyan-Ingush conflict is impossible without reference to the neighboring Ingush republic, where much of the Ingush population is concentrated. Accordingly, throughout the book I frequently refer to the third case as "North Ossetiya/Ingushetiya."[93] The cases were chosen according to the "most different" criteria, since I aim to generalize the findings to Russia's other ethnically defined constituent units.[94] According to this method, if broadly similar phenomena could be observed in the "most different" cases, one would expect the other cases in between to conform to the same pattern. As Adam Przeworski and Henry Teune write, "If the subgroups of the population derived from different systems do not differ with regard to the dependent variable, the differences among these systems are not important in explaining this variable."[95]

The similarities I look for are levels of mobilization in republics with similar local government structures. Alternatively, I seek to explain variations in levels of mobilization by possible subtle differences in local government makeup and relations with nationalist movements. The three republics are broadly similar in terms of the main institutional variable, local government, whose setup in the Soviet and post-Soviet systems was imposed from above by the central ideologues and lawmakers. This factor allows for generalizations about the role of local institutions, while controlling for other variables that make the cases "most different," such as ethnic composition, culture, religion, and economic development.

The republics are drawn from two distinct cultural and geographical regions—the North Caucasus and the Middle Volga. Bashkortostan and North Ossetiya were autonomous republics within the USSR hierarchy and Adygeya was an autonomous *oblast'*. Bashkortostan is one of the wealthiest entities, while Adygeya and North Ossetiya are among the poorest and highly dependent on federal transfers. Adygeya has a very sizeable percentage of the nontitulars— mostly Russians (over 80 percent). Bashkortostan's population is distributed more evenly between the three major ethnic groups—the Bashkirs, Tatars, and the Russians. North Ossetiya has a more sizeable share of the titulars, slightly over 50 percent, while the remaining populations are largely composed of Russian speakers. While the population of the most vocal nontitular group, the Ingush, within North Ossetiya itself is tiny, a large percentage of the Ingush population, displaced to Ingushetiya because of the Ossetiyan-Ingush conflict, continues to have claims to and even maintain homes in the disputed Prigorodnyy district in North Ossetiya.

The three republics had different levels of ethnic mobilization and outcomes of nontitular movements: Adygeya and Bashkortostan are "most similar" on the dependent variable, and North Ossetiya is the deviant case. North Ossetiya witnessed a violent ethnic conflict between the titular Ossetiyans and the nontitular Ingush. In the other two republics relatively low levels of mass-based nontitular activism followed high levels of mobilization between 1990 and 1992. I deliberately chose two republics from within the North Caucasus—one with a peaceful, and another with a violent, outcome—in order to control for the commonly made culture- and history-centered assumptions about the "explosive" nature of the North Caucasus region as a whole and its "age-old ethnic animosities."

The interviews were conducted between 1997 and 2000 on two trips to the republics of Adygeya and Bashkortostan, one trip to North Ossetiya, and several trips to Moscow. In the republics, the interviewees were leaders of nontitular nationalist groups and average activists, contacted according to "snowball sampling," as well as current and past local council deputies. The purpose of the interviews was to establish channels of power, influence, and resource flow between the institutional agencies and the public associations. Accordingly, local councilors and nationalist group leaders were asked similar sets of questions about the nature of their cooperation. The interviews were structured but open-ended.

I also used stenographic records of local council proceedings, combined with the other documents, as a particularly valuable source of data and insights on the role of local councils in "issue framing." Many of the sensitive movement issues were discussed behind closed doors and involved only a handful of activist deputies. Often, a movement statement would be debated word for word and scrutinized for its greater or lesser public appeal and potential to radicalize the movement at large. Comparing the final version of a local soviet statement that would appear in the major local newspaper with the various debated versions thus served as crucial evidence of the impact of local deputies on mass opinion.

In conducting the analysis of interviews and stenographic material, I used the methods recommended in Matthew Miles and Michael Huberman's integrative study of qualitative data analysis. Miles and Huberman suggest both inductive and deductive methods of analysis. I followed each interview with the writing up of a "memo" or a "contact summary sheet" identifying the main ideas and themes suggested by the interviewee.[96] The records of local council proceedings discussing nationalist movements were likewise scanned for major themes. These themes bore on the initial framework of investigation, and helped to identify new ideas on which subsequent interviews should focus. Transcribed interviews were then coded, bearing in mind the broader themes identified in the memo. Miles and Huberman define codes as "tags or labels for assigning units of meaning to the descriptive or inferential information compiled during a study."[97] The process of "clustering" ideas together in such a way allowed for the drawing of parsimonious conclusions and inferences from volumes of complex interview and stenographic material.

Methodological Complexities

The reliance on interviews as the key method of investigation is a subject of some well-known criticism. However, an analysis of local politics makes interviews an indispensable, and indeed, in most cases, the principal source of information and insights on movement activism. Nationalist groups in the republics, for example, often operate in semiclandestine conditions, and their ability to publish materials is limited. Alternative data that could be used to establish the strength of movements and their levels of mass support, such as surveys, are often likewise unavailable because of the restrictive political environment. Indeed, in Adygeya, even a team of researchers from the Russian Academy of Sciences was prohibited from conducting a survey of the republic's ethnopolitical climate. The rationale that the republic functionaries gave to the researchers was their potential to upset "ethnic peace."[98] The feasibility of using other, more systematic methods of data analysis that have been used by social movement scholars is likewise limited. For example, scholars of Western social movements have assessed the intensity of movements and their levels of mass support by examining the indexes of national presses, such as the *New York Times* in the United States.[99]

In Russia, national newspapers give scant coverage to local politics. Local newspapers, however, are a notoriously unreliable source of information. Indeed, a section in chapter 6 of this book is specifically dedicated to the role of "the local newspaper" in denying the existence of political or ethnic opposition; opposition activities simply are not reported, or when they are, it is in a biased and distorted fashion. As a result, interviews and direct observation become the central methodological tools, and the insights derived from them can be fruitful and rewarding. The combination of the use of stenographic records and other printed records with interviews has allowed for a balanced analysis of the movements.

Structure of the Book

Chapter 2 is an historical overview of the origins of the soviets and their role in the Soviet system, particularly as regards the elite career structures and the resources that they controlled. Chapter 3 discusses the historical factors that have led to the republics' ethnic makeup, from Russian colonization and conquest, to the Soviet nationalities policies. It also introduces the cases of Adygeya and Bashkortostan, and describes the nontitular movements and their key actors. Chapter 4 analyses the nontitular movements in Adygeya and Bashkortostan, and the role of the soviets in fostering nontitular mobilization between 1990 and 1992, focusing particularly on their relations with nationalist and other public associations. Chapter 5 examines the Ingush movement, the "most different case," and investigates the role of local governing bodies in fostering or constraining it. Chapter 6 investigates the impact of Yel'tsin's recentralization of local self-government on the administrations' incentive structures and their resource bases, which led to the demise of the movements in Adygeya and Bashkortostan. Chapter 7 provides an overview of local government practices in other regions and republics in order to further generalize about the impact of local government on social activism Russia-wide. The chapter also zooms out of the microlevel of investigation and discusses President Putin's latest institutional reforms. Chapter 8 summarizes the book's findings and conclusions and discusses their implications for broader theoretical debates on local government, federalism, social movements, and ethnic mobilization.

Notes

1. Rogers Brubaker, *Nationalism Reframed: Nationhood and the National Question in the New Europe* (Cambridge: Cambridge University Press, 1996), 46, 54.

2. For a discussion of Russia's ethnofederal structure, see Gail W. Lapidus, "Asymmetrical Federalism and State Breakdown in Russia," *Post-Soviet Affairs* 15, no. 1

(1999): 74-82; and Gail W. Lapidus and Edward W. Walker, "Nationalism, Regionalism and Federalism: Center-Periphery Relations in Post-Communist Russia," in *The New Russia: Troubled Transformation*, ed. Gail Lapidus (Boulder, Colo.: Westview, 1995), 79-113.

3. Skalnik Leff uses this expression in reference to ethnically defined subnational units of the former socialist ethnofederations ("Democratization and Disintegration in Multinational States: The Breakup of the Communist Federations," *World Politics* 51, no. 1 [1999]: 205-35).

4. In Sakha-Yakutiya, for example, where the titulars constitute only 30 percent of the population, by the mid-1990s, 65-70 percent of government ministers were Yakuts. In Adygeya, where the Adyge form slightly over 20 percent of the local population, 80 percent of government executives, and all deans of the universities, were Adyge (Leokadia Drobizheva, "Russians in the Republics of the Russian Federation," paper presented at the seminar "Interethnic Relations in Russia and the Commonwealth of Independent States" [Moscow Carnegie Center, Moscow, 1995]). For a discussion of discriminatory policies in Adygeya, see also Mary McAuley, *Russia's Politics of Uncertainty* (Cambridge: Cambridge University Press, 1997). In Tatarstan, of the nineteen heads of local administrations appointed in 1992, fifteen were ethnic Tatars (McAuley, *Russia's Politics of Uncertainty*, 50). For the practices of gerrymandering and the imposition of electoral legislation ensuring titular overrepresentation in the local assemblies, see Darrell Slider, "Elections to Russia's Regional Assemblies," *Post-Soviet Affairs* 12, no. 3 (1996): 243-64.

5. Of the republics' nontitulars, Russians alone comprise ten million; practically half of them live in republics where they constitute majorities. Drobizheva, "Russians," 121.

6. Sidney Tarrow, *Power in Movement: Social Movements, Collective Action and Politics* (Cambridge: Cambridge University Press, 1996).

7. Survey data also provides evidence to the effect that the nontitulars subjectively feel greater ethnic discrimination or hostility from the titulars. See, for example, Vika V. Koroteeva, *Ekonomicheskie interesy i nationalizm* (Moscow: Rossiyskiy gosudarstvennyy gumanitarnyy universitet, 2000), 213.

8. Samuel P. Huntington, "Democracy for the Long Haul," *Journal of Democracy* 7, no. 2 (1996): 3-13. Skalnik Leff, for example, also noted that the opening of the communist political systems served to "reignite" tensions throughout the region ("Democratization," 206).

9. Tarrow, *Power in Movement*, 3-4.

10. Doug McAdam, *Political Process and the Development of Black Insurgency, 1930-1970* (Chicago: University of Chicago Press, 1982), 25.

11. Valerie Bunce, *Subversive Institutions: The Design and the Destruction of Socialism and the State* (Cambridge: Cambridge University Press, 1999), 10.

12. Alexis de Tocqueville, "Townships, Municipal Administration, State Government," in *Democracy in America*, ed. J. P. Mayer (London: Fontana, 1994); Emile Durkheim, "Anomie and the Moral Structure of Industry," in *Emile Durkheim: Selected Writings*, ed. Anthony Giddens (Cambridge: Cambridge University Press, 1972), 173-88; Emile Durkheim, *Suicide: A Study in Sociology*, trans. George Simpson (London: Routledge, 1952); Giddens, ed., *Emile Durkheim*, 6; Arthur F. Bentley, *The Process of Government* (Cambridge, Mass.: Harvard University Press, 1967); Mancur Olson, *The Logic of Collective Action* (Cambridge, Mass.: Harvard University Press, 1965). See also David B. Truman, *The Governmental Process: Political Interests and Public Opinion*, 2d ed. (New York: Knopf, 1971); and Gustave Le Bon, *Psychologie des Foules* (Paris: Librairie Felix Alcan, 1912).

13. On the role of resources in movement activism, see Beverly Nagel, "Gypsies in the United States and Great Britain: Ethnic Boundaries and Political Mobilization," in *Competitive Ethnic Relations*, ed. Suzan Olzak and Joane Nagel (Orlando, Fla.: Academic Press, 1986), 69-90; Joane Nagel and Susan Olzak, "Ethnic Mobilization in New and Old States: An Extension of the Competition Model," *Social Problems* 30, no. 2 (1982): 127-43; Aldon D. Morris and Carol M. Mueller, eds., *Frontiers in Social Movement Theory* (New Haven, Conn.: Yale University Press, 1992); Herbert Kitschelt, "Resource Mobilization Theory: A Critique," in *Research on Social Movements: The State of the Art in Western Europe and the USA*, ed. Dieter Rucht (Boulder, Colo.: Westview, 1991), 323-47; McAdam, *Political Process*; Doug McAdam, "Tactical Innovation and the Pace of Insurgency," *American Sociological Review* 48 (1983): 735-54; Doug McAdam, John D. McCarthy, and Mayer N. Zald, eds., *Comparative Perspectives on Social Movements: Political Opportunities, Mobilizing Structures, and Cultural Framings* (Cambridge: Cambridge University Press, 1996); and John D. McCarthy and Mayer N. Zald, "Resource Mobilization and Social Movements: A Partial Theory," *American Journal of Sociology* 82, no. 6 (1977): 1212-41.

14. For example, the U.S. Civil Rights movement drew on the coffers of rich liberal sympathizers; Lenin relied on his mother and friends to finance his livelihood and revolutionary movement; and Karl Marx sometimes used Friedrich Engels's funds to write the intellectual foundations of world revolution (Anthony Oberschall, *Social Conflict and Social Movements* [Englewood Cliffs, N.J.: Prentice Hall, 1973]; Isiah Berlin, *Karl Marx* [Oxford: Oxford University Press, 1963]; Craig J. Jenkins and Craig M. Eckert, "Channeling Black Insurgency: Elite Patronage and Professional Social Movement Organization in the Development of the Black Movement," *American Sociological Review* 51 [1986]: 812-29).

15. For example, the French Revolutionary movement was both civic and nationalist, labels which affected its appeal in France and elsewhere; the Soviet and Russian republics' ethnic *nomenklatura* opted for an "ethnic revival" label in its struggle with Moscow over political and economic resources; and the Western white collar establishment sometimes joined the "antiestablishment" bandwagon (Eric Hoffer, *The True Believer: Thoughts on the Nature of Mass Movements* [New York: Harper & Row, 1951]; Daniel S. Treisman, "Russia's 'Ethnic Revival': The Separatist Activism of Regional Leaders in a Post-Communist Order," *World Politics* [1997]: 212-49; Valery Tishkov, *Ethnicity, Nationalism and Conflict in and after the Soviet Union: The Mind Aflame* [London: Sage, 1997]). For an account of the intellectuals' role in fashioning the Russian nationalist ideologies and identities, see Yitzhak M. Brudny, *Reinventing Russia: Russian Nationalism and the Soviet State, 1953-1991*, 2d ed. (Cambridge, Mass.: Harvard University Press, 2000).

16. Olson, *Logic of Collective Action*.

17. On the role of networks and organizations in social movement mobilization, see McAdam, McCarthy, and Zald, eds., *Comparative Perspectives*; Alberto Melucci, "The Symbolic Challenge of Contemporary Movements," *Social Research* 52, no. 4 (1985): 789-816; David A. Snow, Jr., Louis A. Zurcher, and Sheldon Ekland, "Social Networks and Social Movements: A Microstructural Approach to Differential Recruitment," *American Sociological Review* 45, no. October (1980): 787-801; and Jenkins and Eckert. "Channeling Black Insurgency."

18. Kitschelt, "Resource Mobilization Theory," 329.

19 Durkheim argued that cultural and social networks form an important constraint on the behavior of individuals (Durkheim, "Anomie," 173). See also Le Bon, *Psychologie*

des Foules, 5. For classic statements on the "irrationality" of unconstrained mass behavior, see also Neil J. Smelser, *Theory of Collective Behavior* (London: Routledge, 1962); and Talcott Parsons, "Some Sociological Aspects of the Fascist Movements," in *Politics and Social Structure* (New York: Free Press, 1969), 82-97.

20. For an extension and critique of Olson's theory of collective action, see Elinor Ostrom, *Governing the Commons: The Evolution of Institutions for Collective Action* (Cambridge: Cambridge University Press, 1990). For an application of this argument to the explanation of ethnic cooperation versus conflict, see James D. Fearon and David D. Laitin, "Explaining Inter-Ethnic Cooperation," *American Political Science Review* 90, no. 4 (1996): 715-35. On the role of institutions in influencing individual and collective action, see James G. March and Johan P. Olsen, *Rediscovering Institutions: The Organizational Basis of Politics* (New York: Free Press, 1989); and Douglas North, *Institutions, Institutional Changes, and Economic Performance* (Cambridge: Cambridge University Press, 1990). For a discussion of networks in organizational theory, see R. A. W. Rhodes, *Control and Power in Central-Local Government Relations,* 2d ed. (Aldershot, England: Ashgate, 1999). For a discussion of the role of Soviet political institutions and organizations in nationalist mobilization, see Philip Roeder, "Soviet Federalism and Ethnic Mobilization," *World Politics* 43, no. 2 (1991): 196-232. For a recent account of the role of networks in the Bolshevik revolutionary movement and consolidation of power, see Gerald Easter, *Reconstructing the State: Personal Networks and Elite Identity in Soviet Russia* (Cambridge: Cambridge University Press, 2000).

21. Oberschall, *Social Conflict.*

22 On the role of resources in explaining nationalist and other movement activism, see Paul R. Brass, *Ethnicity and Nationalism: Theory and Comparison* (New Delhi: Sage, 1991); Paul R. Brass, *Theft of an Idol: Text and Context in the Representation of Collective Violence* (Princeton, N.J.: Princeton University Press, 1997); and Charles Tilly, *From Mobilization to Revolution* (Reading, Mass.: Wesley, 1978).

23. Tilly, *From Mobilization,* 7.

24. Tarrow, *Power in Movement,* 7; Bert Klandermans, "The Social Construction of Protest and Multiorganizational Fields," in *Frontiers in Social Movement Theory,* ed. Aldon D. Morris and Carol McClurg Mueller (New Haven, Conn.: Yale University Press, 1992), 77-103; and William A. Gamson, "The Social Psychology of Collective Action," in *Frontiers,* 53-76.

25. See Bert Klandermans, *The Social Psychology of Protest* (Cambridge, Mass.: Blackwell, 1997).

26. For a social psychological approach to mobilization, see Ralph H. Turner and Lewis M. Killian, *Collective Behavior* (Englewood Cliffs, N.J.: Prentice Hall, 1957).

27. For examples of the "primordial" approach, see Anthony D. Smith, "Ethnic Identity and Territorial Nationalism in Comparative Perspective," in *Thinking Theoretically about Soviet Nationalities: History and Comparison in the Study of the USSR,* ed. Alexander J. Motyl (New York: Columbia University Press, 1992); and Arend Lijphart, *Democracy in Plural Societies: A Comparative Exploration* (New Haven: Yale University Press, 1977). Most scholars, however, qualify their assumptions about primordialism. For a discussion, see Charles King, "Nations and Nationalism in British Political Studies," in *The British Study of Politics in the Twentieth Century,* ed. Jack Hayward, Brian Barry, and Archie Brown (Oxford: Oxford University Press, 1999), 313-43. For classic "instrumental" accounts of nationalism, see Benedict Anderson, *Imagined Communities: Reflections on the Origin and Spread of Nationalism* (London: Verso, 1983); and Ernst Gellner, *Nations and Nationalism* (Ithaca, N.Y.: Cornell University Press, 1983). On political culture, see Gabriel A. Almond and Sidney Verba, *The Civic Culture: Political Attitudes and*

Democracy in Five Nations (Newbury Park, Calif.: Sage, 1989); and Robert Putnam, *Making Democracy Work: Civic Traditions in Modern Italy* (Princeton, N.J.: Princeton University Press, 1993).

28. David A. Snow, Jr., et al., "Frame Alignment Processes, Micromobilization, and Movement Participation," *American Sociological Review* 51 (August 1986): 464-81; Klandermans, *Social Psychology*; Gamson, "Social Psychology"; William A. Gamson, *Talking Politics* (Cambridge: Cambridge University Press, 1992); William A. Gamson and David S. Meyer, "Framing Political Opportunity," in *Comparative Perspectives*; William A. Gamson and Andre Modigliani, "Media Discourse and Public Opinion on Nuclear Power: A Constructionist Approach," *American Journal of Sociology* 95, no. 1 (1989): 1-37. On the role of the media in framing mass perceptions of a movement, see Brass, *Theft of an Idol*. On the role of the elites versus other actors in mass activism, see Brass, *Ethnicity and Nationalism*; and Anthony Oberschall, "Opportunities and Framing in the Eastern European Revolts of 1989," in *Comparative Perspectives*, 93-121.

29. For a volume that summarizes the state of the discipline on the subject, see McAdam, McCarthy, and Zald, eds., *Comparative Perspectives*.

30. Doug McAdam, John D. McCarthy, and Mayer N. Zald, "Introduction: Opportunities, Mobilizing Structures, and Framing Processes—Toward a Synthetic, Comparative Perspective on Social Movements," in *Comparative Perspectives*, 15.

31. Michael Useem, *Conscription, Protest, and Social Conflict* (New York: Wiley, 1973), 25.

32. Oberschall, *Social Conflict*; Tilly, *From Mobilization*; Peter K. Eisinger, "The Conditions of Protest Behavior in American Cities," *American Political Science Review* 67, no. 1 (1973): 11-28; and Tarrow, *Power in Movement*.

33. Tarrow, *Power in Movement*.

34. McAdam, *Political Process*, 26.

35. For a discussion, see Jerry F. Hough, *The Soviet Prefects: The Local Party Organs in Industrial Decision-Making* (Cambridge, Mass.: Harvard University Press, 1969); Jerry F. Hough and Merle Fainsod, *How the Soviet Union is Governed* (Cambridge, Mass.: Harvard University Press, 1979); Valerie Bunce, *Subversive Institutions*; Carl J. Friedrich, "Totalitarianism: Recent Trends," in *Between Totalitarianism and Pluralism*, ed. Alexander Dallin (New York: Garland, 1992), 16-27; H. Gordon Skilling, "Interest Groups and Communist Politics," in *Between Totalitarianism and Pluralism*, 117-61; H. Gordon Skilling, "Interest Groups and Communist Politics Revisited," in *Between Totalitarianism and Pluralism*, 26; T. H. Rigby, "Politics in the Mono-Organizational Society," in *Between Totalitarianism and Pluralism*, 163-212; T. H. Rigby, "The USSR: End of a Long, Dark Night?," in *The Developments of Civil Society in Communist Systems*, ed. Robert J. Miller (Sydney: Allen & Unwin, 1992), 11-23.

36. Vladimir Tismaneanu, *Reinventing Politics: Eastern Europe from Stalin to Havel* (New York: Free Press, 1993), 170, 175; Robert F. Miller, "Concluding Essay," in *The Developments of Civil Society in Communist Systems*, ed. Robert F. Miller (Sydney: Allen & Unwin, 1992), 130-47.

37. Gregory Gleason, "The 'National Factor' and the Logic of Sovietology," in *The Post-Soviet Nations: Perspectives on the Demise of the USSR*, ed. Alexander Motyl (New York: Columbia University Press, 1992), 1-29. For a critique of post-Soviet scholarship's efforts to break into mainstream comparative political science, see Paul Kubicek, "Post-Communist Studies: Ten Years Later, Twenty Years Behind?" *Communist and Post-Communist Studies* 33 (2000): 295-309.

38. M. Steven Fish, *Democracy from Scratch: Opposition and Regime in the New Russian Revolution* (Princeton, N.J.: Princeton University Press, 1995).

39. Fish, *Democracy from Scratch*, 13.

40. Fish, *Democracy from Scratch*, 27.

41. Fish, *Democracy from Scratch*, 28.

42. Fish, *Democracy from Scratch*, 75.

43. Paul Kubicek, *Unbroken Ties: The State, Interest Associations, and Corporatism in Post-Soviet Ukraine* (Ann Arbor: University of Michigan Press, 1999), 14-18.

44. Jeff Chinn and Robert Kaiser, *Russians as the New Minority: Ethnicity and Nationalism in the Soviet Successor States* (Boulder, Colo.: Westview, 1996), 13.

45. Chinn and Kaiser, *Russians*, 28.

46. Chinn and Kaiser, *Russians*, 32.

47. Chinn and Kaiser, *Russians*, 18.

48. Ian Bremmer, "The Politics of Ethnicity: Russians in the New Ukraine," *Europe-Asia Studies* 46, no. 2 (1994): 261-83.

49. Albert O. Hirschman, *Exit, Voice, and Loyalty: Responses to Decline in Firms, Organizations, and States* (Cambridge, Mass.: Harvard University Press, 1970).

50. For a discussion of the application of Hirschman's theory to empirical studies, see K. Dowding et al., "Exit, Voice and Loyalty: Analytic and Empirical Developments," *European Journal of Political Research* 37, no. 4 (2000): 469-95.

51. In particular, Gorenburg wrote that scholars often underestimate the fact that "nationalist sentiment among the members of a particular ethnic group cannot be assumed to be either constant or randomly distributed," and that select members of the social group itself or in the state play an important mobilizing or identity-creating role. Dmitry Gorenburg, "Not with One Voice: An Explanation of Intragroup Variation in Nationalist Sentiment," *World Politics* 53, no. 1 (2000): 115-42. For a similar argument, see also Elise Giuliano, "Who Determines the Self in the Politics of Self-Determination: Identity and Preference Formation in Tatarstan's Nationalist Mobilization," *Comparative Politics* 32, no. 3 (2000): 295-316.

52. See, for example, Leokadia Drobizheva, "Processes of Disintegration in the Russian Federation and the Problem of Russians," in *The New Russian Diaspora: Russian Minorities in the Former Soviet Republics*, ed. Vladimir Shlapentokh, Munir Sendich, and Emil Payin (Armonk, N.Y.: Sharpe, 1994), 45-55.

53. Chinn and Kaiser, *Russians*; and Paul Kolstoe, *Russians in the Former Soviet Republics* (London: Hurst, 1995). But see Graham Smith and Andrew Wilson, "Rethinking Russia's Post-Soviet Diaspora: The Potential for Political Mobilisation in Eastern Ukraine and North-East Estonia," *Europe-Asia Studies* 49, no. 5 (1997): 845-64.

54. See, for example, Marjorie M. Balzer and Uliana A. Vinokurova, "Interethnic Relations and Federalism: The Case of the Sakha Republic," *Europe-Asia Studies* 48, no. 1 (1996): 101-20; and Svetlana I. Akkieva, "Etnopoliticheskaya i sotsial'no-ekonomicheskaya situatsiya v Kabardino-Balkarii nakanune vyborov 17 dekabrya 1995 goda," in *Razvivayushchiysya elektorat Rossii*, ed. G. A. Komarova (Moscow: Rossiyskaya akademiya nauk, Institut etnologii i antropologii, 1996), 61-89.

55. Skalnik Leff, "Democratization"; Roeder, "Soviet Federalism"; Ronald Gregor Suny, *The Revenge of the Past: Nationalism, Revolution, and the Collapse of the Soviet Union* (Stanford, Calif.: Stanford University Press, 1993); Bunce, *Subversive Institutions*; Lapidus, "Asymmetrical Federalism"; Lapidus and Walker, "Nationalism"; Mark R. Beissinger, "How Nationalisms Spread: Eastern Europe Adrift the Tides and Cycles of Nationalist Contention," *Social Research* 63, no. 1 (1996): 97-146; Mark R. Beissinger, "Nationalist Violence and the State: Political Authority and Contentious Repertoires in the Former USSR," *Comparative Politics* 30, no. 4 (1998): 401-22; Juan J. Linz and Alfred Stepan, *Problems of Democratic Transition and Consolidation: Southern Europe,*

South America, and Post-Communist Europe (Baltimore: The Johns Hopkins University Press, 1996); Treisman, "Russia's 'Ethnic Revival'"; Daniel S. Treisman, *After the Deluge: Regional Crises and Political Consolidation in Russia* (Ann Arbor: University of Michigan Press, 1999). On the role of the state in affecting aspects of social activism in other contexts, see Alfred Stepan, *The State and Society: Peru in Comparative Perspective* (Princeton, N.J.: Princeton University Press, 1978), 14; Harmon Zeigler, *Pluralism, Corporatism, and Confucianism: Political Association and Conflict Regulation in the United States, Europe, and Taiwan* (Philadelphia: Temple University Press, 1988); and G. William Domhoff, *Who Rules America? Power and Politics in the Year 2000* (Mountain View, Calif.: Mayfield, 1998).

56. Claus Offe, "Designing Institutions in East European Transitions," in *The Theory of Institutional Design*, ed. Robert E. Goodin (Cambridge: Cambridge University Press, 1996), 208.

57. Erik P. Hoffmann, "The Dynamics of State-Society Relations in Post-Soviet Russia," in *Can Democracy Take Root in Post-Soviet Russia?* ed. Harry Eckstein, Jr., et al. (Lanham, Md.: Rowman & Littlefield, 1998), 69-101, 82-83.

58. Michael E. Urban, Vyacheslav Igrunov, and Sergei Mitrokhin, *The Rebirth of Politics in Russia* (Cambridge: Cambridge University Press, 1997), 306.

59. Kubicek, *Unbroken Ties.*

60. Anatoliy Kostyukov, "Net mira 'pod kovrom': Zachem na zapade vozrojhdayut kremlinologiyu," interview with Liliya Shevtsova, *Nezavisimaya gazeta*, 12 September 2003, www.ng.ru/ideas/2003-09-12/1_shevtsova.html (accessed 12 September 2003).

61. For a survey of the literature of Russia's political elites, see Vladimir Gel'man and Inessa Tarusina, "Studies of Political Elites in Russia: Issues and Alternatives," *Communist and Post-Communist Studies* 33, no. 3 (2000): 311-29.

62. For a critique of the public opinion survey-based approaches to politics in the post-Communist states, see Grzegorz Ekiert and Jan Kubik, "Contentious Politics in New Democracies: East Germany, Hungary, Poland, and Slovakia, 1989-93," *World Politics* 50, no. 4 (1998): 547-81. Ekiert and Kubik, for example, wrote: "Data on the political activities of nonelite actors are not readily available; public opinion-polls have been routinely used as the sole source of empirical knowledge on the politics of the populace at large," 550.

63. Albert Mabileau et al., "People and Local Politics: Themes and Concepts," in *Local Politics and Participation in Britain and France*, ed. Albert Mabileau et al. (Cambridge: Cambridge University Press, 1989), 9.

64. L. J. Sharpe, "The Growth and Decentralisation of the Modern Democratic State," *European Journal of Political Research,* Special Issue, "Centralisation and Decentralisation: Changing Patterns of Intergovernmental Relations in Advanced Western Societies," 16, no. 4 (1988): 365-80.

65. See Jonathan Fox, "Latin America's Emerging Local Politics," *Journal of Democracy* 5, no. 2 (1994): 105-16. On the Russian Caciquismo, see Kimitaka Matsuzato, "From Communist Boss Politics to Post-Communist Caciquismo," *Communist and Post-Communist Studies* 34, no. 2 (2001): 175-201; and Kimitaka Matsuzato, "Local Elites under Transition: County and City Politics in Russia 1985-1996," *Europe-Asia Studies* 51, no. 8 (1999): 1367-400.

66. Rustow, for example, writes: "It [democracy] must be combined with a strong local government" (Dunkwart A. Rustow, "Transitions to Democracy: Toward a Dynamic Model," *Comparative Politics* 2 [1970]: 339). On the importance of the segmentation of political authority for democracy see also Seymour M. Lipset, "The Social Requisites of Democracy Revisited," *American Sociological Review* 59, no. 1 (1994): 4; Robert A.

Dahl, *Polyarchy: Participation and Opposition* (New Haven, Conn.: Yale University Press, 1971); and Robert A. Dahl, *Who Governs? Democracy and Power in an American City* (New Haven, Conn.: Yale University Press, 1966).

67. A metaphor used by Guiseppe di Palma, *To Craft Democracies: An Essay on Democratic Transitions* (Berkeley: University of California Press, 1990).

68. See Andrew Coulson, "From Democratic Centralism to Local Democracy," in *Local Government in Eastern Europe: Establishing Democracy at the Grassroots*, ed. Andrew Coulson (Aldershot, England: Elgar, 1995), 1-19; Anna Cielecka and John Gibson, "Local Government in Poland," in *Local Government in Eastern Europe: Establishing Democracy at the Grassroots*, ed. Andrew Coulson (Aldershot, England: Elgar, 1995), 23-40; Zoltan Hajdu, "Local Government Reform in Hungary," in *Local Government in the New Europe*, ed. Robert J. Bennett (London: Belhaven, 1993), 208-24; Jan Kara and Jiri Blazek, "Czechoslovakia: Regional and Local Government," in *Local Government in the New Europe*, 246-58.

69. See, for example, Philip Selznick, *TVA and the Grass Roots: A Study in the Sociology of Formal Organization* (New York: Harper & Row, 1966).

70. Stein Rokkan and Derek Urwin, *Economy, Territory, Identity: Politics of West European Peripheries* (London: Sage, 1983), 132.

71. Lynn Avery Hunt, *Revolution and Urban Politics in Provincial France: Troyes and Reims, 1786-1790* (Stanford, Calif.: Stanford University Press, 1978).

72. Theda Skocpol, *States and Social Revolutions: A Comparative Analysis of France, Russia, and China* (Cambridge: Cambridge University Press, 1991), 156.

73. In both France and China, for example, Skocpol suggests that the timing of the revolutions coincided with the granting of special powers to the local assemblies. In all three of her cases of revolution, peasant community structures have also played key roles in mobilization, providing "the organizational basis for spontaneous and autonomous revolts" (Skocpol, *States and Social Revolutions*, 77, 117, 128).

74. For this argument with regard to British local government, see Rhodes, *Control and Power*.

75. For a discussion of the various approaches to local government, see Gerry Stoker, "Introduction: Normative Theories of Local Government and Democracy," in *Rethinking Local Democracy*, ed. Desmond King and Gerry Stoker (London: Macmillan, 1996), 1-27.

76. Skocpol, *States and Social Revolutions*, 29.

77. Skocpol, *States and Social Revolutions*, 29.

78. Skocpol, *States and Social Revolutions*, 31.

79. Gérard Marcou, "New Tendencies of Local Government Development in Europe," in *Local Government in the New Europe*, 56.

80. Robert J. Bennett, "Local Government in Europe: Common Directions for Change," in *Local Government in the New Europe*, 14. See also E. M. Davies, John Gibson, and John Stewart, "Grant Characteristics and the Budgetary Process," in *New Research in Central-Local Relations*, ed. Michael Goldsmith (Aldershot, England: Gower, 1986), 207-24; and Sharpe, "Growth and Decentralisation."

81. Jean C. Oi, *Rural China Takes Off: Institutional Foundations of Economic Reform* (Berkeley: University of California Press, 1999), 12.

82. For a comparative discussion of the role of the size of municipalities in democratic settings, see Bennett, "Local Government in Europe."

83. Putnam, *Making Democracy Work*.

84. On the impact of policing strategies on social movements in different national set-

tings, see Donatella Della Porta, "Social Movements and the State: Thoughts on the Policing of Protest," in *Comparative Perspectives*, 62-92.

85. England's policing is organized at the local council level, although the conflict in Northern Ireland in 1971 resulted in a series of reforms aimed at greater police centralization. See Pierre Birnbaum, *States and Collective Action: The European Experience* (New York: Cambridge University Press, 1988), 170; and Albert Mabileau, "Local Government in Britain and Local Politics and Administration in France," in *Local Politics and Participation in Britain and France*, ed. Albert Mabileau et al. (Cambridge: Cambridge University Press, 1989), 25.

86. For a discussion, see Theodore H. Friedgut, *Political Participation in the USSR* (Princeton, N.J.: Princeton University Press, 1979); and James H. Oliver, "Citizen Demands and the Soviet Political System," *American Political Science Review* 63, no. 2 (1968).

87. Friedgut, *Political Participation*; and Oliver, "Citizen Demands."

88. For a discussion of the similar roles played by local bodies in other communist states, see Rudolf L. Tokes, *Hungary's Negotiated Revolution* (Cambridge: Cambridge University Press, 1996), 126.

89. See Michael E. Urban, *More Power to The Soviets: The Democratic Revolution in the USSR* (Aldershot, England: Elgar, 1990); and Hough and Fainsod, *How the Soviet Union.*

90. Term borrowed from Tilly, *From Mobilization.*

91. On the question of the relative weight of the party versus the central ministries and the soviets, see Stephen Whitefield, *Industrial Power and the Soviet State* (Oxford: Clarendon Press, 1993).

92. Rhodes, *Control and Power*, 79.

93. The empirical part of the investigation is largely based on interviews, observation, stenographic records of local council proceedings, published and unpublished documents of nationalist groups, local newspapers, and lists of local council deputies over time with their professional affiliations. I also used data from the archive of the Ingush Mission in Moscow and that of the human rights group Memorial, which conducted extensive interviews with victims of the Ossetiyan-Ingush conflict. The research was carried out between 1997 and 2000, during which time I spent a total of fourteen months in Moscow, the republics of Bashkortostan, Adygeya, and North Ossetiya. In Bashkortostan and Adygeya, I also supplemented research in the respective regional capitals with fieldwork and interviews in rural localities—two in Adygeya and one in Bashkortostan.

94. For an example of the use of this approach, see David D. Laitin, *Identity in Formation: The Russian-Speaking Nationality in Estonia and Bashkortostan*, Studies in Public Policy, vol. 249 (Glasgow: University of Strathclyde, 1995).

95. Adam Przeworski and Henry Teune, *The Logic of Comparative Social Inquiry*, 2d ed. (Malabar, Fla.: Krieger, 1982), 35.

96. Matthew B. Miles and Michael A. Huberman, *Qualitative Data Analysis: An Expanded Sourcebook*, Second ed. (London: Sage, 1994), 51-2.

97. Miles and Huberman, *Qualitative Data Analysis*, 56.

98. On the reluctance of the Russian political functionaries to solicit public opinion on various policies, see the article with a telling title by Vladimir Shlapentokh, "No One Needs Public Opinion Data in Post Communist Russia," *Communist and Post-Communist Studies* 32 (1999): 453-60.

99. See, for example, McAdam, *Political Process.*

Chapter 2

Local Government and Social Control in the Soviet Union and Post-Soviet Russia

In this chapter I discuss the institutional contexts which led to the emergence of nontitular movements in the early 1990s, when the local governing bodies came to play a central role. Because I take a path-dependent view of local government, arguing that the patterns of interactions between the local bodies and the social agencies in post-Soviet Russia are similar to those that existed under the Soviet system, I here discuss the soviets at some length. The institutional and social contexts fostered by the Soviet nationalities policy and the nationalizing policies of the titular elites in the post-Soviet period will be discussed in the following chapter. This chapter is structured as follows. First, I discuss the evolution of the system of the soviets focusing on their place in the Soviet elite career patterns, their resource base, and their social mobilization functions. I then outline Gorbachev's local government reforms and the resulting shifts in the local bodies' resources and social control.

The Soviets in the Soviet System

The soviets, meaning "councils," from the Russian word *sovet* (advice), were conceived by the Bolshevik ideologues as the primary institutions of government. These bodies, born out of the workers' uprising of 1905, during which time they functioned as strike committees, were greatly appreciated by Lenin, who likened them to the Paris Communes of 1871. After a brief spell of disillusionment with the soviets, which reemerged as a force in early 1917, when the Mensheviks succeeded in capturing power, Lenin returned to his original championship of the soviets, whose mobilizing potential was not lost on the Great Strategist. From October 1917 onwards, the slogan of "All Power to the Soviets!" aided the Bolsheviks in capturing, establishing, and legitimizing power throughout much of the former empire.[1]

In addition to the general populist appeal, the slogan also blended well with the Bolshevik strategies to win the hearts of Russia's numerous minority ethnic groups.[2] It fitted well with the generic conceptions of minority self-government propagated by the Bolshevik ideologues. The nationalities policy underwent numerous changes over the years, and is discussed in the following chapter. At this point, it is important to describe the basic institutional setup that emerged out of these conceptions and strategies and which was further refined under Stalin.[3]

The system that came to be established by 1922, the official date for the creation of the Union of Soviet Socialist Republics (USSR), was a multitiered federation.[4] It was divided into the ethnically defined union and autonomous republics, the autonomous *okruga* (districts) and *oblasti* (regions) within them, and the nonethnically defined *oblasti* and *kraya* (territories). These were further subdivided into the nonethnically defined districts (*rayony*), cities, city boroughs, and settlements (*posyolki*), and villages (*syola*).[5] The soviets were to correspond with these territorial-administrative divisions, with the exception of villages, several of which tended to be clustered within the jurisdiction of one soviet.[6]

Officially, the local government organs proper or *mestnye organy* were considered to be those below the union and autonomous republic levels, starting with *oblast'* and all the way down to the village settlement unit.[7] Although the numbers and sizes of these units changed throughout the Soviet period, for the purposes of this discussion, we will only list the subdivisions within the Russian Soviet Federated Socialist Republic (RSFSR) as they had come to be established by 1989, that is, immediately preceding the period of investigation.[8] In 1989 the RSFSR, one of the Soviet Union's fifteen republics, included the sixteen ethnically defined autonomous republics, five autonomous *oblasti*, and ten autonomous *okruga*, as well as the six nonethnically defined *kraya*, forty-nine *oblasti*, and the cities of Moscow and St. Petersburg. These, with the exception of the latter two entities, were further subdivided into 1,834 rural or district *rayony*, and 1,067 cities,[9] as well as numerous smaller municipal entities. The total number of municipalities before Yel'tsin's dissolution of many soviets in 1993 was 29,445.[10]

The Bolshevik, and later Soviet, official propaganda contrasted the soviets with their Western equivalents of "bourgeois democracy," stressing the soviets' truly representative nature as government "of all the people," ensuring grassroots contact between the average citizen and the state.[11] They were to be popularly elected, and, according to the official ideology, were to combine legislative, executive, and control functions. Even the lowest town or village levels would have their own popularly elected representative assemblies, which would in turn elect the executive bodies, and continue to control and supervise their work. The same would be true for the higher levels, all the way up to the Union. The system was thus officially conceived as a parliamentary one, and was ostensibly to ensure genuine representation of workers, peasants, and other "progressive" social categories, depending on the political expediency of the moment.

At the inception of the Soviet Union, however, and during the maturation of the system, the soviets' role was reduced to those of instruments of party dictatorship, although this assertion must be qualified in reference to the subsequent evolution of the system. Party dominance was achieved through the doctrine of democratic centralism and its institutional manifestations, as well as the *nomenklatura* system of appointments. Democratic centralism ensured a strict top-bottom hierarchy of decision making and subordination, with the lower levels executing decisions of party and soviet agencies above them. The system, leaning heavily towards centralism, defeated the "democratic" premise on which the soviets officially rested. The faithful execution of decisions from above was ensured through the elaborate *nomenklatura* system. Its origins going back to as early as 1922, *nomenklatura* meant the assignment to the various party levels, such as *gorkom*, *raykom*, or *obkom*, authority over appointments to posts considered important.[12] While superficially similar to Western equivalents of bureaucratic agency personnel lists, it had a heavily ideological underpinning, ensuring that only the "right" people gained entry. Significantly, the *nomenklatura* included both appointive and "elective" posts, with heavy gate keeping even for the "grassroots" bodies.[13]

The efficient operation of the *nomenklatura* and democratic centralism ensured that many aspects of the soviets' work had come to be controlled by the Communist Party of the Soviet Union (CPSU)—from nomination to sham election, to appointment of their executives and heads of standing committees, to administrative management of the locales. Where the party did not exercise control and supervision over administrative matters, the central ministries did; they emerged as powerful actors in the context of the Five-Year Plans. In Soviet parlance, the system has become known as embodying the principle of "dual subordination." According to this principle, local administrators were accountable on "vertical" levels to the central ministries or higher soviets, and on "horizontal" levels, to the councils that had elected them. In fact, it has been argued that these soviet executives were almost solely accountable to the local and higher Communist party institutions or central ministries, reducing the role of the soviets in many aspects of local affairs to those of rubber-stamp bodies. Herein lay the fallacy of the "Soviet" state. As Michael Urban aptly puts it,

> The hypocrisy displayed by the regime toward the soviets corrupted the very identity that the regime claimed for itself. For it had never ceased to refer to its domain as "the country of soviets" where lived the *Soviet* people, and always availed itself of this same identity marker in speaking about the order that it had created ("our Soviet way of life," "the new Soviet man," and so forth), even while it had eviscerated the soviets themselves, converting them into lifeless assemblies that resembled governmental institutions in the way that zombies might resemble the living.[14]

Over the course of the development of the Soviet system, these "lifeless assemblies," however, had come to perform an important political function.

They were to be "schools of public administration," allowing a disproportionately large number of citizens to "participate" in government affairs. These
"schools," or local councils alone, that is, excluding the higher union republic
and the all-union bodies, had come to number over 49,500 by the 1970s.[15] In
1985, there were 52,041.[16]

According to Jerry Hough and Merle Fainsod's estimates in 1977, with the
average number of deputies ranging from 33 in the village-level soviets to 78 in
the *rayony*, 134 in the cities, and 218 in the *oblasti*, over 2.2 million people were
drawn into the local council system.[17] The stress on deputy turnover, ensuring
greater levels of participation, and an influx of "fresh" forces at the next elections, as well as the increase in numbers of deputies in the soviets over the years,
served to reinforce further their "participatory" aspect.

While rapid turnover ensured that many would cease to "participate" in
governance once their term ended, for others the soviet would be one of the
channels of entry into the political establishment. Although their opposition to
the party or ministerial line was inconceivable, making many Western observers
question the meaningfulness of their participation, the soviets were the arenas
where the ambitious could make themselves noticeable to those in charge of
nomenklatura. As Jeffrey Hahn, the scholar of the "Soviet grassroots" wrote,
"For the politically ambitious, a good performance in the role of deputy may
attract favorable attention from those in the party seeking new recruits or deciding who to promote."[18]

Evidence on career patterns presented by other scholars of the Soviet political system likewise suggests that those at the top of the regional and indeed all-
union party hierarchies often rose through both party and soviet work.[19] Thus,
T. H. Rigby's typical Politburo member "followed a fairly standard pattern: a
youthful period as a manual worker and/or Komsomol official, sometimes a
spell working for the local soviet or party committee."[20]

True, the soviet channel represented somewhat of a detour entry into the
bureaucratic "ruling class,"[21] the straightforward front-door entry being climbing
along the party ladder. An important feature of the Soviet system, however, was
the overlapping nature of public functions of the political elite and those aspiring
to become part of it. Rigby's typical climber had thus probably combined factory work with part-time soviet deputyship, while simultaneously starting a
party career as an activist or head of a factory party cell. Friedgut, based on his
case study of local government in the city of Kutaisi, thus explains the phenomenon of overlap, which he argues was a general "feature of Soviet life."[22]
He writes: "The limited numbers of those who can be said to be the leadership .
. . mean that the leaders—and those aspiring to be leaders—must take on many
jobs simultaneously."[23] "Such intensive levels of activity," he writes, "appear to
be necessary in a public career."[24]

Other than being mere stepping-stones into the political elite, a degree of
genuine deputy involvement, albeit on a limited scale, in local community governance is uncovered by Friedgut's study. Written in the 1970s, his arguments
dovetailed with those of the pluralist-minded scholars, who gradually recognized

the soviets' greater role as not just representative, but interest aggregation bodies with some decision-making and control capacities.[25]

This existence of agencies other than the Communist party allowing the soviets' participation in decision making, even on a very limited scale, reflected the shift in the soviets' resource base over the years. By "resources," I mean both the soviets' financial revenues and jurisdiction over, as well as an ability to decide on, community matters not reserved for the other agencies. This also encompasses the social resources that the soviets controlled by virtue of the society's overreliance on the soviets in terms of the satisfaction of community needs. The following section explores the soviets' "horizontal" resource base in detail, suggesting a more substantial role for these bodies.

Resources

As mentioned earlier, the soviets, as the main institutions of government, were invested with much formal authority. It extended to performing law-making and executive functions, as well as control over administration, which, while limited to control over the respective administrative locales, was nonetheless substantial.

Russian scholars list a whole range of jurisdictions, including (a) control over land, forests, and other natural facilities; (b) real estate and services; (c) aiding enterprises located on their territories, even if they are formally within the jurisdiction of the central ministries or higher soviets, and supervising their work; (d) supervising *kolkhozy* (collective farms) work; and (e) public safety, law, and order. While their methods of exercising authority were supposed to rely largely on *ubejhdenie* (convincing), according to the Soviet ideologues, if necessary they could also use *prinujhdenie* (enforcement).[26]

In reality, however, this formal authority did not translate into power on many counts.[27] Land, forests, and other natural resources often fell into the jurisdiction of the central ministries, as did real estate, housing, and many other social facilities administered by enterprises subordinate to the ministries.[28] The most important decision-making, executive, and control bodies within the soviets continued to be staffed by local party *apparatchiki*, who combined a formal position in the local party hierarchy with seats on the *ispolkomy* (executive committees) and standing committees of the soviets. It is these bodies, in addition to the ministries, that continued to decide the macro questions of resource allocation and distribution.[29]

Beginning in the 1950s, however, a series of initiatives were undertaken to strengthen the independent resource base of the soviets and their capacity to decide on distributive issues. The initial efforts to strengthen local government were undertaken in the context of Khrushchev's devolution of power from the central ministries to the *sovnarkhozy* and local government bodies proper. The result was an increase in the volume of local facilities controlled by the soviets, most notably in the areas of housing, real estate, and cultural and services facilities.[30] These changes were being introduced against the background of debates on what came to be known as *podmena* or excessive party meddling into local administrative matters at the expense of self-governing bodies.[31]

The gradual devolution of decision making on matters of local significance reflected important changes in the Soviet system, making it largely explicable. Jerry Hough underscores the changes in his study of the "Soviet prefects" by suggesting that although the early prefectorial role leaned more towards ideology and ideological control, it increasingly leaned towards the coordinating and managerial functions as the system matured and the threats of internal ideological challenge diminished, while developmental, consumer services, and other economic prerogatives expanded.[32]

The above premise, which Hough ascribes to the role of the local party boss, could also be well applied to the soviets, with their mobilizing role accompanied by an increasing stress on local administration. It can be further extended to suggest that the diminished ideological function would serve to increase the role of the soviets vis-à-vis the party. Indeed, it would not make sense for the local party boss to intervene into the micromanaging functions of a local soviet deputy, whose functions involved responding to such "raw" demands as repairing a fence or stopping pipe leakage in the neighborhood he represents.[33] Hahn argues that in fact most local government issues in the Soviet Union were simply beyond the need for party authority.[34] While the local "prefect" coordinated, the soviet deputies dealt with the minor day-to-day social, community service, or other issues. We shall see in the following chapters that in terms of resource mobilization for collective action, the latter prerogative is not such a bad thing to have.

It was this micromanaging function of the local soviets, indeed, which ironically made them more important than their local government counterparts in the West. In the context of a state-planned economy and the absence of an autonomous self-aiding civil society, their responsibilities were enormous. "The Soviet citizen," wrote Friedgut perhaps with a degree of irony, "who changes his residence, wants his boots resoled, or wants to buy new clothing will most likely have to deal with an agency of his local soviet."[35] "No problem is supposed to be too personal or too small to take to the deputy," wrote James Oliver, with deputies often engaged in resolving marital and other personal disputes.[36] Oliver wrote that unlike in the Western democracies, in the USSR, where no autonomous groups existed, virtually all "raw" demands had to be processed within the political system.[37] While many citizen requests remained stacked on deputy desks collecting dust for months, Oliver and Hahn found that deputies made genuine efforts to address citizen requests, and could exercise personal discretion in doing so.[38]

This brings us to the final point of this discussion of the soviets' resources. The soviets' involvement with the most mundane local matters, transacted by commercial agencies rather than by the state in countries with market economies, created a system of overdependence on these bodies for the satisfaction of the most basic social needs. While ostensibly weak vis-à-vis the higher agencies, the local soviet thus wielded substantial power and control over local society. This control was reinforced through a system of the soviets' auxiliary agencies in the grassroots. Since we are dealing with the relationship between the state agencies and the social ones, including the organized groups, the social control aspect deserves discussion at some length.

The Soviets and Social Control

The soviets permeated the social fabric via their auxiliary "volunteer" agencies. These were the "volunteer" patrolling groups, neighborhood societies, comrade courts, apartment committees, library councils, and so forth, whose members were recruited from outside, directly from local communities, but whose leadership was drawn from or maintained strong links with the soviets.[39] A detailed description of the "volunteer" agencies is beyond the scope of this introductory survey. Of interest for this discussion is the role of the soviets in fostering social mobilization through these "voluntary" agencies, which involved a large percentage of Soviet citizenry in regime and community activities. Their main purpose was the fulfillment of the soviets' most important function aside from administration, namely what Friedgut calls "mobilized participation." In contrast to "autonomous participation," which springs from the citizenry, mobilized participation involves "actors external to the community, or a select group within it, [as] the sole initiators of participation among the masses, and it is they who establish the legitimate frameworks of participation, determining their agenda and tone."[40] Such controlled social mobilization, through maximum involvement, was essential for the prevention of any activity autonomous from the state, and for that of the emergence of social atomization. Rather than being atomized, as the conventional wisdom holds, Soviet society was highly structured, and it fell to the local soviets to ensure regime-led social organization into controlled networks. The recognition of the importance of this function grew proportionately with the rate of urbanization and the regime's fears of the resulting social atomization. The result was the rise in the numbers of the various "voluntary" agencies attached to the soviets and the role accorded to them.[41]

Friedgut identifies three main specific functions of mobilized participation and of the soviets' "voluntary" agencies in particular: (1) the creation of a community despite the rise in urbanization; (2) the need to give an ideological underpinning to all local campaigns; and (3) the implementation of party policy.[42] Friedgut makes an important point relevant to the first function. The creation of a "community" by organizing people into regime-controlled networks fosters a system of social sanctions and rewards for people who conform or deviate.[43] In fact, certain "voluntary" agencies, such as the "comrades' courts" and the *drujhiny*, specifically dealt with deviating behavior by applying moral sanctions.[44] Others, however, while not concerned with deviant behavior as such, performed the same social pressure functions by virtue of drawing people into networks guided by exemplary regime loyalists from within the soviets. Such a self-reinforcing system made the exercise of coercion redundant. Stephen Whitefield makes the same point in his study of the social impact of the ministerial system. Social loyalty to the regime, he argues, was ensured through a system of material incentives and rewards, accounting for the remarkable passivity of the Soviet citizen.[45]

The second point about ideology feeds into the first one. While the ideological function was largely performed through the bona fide ritualistic acts of mass participation, like May Day demonstrations, ideological coloring was also given to the mundane instances of community administration, like the *subbotniki*. Ideology, constantly projected by the local bodies into the grassroots, served to reinforce community participation and reduce the likelihood of deviation without recourse to coercion. It logically follows that the first two functions, that is, the creation of an organized "community" and the projection of ideology, facilitated the third one, policy implementation.

From a conceptual point of view, the existence and the importance of these three interconnected factors is pertinent in Western contexts as well. Control over networks, often exercised by the local governing bodies even in democratic contexts, and the use of agenda setting, facilitates uncontested policy implementation, while at the same time having the benefit of presenting a given policy as enjoying broad "social" or "civic" support. This premise is still pertinent in post-Soviet Russia: as the subsequent chapters will show, the social penetration role of the local bodies lasted well into the late Soviet and post-Soviet periods. As a result, the question posed by Friedgut two decades ago in the context of Brezhnev's USSR—"How and why do Soviet politics involve the people?"[46]—remains highly pertinent in post-Soviet Russia's local settings if we change the word "Soviet" to "local governing bodies," and is more appropriate than Lester Milbrath's "How and why do people get involved in politics?"[47]

Summary

What were the main outlines of the system of the soviets that evolved over the years leading up to Gorbachev's far-reaching reforms? We can broadly generalize that Gorbachev found a local government system whose formal representative nature was still corrupted by the procedural aspects of elections and candidate nominations, which placed them under party control. It was further undermined by party dominance over the executive arm of the soviet. The soviets, however, had come to play an important role in the recruitment of the Soviet political elite, be it party or administrative. Rather than soviet membership being a mere token step on the career ladder, citizen participation in local bodies became more meaningful as their resource base increased. While the party continued to macromanage, the deputies micromanaged, often in meaningful ways, which increased the sense of their own efficacy, role, and indeed power over local societies. This power stemmed not only from the vast amount of social services they performed, but also from the central role accorded to these bodies in fostering "mobilized participation."

The soviets would, however, continue to remain the party's poor relations in terms of careers and resources short of changing the central bedrock of the system. Were that to happen, it would undoubtedly affect not only the distribution of power and resources between these two institutions, but also the career structures and strategies of the political actors positioned in the various institutional tiers. In particular, it would change the way they manipulated their extant levels of social control under the changed political and ideological circumstances. Despite numerous reforms of the soviets throughout Soviet history, it was not until Gorbachev's ascent to power that the radical transformation of these bodies occurred, achieving the above results.

"All Power to the Soviets!"

Since Gorbachev gave pride of place to political change, it was inevitable that the soviets would feature most prominently on the reformist general secretary's list of priorities.[48] Between his ascent to power in 1985 and 1990 a series of radical proposals involving the soviets were discussed and carried through.

The main thrust of the reforms was a move to competitive elections; the strengthening of the representative branch; and the erosion of democratic centralism. Not originally intended to abolish party power completely, these changes ultimately helped spell the doom of the "leading and guiding force." Soviet political reform combined with the economic changes also shook the foundations on which the ministerial system rested. By default, the soviets became the institutions the Soviet propaganda had hitherto vainly sought to convince the public that they were—the main institutions of the state.[49]

The most crucial event in the reform process was the first nationwide competitive election to the local soviets, held on 4 March 1990. Although candidates were nominated by such establishment agencies as the Communist party, the "volunteer" organizations, enterprises, and worker collectives, there was genuine competition for many seats. However, as was expected, many party first secretaries were successfully elected to the key posts of soviet chairmen. Other lower ranking *apparatchiki* climbing the party or administrative ladder now also considered a "soviet" career at a time when the party was clearly at its nadir. Overall, despite the mixed and more democratic composition of the new bodies, particularly in the liberal urban centers, scholars noted their "colonization" by the former *nomenklatura* elites.[50] By the time the notorious Article 6, enshrining the party's leading role, was finally abolished from the Soviet Constitution in March 1990, party members had already begun to leave the CPSU. As some scholars remarked, the abolition of Article 6 from the Soviet Constitution simply registered the fait accompli.[51] The party, as it had been known, had ceased to exist, while the *nomenklatura* now sought refuge in the reformed soviets.

Despite the reformist thrust of Gorbachev's call to return of all power to the soviets, they were still looked upon through the prism of "mobilized participation." As such, the new legal frameworks and Gorbachev's political language on the soviets endowed them with resources crucial for continued influence over local societies and the fostering of mobilization. The difference, of course, was the nature of the issues they were supposed to address. The preamble to the 1987 law On All-National Discussion of Important Questions of State Life stipulated:

> The development of socialist democracy and of popular self-government pre-supposes the widening of possibilities for each USSR citizen to enjoy the con-stitutional right to participate in the management of state and public affairs, in the discussion of draft laws and *decisions of statewide* and local significance, as well as in major issues of public life.[52] (emphasis mine)

It was the soviets that were charged with ensuring that this popular partici-pation in discussion of issues of "statewide" significance took place. According to the 1990 law On Common Principles of Local Self-Government, the soviets were to function in "close cooperation" with "worker collectives, public associa-tions and movements, [and] create conditions for the realization by each citizen of the USSR of the constitutional right to participate in the management of state and public affairs."[53] The new legislation also placed great emphasis on the so-viets' role in fostering such expressions of direct democracy as referenda, meet-ings, and *skhody* (consultative gatherings of citizens).[54] In addition, it contained provisions for soviet administrations' jurisdiction over public associations, in-cluding over their registration.[55]

At the same time, the 1990-1991 USSR/RSFSR legislation on local self-government contradicted the very premise on which the soviets' reform was based, introducing a potential for conflicts between the various levels of author-ity. The 1990 law On Common Principles did not contain explicit references to democratic centralism and on paper endowed lower soviets with wide-ranging powers. It did, however, stipulate that should conflicts occur between the vari-ous levels, they were to be settled according to laws passed by republic-level legislatures, rather than by the courts. This, according to critics of the law, signi-fied the preservation of a centralist hierarchy.[56]

The 1991 RSFSR law On Local Self-Government contained more refer-ences to democratic centralism, although municipalities were made legally sepa-rate from republic and regional bodies.[57] While local administrations were to be subordinate to the soviets which elected them, they were also to answer to the higher executive organs.[58] Although the lower-level soviets were allowed to challenge, in court, acts of higher organs, they were expected to ensure compli-ance with and the carrying out of stipulations of the superior bodies in the re-spective territories.[59]

Thus, the soviets in Gorbachev's reform program, considering the functions they were endowed with and the preservation of elements of democratic central-ism, were conceived as performing the same mobilizing role they had hitherto performed, albeit for a progressive cause of liberalizing the political system. In the context of an increasing divide between the conservative *nomenklatura* and the democratic forces, the soviets were likely to be used as mobilizing agencies by the various conflicting political forces. The mandate to engage in big politics, as well as the soviets' control over social agencies and other resources, fostered the transgression of these political and institutional conflicts onto the social plane, a subject of discussion in the following chapters.

Local Government in Russia: A Path-Dependent View

The above historical discussion, spanning nearly a century of local government in the Soviet Union, suggests that this ostensibly grassroots institution has been accorded a special *political* significance by the Soviet ideologues. While this point may not appear to be immediately relevant to the central thrust of the book, its pertinence for the post-Soviet period becomes evident when we identify *social mobilization* or *demobilization* for federal or regional regime purposes as a central element in this political role.

Perhaps the term "controlled mobilization" would convey this role more accurately. Controlled mobilization was important for the emerging Bolshevik state and its efforts to consolidate power locally; for ensuring a hold over the exceedingly complex and vast modernizing Soviet society as the system matured; and for fostering support for Gorbachev's radical liberalizing agendas. As the subsequent chapters will show, the federal and regional regimes in post-Soviet Russia continue to regard local government as an instrument of political mobilization or social control much like the Soviet leaders regarded the soviets in the Soviet system.

The difference, of course, is that the nature of the ideologies and agenda projected into the grassroots varied throughout the Soviet and post-Soviet periods, as did the principal agents who controlled such agenda setting. In the Soviet Union, ideology was centralized. Although Gorbachev tried to continue to use the soviets for ideological purposes, his very reforms served to segment and decentralize local power, thereby undermining his efforts. Local governing bodies were bound to become powerful agenda-setting and mobilizing agencies in their own right. They already possessed resources crucial for either fostering or constraining social activism, which I discussed in chapter 1—from being able to provide "selective incentives" to the social agencies—to multiple networks the soviets could rely on if they were to foster social activism—to opportunities for controlling the framing of local agenda setting. This phase lasted until Boris Yel'tsin's recentralization of local government on a regional level served to pass the agenda-setting power on to those who appointed the local executives, that is, the republic and regional regimes. The following chapters investigate the impact of these Soviet legacies, as well as Gorbachev's and Yel'tsin's local government reforms on one aspect of social mobilization: the emergence and death of nontitular movements in the republics.

Notes

1. Vladimir I. Lenin, "The Tasks of the Proletariat in the Present Revolution," in *V. I. Lenin, Collected Works*, vol. 24, 4th ed., trans. Bernard Isaacs (Moscow: Progress, 1964), 21-29. For Marx's original treatment of the Communes, see Karl Marx, "The Civil War in France," in *The Marx-Engels Reader*, ed. Robert C. Tucker (New York: Norton, 1972), 526-76. For a discussion of the distribution of forces within these soviets, see Jeffrey W. Hahn, *Soviet Grassroots: Citizen Participation in Local Soviet Government* (London: Tauris, 1988), 56-9.

2. For a discussion of the national question in Marxist-Leninist thought, and Lenin's strategic choice of appropriate policy lines on the matter, see Walker Connor, *The National Question in Marxist-Leninist Theory and Strategy* (Princeton, N.J.: Princeton University Press, 1984).

3. For comprehensive treatments of the Soviet local government makeup and functions, see Everett M. Jacobs, ed., *Soviet Local Politics and Government* (London: Allen & Unwin, 1983); and L. G. Churchward, *Contemporary Soviet Government* (London: Routledge & Kegan Paul, 1968).

4. The Russian Soviet Federated Socialist Republic (RSFSR), however, was proclaimed earlier, in 1918, together with the first constitution. At the time, it consisted of eight autonomous republics and thirteen autonomous regions. In 1922, a Union treaty was signed incorporating the RSFSR, Ukrainian Soviet Socialist Republic (USSR), Belorussian Soviet Socialist Republic (BSSR), and the Federal Republic of Transcaucasia (FRT), into the new Union of Soviet Socialist Republics (USSR). After the expansion of the original territory to include the borderland entities, the second constitution recognizing the new federal state was adopted in 1924. For the discussion of the evolution of the system and the federalist premises in the various soviet constitutions, see Gregory Gleason, *Federalism and Nationalism: The Struggle for Republican Rights in the USSR* (Boulder, Colo.: Westview, 1990), 46-9.

5. In the 1920s, national rayon and national village soviets were also created on an experimental basis for diaspora groups. These formations, which numbered over 5,000 in the mid-1930s, were abolished in the late 1930s. Paul Kolstoe, *Russians in the Former Soviet Republics* (London: Hurst, 1995), 80.

6. Hahn, *Soviet Grassroots*, 84-5.

7. Hahn, *Soviet Grassroots*, 83.

8. For example, Churchward writes that there were 47,736 local soviets in 1965. This figure is significantly higher than that (29,445) on the eve of Yel'tsin's dissolution of many of the soviets in 1993. Churchward, *Contemporary Soviet Government*, 173.

9. Richard Sakwa, *Russian Politics and Society* (London: Routledge, 1991), 36.

10. By 1999, the number was reduced to 13,669. P. A. Goryunov et al., *Formirovanie organov mestnogo samoupravleniya v Rossiyskoy federatsii: Elektoral'naya statistika* (Moscow: Ves' mir, 1999), 9.

11. Hahn, *Soviet Grassroots*, 12.

12. On *nomenklatura*, see T. H. Rigby and Bohdan Hyrasymiw, *Leadership Selection and Patron-Client Relations in the USSR and Yugoslavia* (London: Allen & Unwin, 1983); and T. H. Rigby, *Political Elites in the USSR: Central Leaders and Local Cadres from Lenin to Gorbachev* (Aldershot, England: Elgar, 1990). For a popular discussion of *nomenklatura*, see Michael Voslensky, *Nomenklatura: Anatomy of the Soviet Ruling Class*, trans. Eric Mosbacher (London: Bodley Head, 1983).

13. Depending on the importance of the post, the authority was vested in one of the party and administrative organs, usually on or above the level of the post within the state or party hierarchy. Voslensky, *Nomenklatura.*

14. Michael E. Urban, *More Power to the Soviets: The Democratic Revolution in the USSR* (Aldershot, England: Elgar, 1990), 2.

15. I. A. Azovkin, *Mestnye sovety v sisteme organov vlasti* (Moscow: Yuridicheskaya literatura, 1971), 45.

16. Hahn, *Soviet Grassroots,* 84.

17. Jerry F. Hough and Merle Fainsod, *How the Soviet Union is Governed* (Cambridge, Mass.: Harvard University Press, 1979).

18. Hahn, *Soviet Grassroots,* 258. Michael Urban, based on his study of Belorussia, also found that the soviets were a particularly high breeding ground for subsequent recruitment into the more prestigious party organs, with both the local party and soviets' organs generating the USSR's "core elite." Michael E. Urban, *An Algebra of Soviet Power: Elite Circulation in the Belorussian Republic, 1966-86* (Cambridge: Cambridge University Press, 1989), 83, 87.

19. See, for example, Hough and Fainsod. *How the Soviet Union is Governed,* 500.

20. Rigby, *Political Elites,* 185-6.

21. For this approach to *nomenklatura,* see Voslensky, *Nomenklatura.*

22. Theodore H. Friedgut, "Community Structure, Political Participation, Soviet Local Government: The Case of Kutaisi," in *Soviet Politics and Society in the 1970s,* ed. Henry W. Morton and Rudolf L. Tokes (New York: Free Press, 1974), 287.

23. In what he suggests was a typical case, "One energetic young man—apparently at the start of a public career—was a member of the bureau of his factory party committee and chairman of the people's control committee in his factory, as well as a key member of a standing committee who had prepared three questions for the Executive Committee and delivered a report to the soviet in the last year, while also taking an active part in the deputies' group to which he was assigned." Friedgut, "Community Structure," 287-8.

24. Friedgut, "Community Structure," 288. Scholars of local councils in communist Poland, in a similar vein, write: "When a factory director is at the same time a member of a committee of the council and of a committee of a party, whom does he represent and where?" Krzysztof Ostrowski and Adam Przeworski, "Local Leadership in Poland," in *Local Politics in Poland: Twenty Years of Research,* ed. Jerzy J. Wiatr (Warsaw: University of Warsaw Institute of Sociology, 1984), 33-65, 39. For a discussion of local government in other communist states, see also Hellmut Wollmann. "Institution Building and Decentralization in Formerly Socialist Countries: The Cases of Poland, Hungary, and East Germany," *Government and Policy* 15 (1997): 463-80.

25. Indeed, Hahn's study of the soviets allowed him to champion a more meaningful role than had hitherto been ascribed to them by Western scholarship. While not underestimating the role of the party and central ministries, he cautiously argued that soviet deputies in fact played more independent roles than had previously been assumed. According to him, genuine grassroots participation in community decision making was also not completely lost under the Soviet system, with soviet-citizen meetings, *skhody* (consultative gatherings of people), deputies' questions, and constituent contacts serving as forums for citizen involvement (Hahn, *Soviet Grassroots*).

26. Azovkin, *Mestnye sovety,* 27-8.

27. For a discussion, see B. Michael Frolic, "Decision Making in Soviet Cities," *The American Political Science Review* 66, no. 1 (1972): 38-52.

28. For a discussion of the role of the central ministries, see Stephen Whitefield, *Industrial Power and the Soviet State* (Oxford: Clarendon, 1993).

29. On the role of the party in local decision making, see Merle Fainsod, *Smolensk under Soviet Rule* (Cambridge, Mass.: Harvard University Press, 1958). See also Peter Rutland, *The Politics of Economic Stagnation in the Soviet Union: The Role of Local Party Organs in Economic Management* (New York: Cambridge University Press, 1992).

30. In addition, a series of legal acts appeared in the 1950s aimed at strengthening the soviets' tax base and giving them greater control over local trade revenues. This was reflected in the increase in local budgets from 4.31 billion rubles in 1946 to 21.1 billion in 1965, with an increase in the overall USSR budget from 14 percent in 1946, to 20 percent in 1965. Friedgut, "Community Structure," 261. Between 1964 and 1968, the soviets' prerogatives were further expanded to include greater control over local consumer goods production, and even the volume and precise items produced in local enterprises—no small feat, considering the planned nature of the Soviet economy. Azovkin, *Mestnye sovety*, 187-94.

31. While the extent of the actual practical outcome of these discussions is debatable, it is noteworthy that they originated among Soviet party ideologues and policy makers, suggesting that they reflected an official line on the matter. Some Western scholars have even cautioned against the oversimplification of the issue of *podmena*, since the same people would sit on these different party and soviet bodies, and it would be difficult to argue who supplants whom (Hahn, *Soviet Grassroots*, 259).

32. Hough used the term "prefects" to refer to the local party first secretaries. Jerry F. Hough, *The Soviet Prefects: The Local Party Organs in Industrial Decision-Making* (Cambridge, Mass.: Harvard University Press, 1969).

33. For a discussion, see James H. Oliver, "Citizen Demands and the Soviet Political System," *American Political Science Review* 63, no. 2 (1968), 467.

34. Hahn, *Soviet Grassroots*, 259.

35. Friedgut, "Community Structure," 263.

36. Oliver, "Citizen Demands," 472.

37. Oliver, "Citizen Demands," 467.

38. Hahn, *Soviet Grassroots*; Oliver, "Citizen Demands."

39. For a discussion, see Robert G. Wesson, "Volunteers and Soviets," *Soviet Studies* 15, no. 3 (1964): 230-49; and L. G. Churchward, *Contemporary Soviet Government*, 182. For a more detailed discussion, see Theodore H. Friedgut, *Political Participation in the USSR* (Princeton, N.J.: Princeton University Press, 1979).

40. Friedgut, *Political Participation*, 30.

41. Friedgut, *Political Participation*, 235-88.

42. Friedgut, *Political Participation*, 236-7.

43. Friedgut, *Political Participation*, 18.

44. Friedgut, *Political Participation*, 243.

45. Whitefield, *Industrial Power*.

46. Friedgut, *Political Participation*, 14.

47. Friedgut, *Political Participation*, 14.

48. For a comprehensive account of Gorbachev's reform strategies and priorities, see Archie Brown, *The Gorbachev Factor* (Oxford: Oxford University Press, 1996), 160-211.

49. For a discussion of Gorbachev's reform of the soviets, see Urban, *More Power to the Soviets*, 21-2; and Seweryn Bialer, "The Changing Soviet Political System: The Nineteenth Party Conference and After," in *Politics, Society, and Nationality inside Gorbachev's Russia*, ed. Seweryn Bialer (Boulder, Colo.: Westview, 1989), 221.

50. James Hughes, "Sub-National Elites and Post-Communist Transformation in Russia: A Reply to Kryshtanovskaya & White," *Europe-Asia Studies* 49, no. 6 (1997):

1017-36. For a discussion of the reform discourse, see Urban, *More Power to the Soviets.* See also Brown, *Gorbachev Factor*, 195.

51. Stephen White, "Pluralism, Civil Society, and Post-Soviet Politics," in *In Search of Pluralism: Soviet and Post-Soviet Politics*, ed. Carol R. Saivetz and Anthony Jones (Boulder, Colo.: Westview, 1994), 5-26.

52. "O vsenarodnom obsujhdenii vajhnykh voprosov gosudarstvennoy jhizni," in *Svod zakonov SSSR* (Moscow: Yuridicheskaya literatura, 1987), 101.

53. "Zakon Soyuza sovetskikh sotsialisticheskikh respublik Ob obshchikh nachalakh mestnogo samoupravleniya i mestnogo khozyaystva v SSSR," *Vedomosti s'ezda narodnykh deputatov SSSR i Verkhovnogo soveta SSSR* 18 (April 1990), 4.

54. "Zakon RSFSR O mestnom samoupravlenii v RSFSR," *Vedomosti s'ezda narodnykh deputatov RSFSR i Verkhovnogo soveta RSFSR* 29, no. 18 (1991): 1166-218; "Zakon Ob obshchikh nachalakh."

55. While this jurisdiction would not last beyond 1992, after which it passed to the respective ministries of justice, it was likely to perform an important political or ideological gatekeeping function at a time when the role of the party's ideological organs was clearly at its nadir.

56. M. A. Krasnov, "Mestnoe samoupravlenie: Gosudarstvennoe ili obshchestvennoe?" *Sovetskoe gosudarstvo i pravo* 10 (1990), 82.

57. See John F. Young, "Zakonodatel'stvo Rossii po mestnomu samoupravleniyu," in *Tret'e zveno gosudarstvennogo stroitel'stva Rossii: Podgotovka i realizatsiya federal'nogo zakona Ob obshchikh printsipakh organizatsii mestnogo samoupravleniya v rossiyskoy federatsii*, ed. Kimitaka Matsuzato (Sapporo, Japan: Slavic Research Center, Hokkaido University, 1998), 118.

58. "Zakon RSFSR O mestnom samoupravlenii v RSFSR," art. 29.2.

59. See for example, "Zakon RSFSR O mestnom samoupravlenii v RSFSR," arts. 55.19 and 65.1. According to one observer, the new law, although it did represent a dawn of the new era in local self-government, at the same time carried the "birth-marks" of the totalitarian state. A. N. Kostikov cited in Young, "Zakonodatel'stvo Rossii po mestnomu samoupravleniyu," 114.

Chapter 3

Ethnosocial Contexts and Grievances

The soviets embodied the ideological postulate of "government by the people," and exemplified another crucial element of the Soviet doctrine: the "flowering of nations."[1] The USSR was a *matryoshka* doll-like federation. Its fifteen union-level republics were in turn subdivided into smaller ethnically defined entities: the autonomous republics, *oblasti* and *okruga*. These entities were lower in status than the union republics, but were nonetheless privileged enough to have enjoyed Stalin's blessing and were officially recognized in the ethnofederal hierarchy. The equivalent of the local "Supreme Soviet" was the key symbol of the titular ethnies' claim to nationhood. Although the body was formally part of local government in the autonomous *oblasti* and *okruga*, it was the highest assembly until 1990, formally combining executive, legislative, and oversight functions. The soviets below the autonomous republic *oblast'* and *okrug* level in cities, districts, towns, and village settlements were subordinate to this Supreme Soviet, while the latter itself was of course subordinate to the higher institutions above. In the Soviet period, the autonomies' Supreme Soviets, perhaps more so than the soviets of other levels, were subject to ethnic quotas privileging the titular ethnies. These quasi parliaments, which after 1990 became legislative institutions in a more meaningful sense, were in the forefront of the "parade of sovereignties." They passed declarations of sovereignty, drafted their own constitutions, and sponsored decentralist laws challenging the federal legislation. For these ethnic entities greater independence from the federal center, however, was not an end in itself. Instead, their key aim was the rapid consolidation of power *within* their territories at a time when political liberalization based on "one person, one vote" threatened to undermine the titulars' quota-based political position locally.

While the titulars controlled the main political bodies in the respective republics, this was not the case with the soviets below them, in areas of predominantly nontitular or mixed residence. In the early 1990s, the local soviets in such areas, particularly in the large urban capitals, emerged as the principal opponents of nationalizing policies. They passed declarations challenging titular nationalism; proclaimed their own miniautonomies; and lobbied Moscow to curb the excesses of the parade of sovereignties. The situation that emerged at the time could best be described as "contending institutions," with the lower-level soviets juxtaposing themselves to the nationalist autonomous republic-*oblast'* and *okrug*-level assemblies. It was a war of institutions in the sense that the respective agencies mobilized their "horizontal" resources to further or oppose nationalist agendas.

These were not merely institutional conflicts, however. The local soviets purported to act on behalf of the respective mass publics and to redress the ethnic grievances that the titulars' nationalist policies served to exacerbate. The institutionalized "ethnic homelands" bearing names of designated ethnic groups in fact embraced extremely diverse ethnic populations; the actual percentage of the titulars in most of these entities did little to legitimize their sense of "ownership" of the quasi polities.[2] In the RSFSR, on the eve of the Soviet Union's disintegration, Russians constituted a majority in twenty out of the thirty-one ethnically defined units; the titular nationalities comprised majorities in only eight, and a plurality in three, of the entities.[3] The ethnic complexity of these areas stemmed from a centuries-long record of migrations, imperial conquests, deportations, and resettlements. Stalin's grand experiment with nation building whereby autonomies were created for some groups and not others, with seemingly little regard to the actual ethnic composition of the respective entities, added another layer of complexity to the autonomies' already intricate ethnic mosaic.[4]

Since grievances represent the basic precondition for collective action, it is important to discuss in some detail the objective historical conditions—political, social, and economic—that have led to the peculiar ethnic makeup of the respective localities, and affect present-day patterns of ethnic interactions. The background facilitates understanding of ethnic mobilization in the early 1990s, but also raises questions as to the subsequent nonmobilization of groups concentrated in areas which have frequently been likened to the Balkans.

The two main cases I chose for the study could not be more "typical"—if such a word can be used to describe the extremely diverse ethnic situations—of the paths taken by Russia's ethnies, whether native or "colonizers." A glance at Russia's political map is enough to show that most of Russia's non-Russian groups are concentrated in two distinct geographic regions—the North Caucasus region in the southwest, and the Middle Volga region in west-central Russia. The history of Adygeya illustrates the fate of the North Caucasus's indigenous mountainous groups, on the one hand, and that of the nonnative settlers, mostly Russians, Cossacks, and Ukrainians, on the other. My third case, also located in the North Caucasus, North Ossetiya/Ingushetiya, illustrates the history and consequences of one of Stalin's many mass deportations, paradoxically the only case with a violent outcome, and is therefore treated in a separate chapter. An excursus into Bashkortostan's history, in turn, illuminates that of the Volga region as a whole, whose nomadic peoples had been subjected to imperial con-

Autonomous Areas in Russia

Autonomous republic
Autonomous oblast (AO)
Autonomous okrug (AOk)

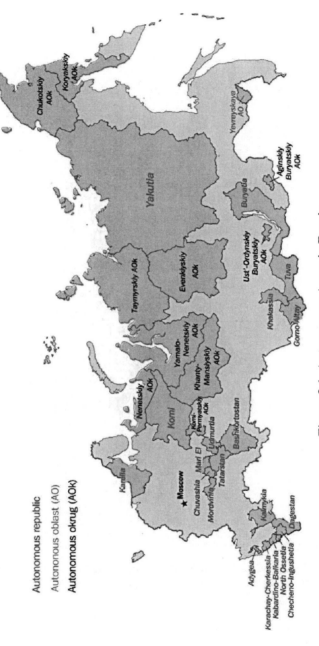

Figure 3.1. Autonomous Areas in Russia

Source: Courtesy of the General Libraries, University of Texas at Austin

Ethnolinguistic Groups in the Caucasus Region

Figure 3.2. Ethnolinguistic Groups in the Caucasus Region
Source: Courtesy of the General Libraries, University of Texas at Austin

quest even before Russia's subjugation of the area, namely by the Tatar-Mongol empire. However historically distant, these events continue to provide rich symbolic material for present-day nationalist discourse, influencing local ethnic grievances and mobilization. In this largely descriptive chapter I provide a setting for subsequent analysis. The introduction of each case is divided into several sections: a brief overview of pre-Soviet patterns of colonization and conquest of the North Caucasus and Volga areas, respectively; Soviet nationality policies and their impact on titular-nontitular interactions, social structure, and elite mobility; the republics' nationalizing policies; and, finally, the nontitular movements that these policies generated.

Adygeya

Adygeya is one of Russia's smallest republics, its territory only 7,600 square miles. It is landlocked in the "red belt's" Krasnodar *kray*, to which it was administratively subordinate as an autonomous *oblast'* until 1990. It is one of Russia's poorest entities, heavily dependent on federal transfers. Of the population of approximately 450,500 people, Russians (including Cossacks) are numerically the largest group, comprising 68 percent, while the titular Adyge make up only 22.1 percent of the local population. The remaining 10 percent of the population are Ukrainians, Armenians, and a number of other smaller ethnic groups.[5] Adyge identity is a recent creation, with the Adyge and the neighboring Kabard, Abkhas, Cherkes, Ybykh, Shapsugs, Abazins, and other groups constituting part of the larger Cherkes identity. Before the Revolution, these groups, whose settlements stretched throughout the Northwest Caucasus, were generically referred to as Circassians.[6] Adyge is a Caucasian branch of the Indo-European language. The major religion is Sunni Islam. However, while the Circassians adopted Islam and rallied around the Naqshbandi Sufi Imam Shamil in the nineteenth century,[7] they maintain many pagan customs and, unlike such areas in the North Caucasus as Chechnya and Dagestan, are known to have been less influenced by Islam.[8]

The numerical weakness of the Adyge in their own republic is the legacy of imperial Russia's Caucasian wars of the early to mid-nineteenth century. The Adyge were the last North Caucasian group to be defeated in the war in 1864,[9] during and after which four hundred thousand Circassian mountaineers, over half the entire population, fled to Turkey, whence many proceeded on to other parts of the Ottoman Empire.[10] While many subsequently returned to Russia, they shared the fate of the North Caucasus's numerous other ethnic groups, whose lands were colonized by the Cossacks.

The Cossacks, a Russian Orthodox warrior caste (*soslovie*), formerly free frontier communities largely composed of escaped serfs, had by the late eighteenth century developed a special relationship with the Russian state, and were granted lands in exchange for their military service and the protection of the expanding frontiers.[11] Although the colonization of the Caucasus by Russian and Ukrainian peasants escaping serfdom dates back to as early as the sixteenth century, the process of Russian colonization began in earnest after the conquest of the area in the nineteenth century. This trend continued throughout the Soviet period, and intensified with the Soviet Union's industrialization and collectivization drives.[12] A special campaign of the late 1920s aimed to relieve pressure from the overpopulated agricultural regions of the European parts of the USSR by utilizing the Adygeyan region's fertile lands and untapped industrial potential.[13] This resulted in a further influx of thousands of Russians and other nonnative groups, who were brought in to develop agriculture, to construct and run the new industrial facilities utilizing the republic's rich timber resources, and who ultimately settled. Industrialization was reflected in the urban-rural distribution of the titular and nontitular groups. By 1970, Adygeya's urban population was overwhelmingly Russian, comprising 84.2 percent, while the Adyge now made up a mere 6.8 percent of the *oblast*'s total urban population, although the trend did begin to reverse itself in subsequent decades.[14]

While the autonomous *oblast'* status, which Adygeya shared with Karachay-Cherkessia in the North Caucasus, was designed to provide special treatment for the culturally distinct groups within the wider Russian-speaking entities, it carried numerous disadvantages compared to the autonomous republics.[15] While not much different from other entities in the North Caucasus with higher status in terms of population and territory, such as Kabardino-Balkariya, as Adyge scholars point out, Adygeya was deprived of such trappings of higher status as a local university and think tanks, and had generally fewer institutions of learning and culture.[16]

That being said, Adygeya did not fail to be an object of Soviet ethnonational construction.[17] Even before the establishment of this and other *oblasti*, ethnic quotas became the norm and were encouraged by the RSFSR bodies bent on sovietizing the North Caucasus. For example, as the Cherkes (Adyge) *oblast'* was being created in 1922, the *oblast' ispolkom* called for "measures to 'Cherkesize' all soviet and administrative organs by drawing the Cherkes mountaineers into the process of Soviet construction, [and] to send as many as possible Cherkes mountaineers to higher educational establishments."[18]

As a low-status entity, however, subordinate to a predominantly Russian *kray*, Adygeya was at a much greater disadvantage in terms of the political situation locally. Efforts were made to ensure an ethnic balance and even an overrepresentation of the ethnic Adyge in local power structures proportionately to their numerical strength, but it was nevertheless Russian speakers who continued to dominate the local economy and political institutions, particularly in the industrial capital city of Maykop and the Maykop *rayon*. For the ethnic Adyge, the only way to advance was to acquire fluency in the Russian language. Many attended universities outside of the autonomy in places like Krasnodar and Rostov, and pursued their careers there. A case in point is Aslan Djharimov, Adygeya's first president, who studied in Krasnodar and began his career as an *apparatchik* there before he was appointed as the *oblast'* party first secretary. At the same time, fewer nontitulars felt the need to acquire fluency in the native language. For the career-minded nontitular, integration into the political elite was through the standard route, discussed in the previous chapter, rather than through knowledge of the titular language.

The above ethnosocial context notwithstanding, in the early 1990s, Adygeya embarked on perhaps one of the most ambitious nationalizing programs of all of Russia's republics. Virtually overnight, large segments of the nontitular population were institutionalized out of politics. Although the Adyge functionaries largely couched the reforms in cultural terms, their key aim was a change in the system of political representation and advancement. For the ambitious nontitular, who had enjoyed such confident positions before the 1990s, the effects were those of "suddenly imposed grievances."[19]

Adygeya declared its exit from Krasnodar *kray* in October 1990, which the latter recognized despite opposition from the Russian speakers in both Adygeya and Krasnodar.[20] Adygeya's exit meant that its policies, most notably those related to political appointments, would henceforth not be subject to Krasnodar's control. It also opened the way for the declaration of sovereignty in June 1991 and the acquisition of a higher republic status, making it institutionally equal to such powerful republics as Tatarstan and Bashkortostan. The RSFSR, which had itself inspired the parade of sovereignties in the context of Yel'tsin's struggle against Gorbachev and the Union, did little to discourage titular nationalism. It promptly recognized the above status changes and symbolic acts, and indirectly encouraged Adygeya's efforts to enhance the titular group's privileged position locally. In September 1991, the Russian Federation issued a special decree on elections to the legislature in Adygeya, which were to be held on 22 December. As a reflection of Yel'tsin's efforts to strengthen executive authority, the decree also urged simultaneous elections to the post of the new republic's chief executive.[21]

The short period allocated for the preparation of the elections fostered a sense of urgency among the native elite for ensuring Adyge predominance in the new legislature. Competitive elections had already been held in March 1990. Political liberalization threatened to further undermine the unspoken policies of affirmative action hitherto practiced with regard to Adyge representation in the *oblast'* power structures. At the same time, the RSFSR stipulation on the elections did contain an ambiguous provision allowing for the reduction of electoral districts "in areas of compact settlements of the indigenous populations."[22]

The RSFSR decree fostered a flurry of activity aimed at ensuring a guaranteed Adyge overrepresentation in the forthcoming elections. Adygeya's Supreme Soviet had already created a constitutional commission, which was to draft a new constitution, and its presidium had been working on a legislative framework for the republic's new power structures.[23] As the elections drew nearer, the constitutional commission advanced a controversial proposal for electoral redistricting. The arrangements it favored were referred to as "parity," implying a fifty-fifty distribution of seats between the Adyge on the one hand, and the non-Adyge on the other. Considering that the Adyge only comprised slightly over 22 percent of the republic's population, the proposed arrangements would have allowed for a significant overrepresentation of the Adyge in the republic legislature at the expense of nontitular groups.

The concept of parity was based on the Bolsheviks' earlier practices of drawing the various ethnic groups into the regime as the Bolsheviks were consolidating power in the Caucasus. The Bolsheviks frequently used the word "parity" in their directives on local institution building. At various periods of Soviet history parity arrangements were practiced in Karachay-Cherkessia and Kabardino-Balkaria, largely as a means to cushion the rivalries of the indigenous elites by drawing them into power-sharing arrangements. While the unspoken policy of affirmative action in Adygeya fostered a system of nominations to the Supreme Soviet whereby rural districts yielded more deputies, thus ensuring Adyge overrepresentation in proportion to its population, full parity was never institutionalized. As elsewhere in the Soviet system, a system of checks also existed in the form of Russian party secretaries who ensured a "fair" representation of the various groups, including the non-Russian nontitulars.

The collapse of the party system with its institutionalized system of ethnic checks and balances, and the carte blanche that the ethnic republics received from the RSFSR in the pursuit of nationalization, threatened to undermine the measure of ethnic consensus and the security that it created for the nontitulars. These institutional proposals were accompanied by strong nationalist rhetoric from the Adyge political elite projected through the *obkom*-controlled presses.[24]

Despite the cautionary notes that accompanied the arguments about the potential benefits of status change and sovereignty to all nationalities in Adygeya, sovereignty was widely presented as a rectificatory measure aimed at arresting the process of cultural and spiritual degradation of the Adyge, increasing the fairness in political appointments for the indigenous population, and "genuine equality" of representation in legislative bodies.

The opening paragraph of the sovereignty declaration reads: "On behalf of the multinational people of Adygeya . . . acknowledging responsibility for the *destiny of the Adyge nation*, all nationalities . . . [The session of the *oblast'* soviet] solemnly declares state sovereignty of the Soviet Socialist Republic of Adygeya" (emphasis mine).[25] The first article established the "inalienable right of the Adyge nation for self-determination" as the basis for the declaration of sovereignty.[26]

An independent Adyge nationalist organization, Adyge Hase, reinforced the nationalist rhetoric. According to Djharimov's own statements, actively supported by the *obkom*,[27] Adyge Hase became a key social spokesman for Adyge sovereignty and nation building, legitimizing the otherwise *nomenklatura*-led process. It enjoyed regular access to the *obkom* press organ, *Adygeyskaya pravda*, publishing controversial historical exposés on the nineteenth-century "genocide" of the Adyge people and maps showing indigenous settlements stretching from the Black Sea to the Caspian, and demanding radical ethnically based changes in Adygeya's institutional makeup. Adyge Hase's congresses enjoyed the attendance and support of senior party figures, including Djharimov.

The Nontitular Movement and Its Actors

The Soviets

The nationalizing policies generated a "countermovement" with a variety of actors.[28] The lower-level soviets emerged as the principal fora for debates on the pressing political issues of the day. When, in September 1990, the *oblast'* Supreme Soviet mandated the discussion of the issue of raising Adygeya's status in local soviets, it was conceived as no more than a bureaucratic formality rather than a genuine solicitation of views of the lower bodies and their constituencies. Indeed, such Soviet-style references to the need for "explanatory work," *raz'yasnitel'naya rabota*, to be carried out by the soviets, suggested their continued perception as the regime's instruments for political mobilization. This was evident from the subsequent dismissal of the results of the "discussions" on the grounds that issues of *oblast'* significance should be decided by the *oblast'* Supreme Soviet.[29] Altogether, however, out of the fifty-two soviets, seventeen, including all thirteen soviets of the mostly Russian Giaginsk *rayon*, voted against the presidium's decision to raise Adygeya's status.[30]

Although the predominantly Russian Maykop and Giaginsk *rayon* soviets ultimately voted in favor of the status change, they did so after protracted publicly aired debates and deliberations. These, despite differing opinions, fostered consensus points with regard to the matter among the mostly Russian soviets' deputies. Although many deputies justified their consent to exit with economic arguments after years of "exploitation" by Krasnodar, they expressed indignation at the apparent disregard for the lower soviets, a sentiment reinforced by the subsequent dismissal of the results of the "consultations."[31] While the Maykop city soviet opted for a "voice" within the *oblast'*, the Maykop *rayon* soviet, where Russians comprised over 84 percent of the population,[32] threatened to "exit." By a very slight majority of 50.2 percent, the soviet voted in favor of secession of the *rayon* to Krasnodar *kray*, although the decision remained at the level of a declaration.

The city of Maykop, as well as the Maykop and Giaginsk *rayon* soviets, re-emerged as the main challengers to the *oblast'* bodies on the eve of the elections to Adygeya's new legislature. The Deystvie (Action) group of the Maykop city soviet was a particularly vocal opponent of the parity proposals. Originally founded with the goal of increasing "real influence of the soviets, and the development of local self-government," it subsequently became the key focal point of opposition to the *oblast'*-led Adyge nationalism. The group's effective control over the newspaper *Maykopskie novosti* facilitated public agenda setting in juxtaposition to the increasingly nationalist *Adygeyskaya pravda*. Deystvie also actively cooperated with the burgeoning public associations, and sponsored regular meetings, "roundtable discussions" and other fora for mobilization and the influence over public opinion. On the eve of the elections, it participated in the founding of the Democratic Block, an umbrella organization uniting local soviet deputies and public associations, headquartered in the Maykop city soviet. It also actively sought federal influence over republic decision making. In one particularly effective and highly publicized instance, Deystvie was able to involve Oleg Rumyantsev, a prominent Russian liberal and one of the drafters of the federation's new constitution, in Adygeya's antinationalist cause. Rumyantsev, who visited Adygeya amidst the parity controversy and met with Maykop soviet deputies and public associations, subsequently published a large article in Moscow's daily *Nezavisimaya gazeta* likening proposed parity to a form of "apartheid." The article was duly reprinted in *Maykopskie novosti.*

In the end, the Maykop soviet and the democratic public associations allied with it proposed to engage in "mutual consultations" with the *oblast'* soviet, and to come up with a compromise solution regarding the ethnicity of the various candidates rather than agreeing on rigid institutional quotas. The *oblast'* presidium, however, insisted on ensuring a minimum 50 percent representation for the Adyge. The result of the standoff between the opposition and the *oblast'* soviet was that Adygeya's Central Electoral Commission (CEC), charged with carrying out districting, preserved virtually intact the previous electoral districts with a roughly equal number of electors.[33] Despite the pressure from the *oblast'* soviet, CEC refused to back down. One reason for CEC's decision was the success of the Maykop soviet's political campaign against institutionalized parity. A group of deputies traveled to Moscow on behalf of the Maykop soviet and the broader public to ascertain the constitutionality of the parity decision.[34]

In November 1991 an extraordinary session of the Maykop city soviet, backing its claim with the results of consultations in Moscow, declared the *oblast'* decision to declare CEC districting unconstitutional and demanded control over the election of deputies from the city to ensure they were carried out "on a democratic basis." Consequently, elections were carried out according to the existing districting, although compromises between nominating organizations did yield a roughly fifty-fifty distribution of seats between the Adyge on the one hand, and the non-Adyge deputies on the other.[35]

Significantly, the soviet chairmen in two predominantly Russian areas, the Maykop city and Maykop *rayony*, who still combined their posts with those of local party first secretaries, allied with the opposition forces, cautioning against exit, the elevation to republic status, and parity. In an address to the extraordinary session of the *oblast'* soviet, Krokhmal', the chairman of the Maykop *rayon* soviet, justifying the soviet's decision, demanded "respect for the opinions of the deputies" against the officially imposed views. "Although I support the decision of the *oblast'* soviet presidium [on the change of *oblast'* status]," he maintained, "I have certain doubts: is the population of the whole *oblast'* ready to accept it painlessly? Perhaps, as many will agree, they won't. A certain proportion of the population is intimidated by the events taking place in the country as regards interethnic relations."[36]

Lev Simatov, the chairman of the Maykop city soviet, likewise criticized the hasty sovereignty decisions and the subsequent proposals for institutional change. While leaders of Deystvie criticized him for excessive wavering when decisive action was needed, in many public statements Simatov endorsed the opposition's critique of the proposed ethnically based institution building.[37] He was one of the envoys who traveled to Moscow on behalf of the Russian speakers to lobby against the proposed parity-based elections.

Public Associations

Besides the soviets, a number of public associations emerged as voices for nontitular interests. One was the Grajhdanin (Citizen) discussion club, which was formed prior to the March 1990 elections, during which time it remained a classical "sofa" organization of the kind described in other accounts of *perestroyka*-era activism, uniting a handful of friends and relatives of the original founder. The title of the group, founded by a high school teacher, was telling in that it stressed the inclusiveness of its membership and generally civic and democratic agendas. The group enjoyed limited publicity, and had difficulty obtaining access to the one official press organ, the *obkom*'s *Adygeyskaya pravda*. Following the March elections, the group became increasingly vocal, allying itself with the Maykop soviet's democratic wing, and made regular public statements in the soviet's newly founded press organ, *Maykopskie novosti*.

In addition to Grajhdanin, several other public organizations, hitherto concerned with cultural issues or specifically founded to counter Adyge nationalism, became active. The years 1990-1991 saw the emergence of various Cossack associations.[38] At first stressing the rebirth of the Cossack cultural legacy and traditions, these organizations became actively engaged in the political process, staging demonstrations against the sovereignty declaration and the proposed constitution.[39] Civic-minded associations joined the nationalist fray. Grajhdanin moved to the right, from the more moderate focus on democracy and human rights, to championing the cause of Adygeya's nontitulars. It became one of the founding organizations of the Union of Slavs of Adygeya, established in September 1991 at the height of the controversy over electoral districting. The founding conference boasted over 400 delegates. Blessed by a Russian Orthodox priest, attended by Cossacks in traditional attire, and featuring speeches about the need to protect the *oblast*'s Slavic populations, the conference symbolized the deepening of the political cleavage between the titular group on the one hand, and the *oblast*'s Slavic populations on the other.[40]

Summary

Between September 1990 and the December 1991 elections, which witnessed a peak of public activism, one can speak of a movement uniting a number of actors. The soviets in the areas of nontitular concentration, such as Maykop city, as well as Maykop and Giaginsk *rayony*, emerged early in the process as a political force with the potential to shape public opinion thanks to the press access they enjoyed and to the *oblast'* body's recognition of a measure of legitimacy of these institutions in shaping policy outcomes. To a certain degree, the soviet chairs backed these bodies. Their cautious pronouncements against sovereignty spoke of an unprecedented willingness to challenge republic-level party and soviet bodies. Within the soviets, a core of more radical deputies emerged, such as the Deystvie faction in the Maykop city soviet. These deputies acted in tandem with the social actors, the public associations that sprung up at the time of the controversial debates on Adygeya's status and institutional change. While they failed to prevent the adoption of the declarations concerning status and sovereignty, together these actors were successful in temporarily blocking parity in December 1991, a potentially major institutional change that would have significantly underrepresented the nontitulars in the republic's legislature. The respective roles of the various actors in affecting movement outcomes will be discussed in the following chapter. The next section introduces the republic of Bashkortostan and provides an account of the nontitular movement there, which broadly paralleled that in Adygeya in terms of the key movement actors and their strategies.

Bashkortostan

The Republic of Bashkortostan is located at the junction of the Urals and Volga, Povoljh'e geographic regions. Russia's most populous republic, it is also one of the wealthiest in terms of natural resources, most notably petrochemicals. Russians comprise 39.9 percent of the population of over four million, with Tatars and Bashkirs making up 28.4 and 21.9 percent, respectively. The remaining population consists largely of the Chuvash, Mariy, and Ukrainians.[41] The titular Bashkirs profess Sunni Islam, although, as in Adygeya, while reinforcing their identity vis-à-vis the Slavic settlers and conquerors, it has never taken a very strong hold on the population. Created in 1919, the Bashkir Autonomous Soviet Republic began as a much smaller territory, referred to as Malaya Bashkiriya, Lesser or Little Bashkiriya, the southern part of contemporary Bashkortostan. Its capital was in the formerly Ufa *guberniya* (region) town of Sterlitamak. At the time of the secession of the whole of Ufa *guberniya* to the republic in 1922, Bashkortostan acquired the largely Russian-populated Ufa as its capital, as well as the areas of ethnic Tatar concentration in the north. The establishment of Bashkortostan as a separate administrative entity with borders that did not even roughly correspond to the ethnic distribution within it reflected the diversity of Bashortostan's ethnic makeup, as well as political expediencies of both the Bolsheviks and the native nationalist leaders.

The Middle Volga, distinct from the Upper and Lower Volga areas, is one of Russia's most ethnically diverse areas, next only to the North Caucasus, with interspersed settlements of speakers of three distinct language groups, Finno-Ugric, Turkic, and Slavic.[42] The Bashkirs are a Turkic group. Their Turkic or Uralic ancestors settled in the Southern Urals around the ninth to tenth centuries.[43] The Tatars and Chuvash are other distinct Turkic groups in the Middle Volga area. The Finno-Ugric groups include the Mariy, Udmurts, and Mordvinians. The Slavic community is largely Russian, but there are sizeable Ukrainian and Belorussian populations.[44]

The Bashkirs were nomadic with no record of independent statehood, which made them vulnerable to cultural, religious, and linguistic influences by the region's sedentary and politically dominant groups, most notably the Volga Bulgars. In 1236, the Golden Horde conquered the Bashkir tribes. The Tatar Mongol conquerors, ethnically descendant from Turkic, Mongol, and other Siberian groups, had a policy of religious and cultural tolerance, adopting Islam and cultural practices from the Volga Bulgars.[45] While the Golden Horde did not practice a policy of assimilation, Tatar cultural and political dominance, combined with the spread of Islam, fostered a Tatarization of the smaller nomadic communities within the Tatar-Mongol state.[46]

This trend did not end with the Russian conquest of Kazan in 1552, following which the Bashkirs voluntarily joined the Russian state in 1557, signing treaties to that effect.[47] In fact, Tatarization of the Middle Volga intensified under Catherine the Great in the late eighteenth century. Catherine and her successors believed in religious tolerance, especially for Islam. Moreover, they relied on Tatar administrators and educators to maintain Russian control of the area, and encourage the nomads to settle.[48] By the time of the Bolshevik Revolution, over a third of Bashkirs claimed Tatar as their native tongue.[49] As I will discuss later, this factor complicated relations between the two ethnically close groups through the centuries.

While the Middle Volga had already become a destination for Slav peasants escaping serfdom, the fall of Kazan brought a hitherto unprecedented influx of Russian settlers, a trend which increased in the Tsarist and Soviet periods.[50] In fact, the Bolsheviks' administrative policies further increased the proportion of the republic's non-Bashkir populations, Slavic and otherwise. Bashkortostan, as has already been noted, had originally been a much smaller entity, with a proportionally larger Bashkir population: Lesser Bashkiriya included only the Southern Urals' southern and southeastern parts of what is now Bashkortostan.

While some Bashkir leaders advocated alliance with the Tatars in striving for the larger entity and proposed a Volga-Urals state or joint Tatar-Bashkir republic,[51] such a policy was not favored by Akhmed Zaki Validi, a Bashkir nationalist leader and key proponent of a separate polity. It is with him that the Bolsheviks chose to deal, reaching an agreement in 1919 which created what ultimately became the RSFSR's first republic, the Bashkir Autonomous Soviet Republic. The new entity, however, was a backwater, a largely rural and heavily forested area with virtually no urban settlements. The capital city was a small provincial town. Efforts to root Soviet power in Bashkortostan were hampered by its slow economy, but were progressing much faster in the urbanized neighboring Ufa *guberniya*. The Bolsheviks decided to merge the two areas together.[52] Politically and economically, this merger was a significant gain for the Bashkirs. In addition to acquiring developed cities, such as Ufa, they also gained the two mostly Tatar Belebeevskiy and Birskiy *uezdy* (districts). There were supposed to be plebiscites held among the populations of these districts, blocked by the new Bashkir leaders, as to whether they wanted to remain part of Bashkiriya or join the newly created Tatar republic. Since the plebiscites never happened, relations between the two Turkic groups became further strained.[53] The merger resulted in a greater ethnic imbalance, with Russians comprising 40 percent, and Tatars and Bashkirs approximately 25 percent each in Greater Bashkiriya.[54]

As in Adygeya, the urban-rural divide compounded the ethnic cleavage between the various groups throughout much of the Soviet period. By 1989, the Bashkir Autonomous Soviet Socialist Republic (BASSR) had the smallest percentage (7.9) of titular urban dwellers compared to the other republics.[55] As Bashkortostan is one of Russia's more developed industrial centers, with much of the industry concentrated in Ufa and its environs, with blue- and white-collar workers drawn from the Russian populations, with some exceptions, the cities were largely Russian speaking. By the late 1950s only one of every twenty Ufa city dwellers was a Bashkir.[56] The trend only began to reverse in the 1960s when growth rates of the Bashkir populations in the cities and their migration to urban centers exceeded those of the Russian speakers. Even in 1989, however, Ufa, with 54.2 percent Russians,[57] was one of only three autonomous republic capitals, the other two being Kazan and Groznyy, where Russians were still a majority, albeit a slight one.[58]

As with the other titular ethnies, the Bashkirs of course did benefit from the standard package designed for the promotion of titular ethnies. Autonomous republic status entitled Bashkortostan to higher-learning institutions, think tanks, and better facilities for native language instruction. Although by the 1970s, Russian language instruction was increasingly squeezing out native languages in urban schools, Bashkortostan was one of two republics in Russia with several schools maintaining titular language instruction from the first to the last grade.[59] In addition, ethnic quotas were put in place to ensure Bashkir representation and advancement in the party and soviet bodies.

By 1990, Bashkirs occupied almost 45 percent of the *rayon* and city-level "prefectorial" and *ispolkom* chair posts within the republic, compared to the Russians' roughly 30-plus percent, and the Tatars' not quite 20 percent.[60] The pre-1990 Supreme Soviet had 40.3 percent Bashkirs, significantly overrepresenting the titular group at the expense of the other two largest groups, in proportion to its total population.[61]

Despite the prima facie privileged position of the titular group, the two other largest groups, the Russian speakers and Tatars, had integrated well, and in some areas enjoyed predominance. Russians continued to dominate industry, mostly concentrated in the capital city, Ufa. The Tatars had always enjoyed a cultural predominance in the region over the other native groups, hence their high educational and professional achievements in the Soviet period. The rate of Tatar representation in the political structures and in other spheres is actually substantially higher than the official figures cited above suggest.

The Bashkirs' status as titulars encouraged many Tatar speakers to take up Bashkir nationality in their passports, and ensure that their children did the same. The result was a significant percentage of what became known as "paper Bashkirs," privately maintaining Tatar identities, but officially listed as Bashkir. While the Tatars blamed them for the resulting "Bashkirization," the Bashkirs argued that in fact these assumed official identities served to perpetuate centuries' long Tatarization; the Tatars, they alleged, continued to dominate in the republic under an assumed Bashkir identity. In areas of predominantly Tatar concentration in the northwest of Bashkortostan, they pointed out that an opposite trend had been observed in the 1960s and 1970s, when (mostly Tatar) heads of administrations encouraged Tatar-speakers who maintained Bashkir identities to assume "paper" Tatar nationality.[62]

Thus, Bashkortostan, despite its higher status in the Soviet ethnofederal hierarchy compared to Adygeya, was broadly similar to the Caucasian republic in a number of respects. First, the titular group in both the entities was at a significant numerical disadvantage, slightly over 20 percent, compared to the nontitulars. Second, despite the Bolsheviks' efforts at modernization, the titular groups remained culturally subordinate to the larger nontitulars, the Russians and, in the case of Bashkortostan, Tatars. Russian remained the lingua franca, the language of advancement here and in Adygeya. Tatar, a regional lingua franca in Bashkortostan before the Revolution, maintained its status as the language of the Turkic intelligentsia. Both languages had greater status thanks to their rich literary heritage. Finally, despite a growing trend of urbanization among Bashkirs, Russian speakers continued to predominate in the cities, particularly in the capitals, occupying positions of power and influence within the urban political, managerial, and educational hierarchies. Despite republic-level political structures being overrepresented by the titular group, the Soviet cadre policy ensured continued entry and integration of the other groups into the political establishment. As in Adygeya, in Bashkortostan this situation would begin to change substantially in 1990.

Following on the heels of Tatarstan, Bashkortostan advocated that year a radical decentralist line vis-à-vis the center. It was in Bashkortostan that Yel'tsin famously uttered, "Take as much sovereignty as you can swallow,"[63] which the republic did, adopting a sovereignty declaration in October 1990, and enacting a number of legal and institutional changes to substantiate it. Invoking the defunct 1919 "treaty" with the Bolshevik state, the Bashkir Supreme Soviet also advocated treaty-based relations with Moscow, as well as the supremacy of Bashkir laws over federal ones. Bashkortostan became the only republic to sign the Federal Treaty with a special clause recognizing the republic as a subject of international and foreign economic relations and its right to determine the issues of budget and taxation, to establish its own legislation and judiciary.[64] Despite the nontitulars' widespread criticism of the various draft declarations presented for "public discussion," the final version of the sovereignty declaration preserved some of the more criticized initial provisions. These included a statement to the effect of the supremacy of Bashkir laws over federal ones, and a stress on the

Bashkir nation as the primary bearer of sovereignty within the republic. In particular, the final version contained a preamble recognizing the "inalienable right of the Bashkir nation to self-determination." Similar provisions appeared in the drafts of the new constitution proposed the same year.[65]

A more controversial proposal concerned the official status of the republic's languages. Bashkir appeared as the sole official language in a draft of the sovereignty declaration, Russian having been demoted to a language of "international communication."[66] Although the final draft declaration of state sovereignty did not refer to any official languages, the Supreme Soviet once again placed the issue on the agenda in 1991. The draft language law, prepared over 1991-1992, stipulated: "Bashkir is the state language of the republic of Bashkortostan as the language of the people, which . . . is compactly residing on this territory as a separate ethnie and which gave the name to this republic."[67] While Russian would be the second official language, the elevation of Bashkir to the status of state language made this fact irrelevant considering that few Russian speakers were fluent in Bashkir and therefore would not be eligible for public office. Not only did the law implicitly mandate fluency in Bashkir as a criterion for eligibility for office, but it also made no mention of Tatar as a possible third official language, a fact seized upon by Tatar nationalist groups as an insult. Unlike the sovereignty declaration and the emotionally charged struggle over the definition of the republic's political symbols, the language provisions had immediate implications for Bashkortostan's population. According to the 1989 census, 78.5 percent of Bashkirs and 83 percent of Tatars were fluent in Russian. Conversely, a mere 0.1 percent of ethnic Russians claimed to be bilingual in Russian and Bashkir four years later, while 2.6 percent of Tatars claimed equal fluency in Bashkir and Tatar.[68] The law would have excluded the majority of the republic's population from eligibility for public office. In this respect, the draft language legislation was similar to Adygeya's proposed legislative parity arrangements.

As in Adygeya, the nationalist rhetoric surrounding titular reforms further intensified the already emotionally charged political atmosphere. While arguing the economic rationale for sovereignty, the Bashkir *nomenklatura* actively sponsored and courted radical Bashkir nationalist opposition groups, such as the Bashkir National Center, Bashkirskiy natsional'nyy tsentr (BNTs), reinforcing the nationalist aspects of the sovereignty process. Legislative sessions debating sovereignty and the Federal Treaty were picketed by hundreds of Bashkir villagers, brought to the capital on public buses, and chanting radical nationalist slogans. As a result, despite the Supreme Soviet's denial of sponsorship of the nationalist opposition, advocacy of sovereignty became linked with aggressive Bashkir nationalism calling for the Bashkirization of appointments, education, and culture.

The nationalist reforms and rhetoric generated a "countermovement" uniting both Russian and Tatar groups.[69] Its activities spanned both the Ufa capital and the peripheral Tatar localities; its actors included public associations, democratic umbrella organizations, soviet deputies, and the press. Although, as in Adygeya, the movement was short-lived, it boasted significant gains from the republic establishment. While it could not curb the adoption of a sovereignty declaration institutionalizing Bashkir predominance locally on a symbolic level, the movement has taken credit for blocking the most substantial tangible tool for curbing or expanding political advancement, namely, the language law.

The Nontitular Movement and Its Actors

The Soviets

As in Adygeya, the Bashkortostan soviets below the level of republic in areas of predominantly Russian and Tatar residence became the principal contestants of the nationalizing projects. Here too, the liberal urban administrative center led the process. Between March 1990 and 1992 the Ufa soviet emerged as the most vocal critic of the Bashkir Supreme Soviet, especially of the sovereignty declaration and proposed language legislation. Shortly after the elections, the soviet sought to define its identity in juxtaposition to the higher body along a number of dimensions. While the Ufa soviet was arguably more democratic, the Supreme Soviet, it was alleged, was packed with old-style *nomenklatura*. The Ufa soviet was "the conscience of the city," while the Supreme Soviet was a "bastion of reaction." When Bashkortostan joined the "parade of sovereignties," the Ufa soviet increasingly became identified with the "antisovereignist" cause, while the republic presidium and the Supreme Soviet were conversely associated with support for greater sovereignty from Russia.

Internal mobilization, initially manifested in the form of isolated statements by individual Ufa soviet deputies using their prerogative of "voice" in the soviet newspaper *Vechernyaya Ufa* (*VU*), progressed to include first a small group of deputies, and then majorities sufficient to back the soviet's statements and actions against the republic bodies. Anecdotal evidence of the intensity of the institutional opposition may be found in the republic leadership's criticism of the Ufa soviet's stand as "the war of the Ufa soviet" or "Ufa city authorities' crusade"[70] against Bashkir sovereignty and related legislation.

The soviet linked the issue of sovereignty with potential consequences for the nontitular populations and the discriminatory language and other legislation that had already come up on the agenda. "The next step after adopting the declaration of sovereignty," warned a soviet deputy in a *VU* editorial "will be the adoption of a constitution, then, as the Baltic experience shows, a citizenship law, the law on state languages. . . . That, in turn, will raise the question of whom to consider the citizens of a new Bashkiriya: those who were born here, those who lived before the union with Russia, or the Bashkirs?"[71]

Shortly after the publication of the draft sovereignty declarations, the soviet held a special session to discuss the document. Lacking "sufficient arguments for the declaration," the majority of the deputies voted to adopt an official "Decision."[72] The "Decision" questioned, among other things, those provisions of the declaration deemed inappropriate given the "peculiar ethnic composition" in the republic.[73]

An open letter addressed to Yel'tsin, entitled "Who Needs a Union Status?" with forty deputies as signatories, was featured in *VU*. "In reality," the statement read, "the concern is not for the good of the people, but for the former elite and that part of it which will shortly be made redundant."[74] Similar motions were subsequently passed in some of the other lower soviets, such as the Oktyabr'skiy *rayon* soviet, whose deputies overwhelmingly deemed the change of Bashkortostan's status "inappropriate." Between October 1990 and early 1991, both the Ufa and Oktyabr'skiy *rayon* soviets, challenging the republic Supreme Soviet's right to legislate on Bashkirya's status, called for popular referenda on sovereignty.[75]

The Ufa soviet also used its prerogatives to challenge specifically the proposed language law. Numerous statements against the law appeared in *Vechernyaya Ufa*. In addition, the soviet's deputies actively lobbied the Supreme Soviet in an effort to block the law in its proposed form. Since Ufa deputies were entitled to attend the sessions of the Bashkir Supreme Soviet, groups of activist deputies would be delegated from the soviet to attend discussions of the language law. Murtaza Rakhimov, the Supreme Soviet chair, attempted to obstruct their input at one point during deliberations.

While they had been assured of the right to make a statement before the session, the agenda was subsequently altered, preventing them from coming to the floor. A note was sent to Rakhimov: the deputies threatened to stage a walkout in full view of the media present in the hall. Threats to hold referenda and demonstrative pressure tactics allowed the soviet subsequently to take credit for shelving the language legislation.

As in Adygeya, much of the soviet engagement with these issues was carried out by a group of activist deputies. They represented a minority of the soviet body, but managed to get enough votes for several initiatives and statements. These statements were frequently endorsed by the soviet chairman, Mikhail Zaytsev, giving them weight. While Zaytsev was required by the soviet statute to sign any motions passed by a majority of deputies, he also issued mild criticism of his own on the language legislation. More often, however, he took no active role and was silent on the controversial nationalizing legislation.

Public Associations

The Ufa and other opposition soviets fought the antisovereignty battle on the pages of their respective press organs, in the soviet meeting halls, and the Bashkir Supreme Soviet, to which they had access as "observers." They also sought to use the legitimate institutionalized channels of soliciting public opinion and involvement, like referenda. In contrast, the independent public associations rallied people on the streets, in the "palaces of culture," and at protest demonstrations. At the same time, they enjoyed access to official agencies like the Ufa soviet sessions and its press organ, *Vechernyaya Ufa.*

The main public spokesman for Tatar interests was the Tatar Public Center, Tatarskiy obschchestvennyy tsentr (TOTs). Founded in 1988 by an Ufa think tank affiliate, Kerim Yaushev, it was not very active or important until 1990, when it finally obtained official registration. At the height of its success, in 1990-1991, it claimed hundreds of members, although public associations throughout Russia then tended to exaggerate their memberships, and there is no reason to suggest that TOTs did not do the same. It also boasted representation throughout the Tatar areas of the republic and in Ufa, in addition to the group of Ufa-based activists.

The center's statements in defense of Tatar rights appeared frequently in *VU.* It held a number of congresses and protest acts against the proposed language law and other expressions of "Bashkirization" both in the capital city and the western and northwestern areas of the republic bordering on Tatarstan. In June 1990, a TOTs Kurultay (Congress) with delegates from around the republic and from neighboring Tatarstan called for the "equality of all peoples of the republic of Bashkortostan."

During Yel'tsin's summer visit to the republic that year, TOTs appealed to him against Bashkiriya's sovereignty in its proposed form. A special plenary meeting strongly came out against sovereignty for just one, Bashkir, nation. TOTs also called for a Tatar national autonomy and equality of language status and, together with the Ufa soviet, urged a referendum on sovereignty. When the Bashkir Supreme Soviet debated the sovereignty declaration, TOTs staged a protest demonstration outside the Supreme Soviet building, bringing people from all over the republic. These mass acts and public opinion framing allowed it, too, to take credit for the subsequent shelving of the language law. When asked about the greatest achievement of the Tatar Public Center, a TOTs activist maintained, "When they say: What is your biggest success, I say: We [TOTs] did not allow the Tatar language to die."[76]

The Russian speakers lacked an ethnically based organization until early 1992, when the public association Rus' was established. Founded by Alexander Arinin, a former *obkom* secretary for ideology, who was also a university professor, its original aims included the preservation of the republic's Slavic heritage and culture. It did not take very long, however, for Rus' to reorient itself to political aims.

Rus' and TOTs became allies in the movement against the language law, coming out with joint public statements and staging protests together. Both of these organizations participated in the Congress of Democratic Forces, a movement uniting Ufa soviet deputies and a number of democratically oriented public associations. Rus' claimed memberships and cells in both the capital and the other cities with a significant Russian presence. When Arinin ran for the Bashkir Supreme Soviet elections in 1992, he claimed to represent the disaffected Russian speakers and campaigned for nontitular rights.

Summary

Between 1990 and 1992, we identify a number of local agencies opposed to Bashkir sovereignty and language legislation. Whatever their actual influence on public opinion and levels of mass mobilization, these actors made regular public appearances and statements establishing themselves as "the opposition movement." The fact that their statements appeared in the Ufa soviet's daily *Vechernyaya Ufa* served to confer "legitimacy" upon them and provided them with regular exposure. One group of actors were the soviet deputies in the capital city of Ufa, as well as those in the lower-level soviets of the city boroughs and soviets in areas of ethnic Tatar concentration. The Ufa city soviet chair, Zaytsev, who frequently appeared as a signatory to the Ufa soviet statements, was in this group of council officials, although his position seems to have been ambivalent. These actors further legitimized their position with references to the opinions of public associations and the wider publics. The Ufa soviet claimed to be the "conscience of the city," and cited the opinions expressed at the enterprises of its deputies' constituencies. TOTs and Rus' claimed the support of scores of Russian and Tatar speakers, respectively, throughout the republic. Although these organizations acted together with the councils and used each other's backing to validate their claims, they took separate credit for the ultimate achievement of movement goals.

Conclusion

Imperial conquest, migrations, and Soviet nationalities policies produced a peculiar composition in Russia's ethnically defined republics: the titular groups, often at a numerical disadvantage, nevertheless enjoyed symbolic and substantive privileges locally. In the Soviet period, however, a system of checks existed on the policies of "nativization" or "indigenization," a system made possible by the *nomenklatura* method of appointments. The titulars, the ethnic Russians, and the other nontitulars could therefore take the standard route into the political elite discussed in the previous chapter, through the local party organs and the soviets. The onset of nationalizing policies in the republics caught the nontitulars by surprise. Indigenization would now be pursued unchecked; it was to be institutionalized in republic legislation, its message reinforced by the nationalist rhetoric of the titular groups. These republic-specific developments only compounded the changes already occurring in the hitherto standard routes of career advancement, such as the collapse of the party system, reinforcing the grievances of the nontitular groups. It is not surprising, then, that nontitular movements emerged to challenge the nationalizing policies. The preceding discussion of the movements raises two sets of questions. The first concerns the respective role of the social versus institutional agencies in fostering or constraining mobilization. The second set of questions is related to the variable role of the respective agencies in the choice of movement strategies ultimately affecting movement outcomes. These questions are examined in the following chapter.

Notes

1. The key canons of the policy were the promotion of the indigenous cadre, in something resembling affirmative action, and the development and promotion of titular cultures and languages, while also encouraging bilingualism and Russification. For an overview of the Soviet nationality policies, see Viktor Zaslavsky, "Successes and Collapse: Traditional Soviet Nationlities Policy," in *Nations and Politics in the Soviet Successor States*, ed. Ian Bremmer and Ray Taras (Cambridge: Cambridge University Press, 1993), 29-42; Henry Huttenbach, ed., *Soviet Nationality Policies: Ruling Ethnic Groups in the USSR* (London: Mansell, 1990); Rachel Denber, ed., *The Soviet Nationality Reader: The Disintegration in Context* (Boulder, Colo.: Westview, 1992); Robert J. Kaiser, *The Geography of Nationalism in Russia and the USSR* (Princeton, N.J.: Princeton University Press, 1994); Ronald Gregor Suny, *The Revenge of the Past: Nationalism, Revolution, and the Collapse of the Soviet Union* (Stanford, Calif.: Stanford University Press, 1993); and Paul Kolstoe, *Russians in the Former Soviet Republics* (London: Hurst, 1995), 71-104. On language policies in the USSR, see Simon Crisp, "Soviet Language Planning," in *Language Planning in the Soviet Union*, ed. Michael Kirkwood (London: Macmillan, 1989), 23-45; Michael Kirkwood, ed., *Language Planning in the Soviet Union* (London: Macmillan, 1989); and Barbara A. Anderson and Brian D. Silver, "Equality, Efficiency, and Politics in Soviet Bilingual Education Policy, 1934-1980," *American Political Science Review* 78, no. 4 (1984): 1019-39. For a discussion of the affirmative action policies and their results, see Valery Tishkov, *Ethnicity, Nationalism and Conflict in and after the Soviet Union: The Mind Aflame* (London: Sage, 1997); and Kaiser, *Geography of Nationalism*, 243. For a discussion of ethnic competition in the context of modernization in the USSR, see Teresa Rakowska-Harmstrone, "Minority Nationalism Today: An Overview," in *The Last Empire: The Nationality and the Soviet Future*, ed. Robert Conquest (Stanford, Calif.: Hoover Institution Press, 1986), 235-64; Kaiser, *Geography of Nationalism*, 257; Tishkov, *Ethnicity*, 86; John H. Miller, "Cadres Policy in Nationality Areas: Recruitment of CPSU First and Second Secretaries in Non-Russian Republics of the USSR," *Soviet Studies* 29, no. 1 (1977): 3-36, 110; and Philip Roeder, "Soviet Federalism and Ethnic Mobilization," *World Politics* 43, no. 2 (1991): 196-232.

2. This is not to deny, however, that ethnic predominance of the titular groups played a strong role in border delimitation, although many scholars believe that the Bolsheviks were guided by "divide and rule" logic. For the "divide and rule" argument, see, for example, Aleksey Zverev, "Etnicheskie konflikty na Kavkaze, 1988-1994" in *Spornye granitsy na kavkaze*, ed. Bruno Koppieters (Moscow: Ves' mir, 1996), 69; Walker Connor, *The National Question in Marxist-Leninist Theory and Strategy* (Princeton, N.J.: Princeton University Press, 1984), 304; and Robert Conquest, *The Nation Killers* (London: Sphere, 1972), 43-44. For an alternative view, see Lee Schwartz, "Regional Population Redistribution and National Homelands in the USSR," in *Soviet Nationalities Policies: Ruling Ethnic Groups in the USSR*, ed. Henry Huttenbach (London: Mansell, 1990), 134-7; Kaiser, *Geography of Nationalism*, 111-2; and Kolstoe, *Russians*, 79. Schwartz wrote, for example: "The nationality jurisdictions were planned to include, within the borders of a single uninterrupted landmass, as much of an ethnic group's homogenous union-wide population as was feasible" ("Regional Population," 134). It appears that the

dispersed nature of ethnic settlements, considering Russian migrations even before the Revolution, would make precision impossible in such an undertaking, if it is at all possible elsewhere.

3. Richard Sakwa, *Russian Politics and Society* (London: Routledge, 1991), 177.

4. It is also worth noting that the intensity with which indigenization was pursued and the social position of the various ethnic groups varied according to the status that these units occupied within the Soviet ethnofederal hierarchy, a factor which continues to impact upon present-day interethnic relations in these entities. In addition to the USSR's failure to grant the RSFSR's constituent autonomies the right to secede, they were denied a number of other advantages that the Union entities enjoyed. These ranged from fewer opportunities for native cultural and linguistic development, to a lower intensity of the pursuit of local affirmative action. Titular language training is a case in point. Robert Kaiser wrote: "Below the union republics, the members of most national communities with autonomous republics, oblasti, and okruga had significantly fewer opportunities to study in their native languages" (*Geography*, 257). According to Valery Tishkov, by the 1970s there were only two autonomous republics in the RSFSR where native instruction went from first through tenth grades. Even in Tatarstan, a republic that had almost gained Union status in the early Soviet period, by 1978, only one "national Tatar" high school existed in Kazan (*Ethnicity*, 86).

5. Michael McFaul, and Nikolay Petrov, eds, *Politicheskiy al'manakh Rossii 1997*, vol. 2 (Moscow: Moscow Carnegie Center, 1998).

6. These tribal divisions within the more generic identity are now reflected in the Adyge flag, which has twelve stars on it representing the major Cherkes tribes. On the history of the Adyge peoples, languages, and tribal distinctions, see Yu. D. Anchabadze and N. G. Volkova, *Narody Kavkaza* (Moscow: Rossiyskaya akademiya nauk, Institut etnologii i antropologii, 1993).

7. The Muridist religious movement originated in the 1820s in Dagestan. United by the spiritual leader Kazi Mulla, it rallied the mountaineers and the Caucasus land-owning elite against the Russian policy of the confiscation and transfer of land to the Cossacks. Kazi Mulla was succeeded by Shamil, who was only defeated in 1859, after years of resistance to Russia. He was then introduced to the court in St. Petersburg, and later allowed to live in the city of Kaluga until his trip to Mecca in 1871, during which he died (Hugh Seton-Watson, *The Russian Empire: 1801-1917* [Oxford: Clarendon, 1967], 290-417).

8. The fact that even in the 1990s Adygeya virtually lacked indigenous Muslim clergy testifies to this assertion (N. D. Pchelintseva and L. V. Samarina, *Sovremennaya etnopoliticheskaya i etnokul'turnaya situatsiya v Respublike Adygeya*, Issledovaniya po prikladnoy i neotlojhnoy etnologii, vol. 47 [Moscow: Rossiyskaya akademiya nauk, Institut etnologii i antropologii, 1993], 12). A scholar of Islam notes that in fact, while the Arabs first introduced Islam in the Caucasus in the seventh century, and it was subsequently spread by the Golden Horde in the twelfth and thirteenth centuries, and later, by the Ottomans, in the sixteenth and seventeenth centuries, it maintained weak hold on most of the local populations even in the early nineteenth century, affecting the elites, but not the mostly animist common people (Ira Lapidus, *A History of Islamic Societies* [Cambridge: Cambridge University Press, 1993], 815). Another scholar notes the facts of resistance of the khans, or local princes, who felt a threat to their rule, and the village elders, as well as ordinary populations, who regarded the spread of Islamic order as an encroachment on the traditional customs and legal systems, or *adat*. Shamil's success is attributed less to the locals' Islamic fervor than to their reaction against the Russian Ge-

neral Yermolov's brutality (Semyon Esadze, *Istoricheskaya zapiska ob upravlenii Kavkazom*, vol. 1 [Tiflis, Georgia: Guttenberg, 1907], 36, 40).

9 Chechnya, notably, was the second last to be defeated, in 1859 (S. I. Bruk and Valery Tishkov, "Rossiya: Formirovanie territorii gosudarstva," in *Narody Rossii: Entsiklopediya*, ed. Valery Tishkov [Moscow: Nauchnoe izdatel'stvo Bol'shaya rossiyskaya entsiklopediya, 1994], 14).

10. While the Circassians were not forced to leave, many refused to resettle to the areas on the plains assigned to them by the Russians; they preferred the second option of immigrating to Turkey by the deadline of 1864, within a period of only two and a half months (Seton-Watson, *The Russian Empire*, 417). The North Caucasus mountaineers were in the state category of *inorodtsy*; like Jews and most of the empire's nomadic groups, they were allowed to maintain their own legal systems and self-rule. Should they settle on land, their status changed to that of regular Russian subjects. Richard Pipes notes that because of this, the nomadic peoples were generally treated with greater respect (Richard Pipes, *The Formation of the Soviet Union* [Cambridge, Mass.: Harvard University Press, 1964], 6).

11. Their role increased in the context of Catherine the Great and her successors' conquests of the strategically important areas between the Black and Caspian seas. For a general account of Russia's expansion in the South, see Nicholas V. Riasanovsky, *A History of Russia*, 5th ed. (Oxford: Oxford University Press, 1993), 263-389; Seton-Watson, *The Russian Empire*, 290-417; and Michael Rywkin, *Moscow's Lost Empire* (Armonk, N.J.: Sharpe, 1994), 42-5. For an account of Russian incorporation and modes of administration of the North Caucasus, see Esadze, *Istoricheskaya zapiska.*

12. This process followed the establishment of the first diplomatic relations and a Russian military presence, after the marriage of Ivan the Terrible to a Kabardian princess. On the history of diplomatic relations with the North Caucasus peoples, see G. A. Kokiev, "Snosheniya Rossii s narodami severnogo Kavkaza," in *Iz istorii vzaimootnosheniy Dagestana s Rossiey i s narodami Kavkaza* (Makhachkala: Dagestanskiy filial Akademii nauk SSSR, 1982). In time, the North Caucasus became one of the most favored destinations, with 22.8 percent of all of Russia's settlers choosing the area by the late nineteenth and early twentieth centuries. See Bruk and Tishkov, "Rossiya: Formirovanie territorii gosudarstva," 60.

13. E. A. Zuykina, "K voprosu o russkikh v sisteme mejhnatsional'nykh otnosheniy na severnom Kavkaze," in *Severnyy Kavkaz: Vybor puti natsional'nogo razvitiya*, ed. N. F. Bugay (Maykop, Russia: Meoty, 1994), 127-39.

14. B. N. Kazantsev, "Severnyy Kavkaz: Sotsial'no-demograficheskie problemy gorodskogo naseleniya, pyatidesyatye-shestidesyatye gody," in *Severnyy Kavkaz*, 219-35, 225; Pchelintseva and Samarina, *Sovremennaya*, 1.

15. While the Adyge were fortunate to escape the fate of some of the other North Caucasus groups who were deported in 1944—Stalin reportedly having said, "The Caucasus without the Adyge is not the Caucasus—they shared the experience of numerous administrative changes in their status. This in turn reflected the settlement patterns of the Adyge resulting from Russian colonization of the area, and efforts to create or reinforce ethnic identities of the respective groups. Adygeya started in 1922 as a Cherkes (Adyge) autonomous *oblast'*, was later renamed into the Adyge (Cherkes) republic, and in 1928 into the Adyge republic. Between 1922 and 1924 it was an administrative entity directly subordinate to the USSR. It was then part of the North Caucasus *kray* until 1934, Chernomorskiy *kray* until 1937, and Krasnodar *kray* until its declaration of sovereignty in 1991. The current capital city Maykop, the Maykop *rayon*, and the mostly Russian-speaking Giaginsk administrative *rayon* were initially made administratively part of

Krasnodar *kray*, and were only added to Adygeya in 1936 and 1962, respectively (McFaul and Petrov, eds., *Politicheskiy a;'manakh Rossii 1997*, 66).

16. The original all-Russia Central Executive Committee, Vserossiyskiy tsentral'nyy ispolnitel'nyy komitet (VTsIK), decree of 1925 on administration in the North Caucasus autonomous *oblasti* allowed them to be independent vis-à-vis the *kraya* in internal and judicial matters, budget, and culture, and allowed them to have representations in Moscow. The 1928 decrees on the formation of the Adyge *oblast'* and the relations between the *kraya* and entities forming part of them contained principles militating against subordination of the power and administrative bodies. The RSFSR and the USSR constitutions did not have provisions stipulating the subordination of autonomous *oblasti* to the *kraya*, and the former were made subjects of the Russian federation on a par with other entities. These powers, however, were progressively curbed both de jure and de facto. Branches of the respective Krasnodar agencies, for example, administered the judiciary (A. S. Buzarov and K. K. Khutyz, "Totalitarizm i natsional'nye otnosheniya: Uroki i sovremennost' [Na primere stanovleniya gosudarstvennosti adygskikh narodov severnogo Kavkaza]" in *Severnyy Kavkaz*, 16-17).

17. On the establishment of Soviet power in the North Caucasus in the early 1920s see T. P. Khlynina, "Adygskie narody Kubanskoy oblasti: Problemy sovetizatsii (Nachalo 20-kh godov)," in *Severnyy Kavkaz*, 100-12.

18. Numerous other forms of ethnic representation were debated in the 1920s, such as the creation, in the severo-kavkazskiy *kray*, of a two-chamber *ispolkom*. The second chamber was to be the "chamber of nationalities" composed on a parity basis and possessing veto powers. These proposals did not materialize, however (N. F. Bugay, "Dvadtsatye gody: Stanovlenie demokraticheskikh form pravleniya na severnom Kavkaze," in *Severnyy Kavkaz*, 89, 91).

19. Term used by Bert Klandermans, *The Social Psychology of Protest* (Cambridge, Mass.: Blackwell, 1997), 40.

20. Aslan Djharimov, *Adygeya: Ot avtonomii k respublike* (Moscow: Autopan, 1995), 26-7.

21. "Postanovlenie prezidiuma verkhovnogo soveta RSFSR O poryadke i srokakh provedeniya vyborov narodnykh deputatov v Sovetskoy sotsialisticheskoy respublike Adygeya v sostave RSFSR," *Sovetskaya Adygeya (SA)*, 4 October 1991, 1; see also "O postanovlenii Verkhovnogo soveta RSFSR ot 11 Oktyabrya 1991 O glavakh ispolnitel'noy vlasti respublik v sostave RSFSR," *SA*, 29 October 1991, 1.

22. "O postanovlenii Verkhovnogo soveta RSFSR ot 11 Octyabrya 1991 O glavakh ispolnitel'noy vlasti respublik v sostave RSFSR," *SA*, 29 October 1991, 1.

23. "Reshenie pyatoy sessii Soveta narodnykh deputatov Adygeyskoy avtonomnoy oblasti ot 28 iyunya 1991 goda" (Djharimov, *Adygeya*, 204).

24. In his advocacy of exit from the *kray*, Aslan Djharimov maintained: "Local power structures, in essence, were deprived of the right to independently decide on issues related to the development of culture, the study of mother tongue" ("Za obnovlenie i sozidanie." *Adygeyskaya pravda [AP]*, 30 May 1990, 1).

25. Appendix 2, "Deklaratsiya O gosudarstvennom suverenitete Sovetskoy Sotsialisticheskoy Respubliki Adygeya" (Djharimov, *Adygeya*, 205).

26. Djharimov, *Adygeya*, 205-6.

27. Djharimov, *Adygeya*, 19-20.

28. Term used in Mayer N. Zald and Bert Useem, "Movement and Countermovement Interaction," in *Social Movements in an Organizational Society*, ed. Mayer N. Zald and John D. McCarthy (New Brunswick, N.J.: Transaction Books, 1987), 247-72.

29. "Navstrechu sessii oblastnogo soveta narodnykh deputatov," *AP*, 4 October 1990, 1.

30. "Navstrechu," *AP*, 4 October 1990, 1.

31. See, for example, "Vybor sdelan v interesakh vsekh jhiteley," *AP*, 10 October 1990, 3.

32. Pchelintseva and Samarina, *Sovremennaya*, 5.

33. "Postanovlenie TsIK Ob obrazovanii izbiratel'nykh okrugov po vyboram narodnykh deputatov VS SSRA,"*AP*, 18 October 1991, 2.

34. "V poiskakh vykhoda iz tupika," *Mayopskie novosti* (*MN*), 6 November 1991, 1.

35. "Chto skajhet tretiy tur," *AP*, 30 January 1992, 1.

36. "Vybor sdelan v interesakh vsekh jhiteley," *AP*, 11 October 1990, 3.

37. Personal interview with activist deputy, Moscow, 24 May 1999.

38. "Novaya kazachya organizatsiya," *AP*, 30 November 90, 1; "Byt'v Mayope kazachestvu," *MN*, 8 February 1991, 3.

39. The Cossacks maintained loose criteria for joining their ranks, allowing the entry of *inorodtsy* or *pripisnye kazaki*, rather than the strictly *potomstvennye* Cossacks (Pchelintseva and Samarina, *Sovremennaya*, 5).

40. "Soyuz slavyan Adygei," *SA*, 10 October 1991, 1.

41. McFaul and Petrov, eds., *Politicheskiy*, 82.

42. Evgeniy Busygin, "Russkie v mnogonatsional'nom povoljh'e," in *Yazyk i natsionalizm v postsovetskikh respublikakh*, ed. M. N. Guboglo (Moscow: Rossiyskaya akademiya nauk, Institut etnologii i antropologii, 1994), 35.

43. D. V. Vorob'ev and D. V. Grushkin, *Ideya natsional'noy gosudarstvennosti i problemy etnicheskoy diskriminatsii v respublike Bashkortostan* (Moscow: Zven'ya, 1999), 9; Ron Wixman, "The Middle Volga: Ethnic Archipelago in a Russian Sea," in *Nations and Politics in the Soviet Successor States*, ed. Ian Bremmer and Ray Taras (Cambridge: Cambridge University Press, 1993), 426.

44. Busygin, "Russkie," 35.

45. Wixman, "Middle Volga," 425.

46. Wixman, "Middle Volga," 426.

47. Vorob'ev and Grushkin, *Ideya*, 9; Il'dar Gabdrafikov, *Respublika Bashkortostan: Model' etnologicheskogo monitoringa* (Moscow: Rossiyskaya akademiya nauk, Institut etnologii i antropologii, 1998), 93.

48. Wixman, "Middle Volga," 426.

49. Wixman, "Middle Volga," 430.

50. The expropriation of nomadic grazing lands by the Russian peasants, the state, and the Russian Orthodox Church provoked hostility of the Bashkir nomads, causing a number of uprisings throughout the seventeenth and eighteenth centuries. The Volga or "Mother Volga" in time became etched in the Russian mind as symbol of Russia and Russianness, much to the displeasure of Tatars and Bashkirs alike, who now struggle to appropriate the Turkic name for the river—Idel'—as a symbol of the local nationalist identities (Vorob'ev and Grushkin, *Ideya*, 9).

51. Gabdrafikov, *Bashkortostan*, 93.

52. With the exception of the Menzelinskiy *uezd*, which went to Tatarstan, in 1922 (Gabdrafikov, *Bashkortostan*, 94).

53. Gabdrafikov, *Bashkortostan*, 94.

54. Gabdrafikov, *Bashkortostan*, 94.

55. Michael Guboglo, ed., *Etnopoliticheskaya mozayka Bashkortostana* (Moscow: Rossiyskaya akademiya nauk, Institut etnologii i antropologii, 1992), 49.

56. Gabdrafikov, *Bashkortostan*, 94.

57. Vorob'ev and Grushkin, *Ideya*, 10.

58. Guboglo, ed., *Etnopoliticheskaya*, 50.

59. Tatarstan was another one (Tishkov, *Ethnicity*, 86). Following the Communist Party of the Soviet Union (CPSU) directive On the Improvement of Russian Language Instruction in Schools, many schools dropped native language instruction in favor of Russian in schools with predominantly Tatar, Mariy, Chuvash, and other non-Bashkir students (Gabdrafikov, *Bashkortostan*, 83).

60. Vorob'ev and Grushkin, *Ideya*, 39.

61. Guboglo, ed., *Etnopoliticheskaya*, 293.

62. Vorob'ev and Grushkin, *Ideya*, 12.

63. "Blagotvoritel'nost' nachinaetsya doma," *Vechernyaya Ufa* (*VU*), 14 August 1990, 1. Yel'tsin also made the same statement in Tatarstan during his tour of the Middle Volga region.

64. Gabdrafikov, *Bashkortostan*, 38.

65. The final adopted version dropped them, however, referring to the "multinational people," rather than to the sole Bashkir right to self-determination. Vorob'ev and Grushkin, *Ideya*, 27.

66. Gabdrafikov, *Bashkortostan*, 78.

67. Vorob'ev and Grushkin, *Ideya*, 54.

68. Gabdrafikov, *Bashkortostan*, 81.

69. Zald and Useem, "Movement and Countermovement Interaction."

70. M. Kul'sharipov, "Edinaya i nedelimaya?" *Vechernyaya Ufa* (*VU*), 4 October 1990, 2.

71. "Vozmojhny varianty," *VU*, 10 September 1990, 2.

72. "Resheniya IV (vneocherednoy) sessii Ufimskogo gorodskogo soveta narodnykh deputatov XXI sozyva O proekte Deklaratsii O gosudarstvennom suverenitete Bashkortostana," *VU*, 23 August 1990, 1.

73. "Resheniya," *VU*, 23 August 1990.

74. "Komy nujhen soyuznyy status?" *VU*, 14 August 1990, 1.

75. See "Obrashchenie k narodnym deputatam VS BASSR," *VU*, 8 October 1990, 1; and "Tol'ko posle referenduma," *VU*, 1 February 1991, 1.

76. Interview by author with Tatar activist, tape recording, summer 1998.

Chapter 4

The Soviets and Nationalist Movements, 1990-1992: Setting the Limits of Contention

Local ethnic activism in the republics touches upon debates that run through several bodies of literature, identified in the first chapter. The various theoretical approaches relevant to the topic of this book concern the role of the social versus the state agencies and the elite actors within them, in affecting social and political change. Local governing institutions raise a particularly intriguing set of questions. Are they to be considered as the bona fide grassroots agencies aggregating and articulating the preferences of the local communities? Were this so, the explanation for their involvement in nontitular activism would be a straightforward one. Alternatively, are they to be regarded as agencies of the state and the vehicles for the exercise of elite power? Whether they are elite agencies or not, to what extent do they facilitate or constrain ethnic or social activism?

These questions are addressed in this chapter, which investigates the role of the local soviets in Adygeya and Bashkortostan in the period between 1990 and 1992, mainly focusing on the republics' respective capital cities, Maykop and Ufa. It is based on an investigation of the composition of the two councils and the republic-level Supreme Soviets, the public statements of capital city councils, and a series of in-depth interviews with a limited number of actors—activists of nontitular public associations (PAs) and deputies in the Maykop and Ufa city soviets.

This methodology allows for a nuanced analysis of the links between the social agencies and local governing institutions, which would not have been possible with a large sample of cases. The goal, however, is not to present "thick descriptions" of nontitular activism peculiar to the two republics, but rather to generalize to the other republics; Adygeya and Bashkortostan are "most different" cases in terms of their ethnic composition, relations with the federal center, size, their former status in the Soviet federal hierarchy, and many other parameters. The chapter finds the republics to have broadly similar patterns of interactions between the soviets, the organized social agencies, and the broader publics. These similarities in turn allow for making further inferences about the role of the local soviets in affecting social activism, and about the nature of state-society relations in Russia in general.

The chapter is structured as follows. First, it examines the composition of the two city soviets and contrasts them with that of the republic legislatures. Second, it discusses the incentives for the deputies' participation in the opposition movement, but also for cooperating with the diverse social and institutional actors. Third, it analyses the authoritative relationships between the councils and public associations. Fourth, it seeks to establish the distribution and input of resources needed for mass mobilization, between the various agencies. Finally, it addresses the broader question about the impact of the institutional actors on ethnopolitical and social dynamics in light of the available evidence.

The City Soviets

The composition of the capital city soviets differed along a number of dimensions from the republic Supreme Soviet legislatures, which the lower soviets opposed and identified with the titular nationalizing projects. The degree to which the lower-level city soviets were representative of the nontitular constituencies on whose behalf they acted, compared to the republic-level bodies, permits generalizations on the role of these agencies in nontitular movement activism. The differences in the respective council compositions are discussed below.

In the Adyge *oblast'* soviet almost 40 percent of the deputies elected to the 125-strong assembly came from the party *apparat* and senior managerial positions.[1] The single largest category in the assembly, thirty-four individuals, or over one-quarter of the deputies, represented the senior managerial cadre with the status of enterprise or *kolkhoz* managers. While workers, with twenty-one deputies, were the second largest category, reflecting the continued late Soviet policy preoccupation with ensuring working-class representation, the third largest group of deputies came from the soviet executive bodies with the status of senior executives.

In contrast, in the Maykop city soviet, which had the same number of deputies as the *oblast'* assembly, workers represented the largest category, with twenty-six deputies, comprising over 20 percent of the deputy corps. Although senior managers also performed well in the elections, with this category represented by twenty deputies (16 percent), a significant cumulative percentage of the deputy seats went to those in such professional categories as the lower managerial cadre (below the status of enterprise director), engineers, teachers, and doctors. Representation in the capital city soviet is also more broadly spread between the various social categories.

In terms of the ethnic composition, the *oblast'* body had an overrepresentation of the titular group relative to its overall weight in the republic. The Russian speakers nevertheless constituted a majority within the entity, occupying approximately 54 percent of the seats. In the Maykop city soviet, in contrast, the proportion of ethnic Adyge was slightly over 18 percent, the assembly being overwhelmingly Russian. In terms of the party affiliations, 28 percent of the city council deputies were either *bespartiynye* (no party membership) or identified as Komsomol members, compared to the *oblast'* body's mere 11 percent in the category, with over 88 percent party members.

The Bashkir Supreme Soviet was a sizeable body with almost 300 deputies.[2] It was even more skewed than the Adyge Supreme Soviet towards managers and high-ranking party figures. Managers, that is, those in the rank of enterprise or *kolkhoz* (collective farm) director comprised almost 33 percent of the Supreme Soviet's deputy corps. Senior party functionaries in the "prefectorial" positions, as well as those with the status of secretary of the republic or capital city levels comprised 18.6 percent, bringing the representation of managerial and party *nomenklatura* to over 50 percent in the body. The third largest category, with 13.9 percent, were the various level *ispolkom* chairmen, also referred to here as heads of administrations (HAs).

The Ufa soviet, in contrast, had a negligible representation of senior party figures, less than 1 percent. Senior managers, with slightly over 10 percent, ranked third in the city body after workers (the largest category), with 21.3 percent, and the lower managerial cadre (20.8 percent). The Ufa soviet had a significant representation of engineers (8.1 percent) and educators, many of which were university professors and heads of university academic departments, while heads of educational establishments comprised 4.6 percent.

Before I begin the discussion of the above electoral results it is important to note that many of the differences stemmed from the variable power bases of the republican versus the city actors. The republican elites' power base lay largely in the rural areas, where titular populations tend to reside, in contrast to the large

Table 4.1. Composition of Maykop and Ufa City Soviets, 1990

Deputy category	Maykop (%)	Ufa (%)
Soviet administration official	5.6	4.1
Engineer	4.0	8.1
School head	6.4	4.6
Hospital head	0	3.6
Lower-level manager	7.2	20.8
Manager	16.0	10.2
Worker	20.8	21.3
Public association member	7.2	3.6
Teacher	7.2	8.6
Lower-rank party official	5.6	4.1
Military	4.8	0
Other	15.2	11.2

Sources: Compiled from *Adygeyskaya pravda* and *Sovetskaya Bashkiriya*

cities, where nontitular populations are usually concentrated. Subsequent elections to the republic and local assemblies have tended to reproduce this "urban versus rural" split, with republic-level bodies even resorting to gerrymandering and other manipulative practices to ensure the overrepresentation of the rural areas at the expense of large cities, a practice that was significantly more pronounced than in the nonethnically defined regions.[3]

However, the composition of republic/*oblast'*-level and city councils indicates that ethnicity was but one cleavage line distinguishing the two sets of institutional bodies. On the face of it, the city councils were more representative of the broad social constituencies. This reflected the generally more competitive nature of elections at lower levels. The basic investigation reveals that the cities had a more even distribution of seats between the various professional and social categories and a larger-than-token representation of workers, as well as significant numbers of what may be broadly referred to as the "intelligentsia" and "professionals."

Such basic conclusions are in line with the other studies of the first democratically elected soviets. Jeffrey Hahn, for example, found that in Yaroslavl the *apparatchiki* did much better at the *oblast'* than at the city level, the *apparatchiki* referring to senior party and state officials.[4] He wrote that in the city body "a much greater number of deputies came from the ranks of service personnel, including professionals."[5]

Hahn, however, does not specify what social categories he subsumes under the "professionals" label. James Hughes in his analysis of the regional elite in the post-1990 regional legislatures also includes the "professional" category,[6] while Darrell Slider includes that of the "intelligentsia."[7] Disaggregation of the professional and intelligentsia categories, however, allows for a more nuanced analysis of the council makeup. The above scholars distinguish between the intelligentsia and professional categories on the one hand, and the party and state apparat and managerial cadre on the other, in the sense that the former did not belong to the narrow *nomenklatura* elite and did not possess the trappings of power associated with such a status. A closer look at the professional and intelligentsia categories, however, paints a different picture. Heads of schools and medical establishments, for example, may be included in the above two categories. While they may not belong to the narrow elite, they possess resources crucial for the purposes of this discussion in the sense that they are in positions of power and influence within large social and professional networks.

A closer scrutiny of the Maykop and Ufa city councils from the above point of view reveals that the city councils had significant numbers of people with influence in large social networks, as well as other "notables," whose positions served as traditional stepping-stones into the higher *nomenklatury.* The heads of medical and educational establishments, as well as engineers, belong to the above categories. Over the course of Soviet history these professions were becoming an increasingly important prerequisite for entry into the higher elite as the system laid greater stress on education and technocratic skills. Another point not immediately evident from deputies' affiliations is the presence of the quintessential "activist" deputies, identified in Friedgut's studies of Soviet community politics.[8] These were often drawn from the working class, and their entry into the establishment was by working themselves up through activism in the various enterprises' Komsomol and party cells. Theories of mobilization would suggest that these actors would have had particularly strong incentives to oppose the titular nationalizing projects, considering their implications for traditional elite mobility. They are also likely to possess crucial mobilizational resources because of their control over social and professional networks.[9]

The Activist Deputies

Not all deputies regularly engaged in nontitular movement activism. My discussion of the republic movements has indicated that in both capital cities only a core of activist deputies pursued movement activities and made public statements. It is the fact that they were able to ensure a majority vote on a given motion, as well as the signature of the soviet's chairman, which fostered the identification of the soviets with the opposition.

In Adygeya this activist group centered on the Maykop soviet's Deystvie faction. In Bashkortostan, a core group of about twenty deputies in the Ufa soviet attached their names to public antisovereignty statements, which appeared in the soviet's press organ *Vechernyaya Ufa*. Another two or three regularly came up with separate editorials in *VU*. Bashkortostan's activist core of twenty-three deputies who attached their names to public antisovereignty statements largely consisted of local "notables." This group included three engineers and three individuals occupying lower managerial posts. Seven held senior posts in industry, the media, and education. It also included the senior editor of an establishment newspaper, *Sovetskaya Bashkiriya*, the dean of a petroleum institute, heads of engineering and construction enterprises, a school headmaster, and a hospital head. Out of the list of twenty-three, only four were workers. This contrasts with the proportionally larger percentage of the worker category, in fact the single largest category, in the Ufa soviet as a whole. The list may be misleading, since frequently out of a list of signatories, only a small number of individuals identified themselves by name; the rest would be included as "other signatories." It does, however, give an indication of the social makeup of some of the more active individuals in the opposition.

In Adygeya, the activist Deystvie group was founded by and associated with the council deputy Valentin Lednev. Lednev had made his career in the trade unions. He had also been "elected" to the Maykop soviet before 1990, and by the time he was again elected to the Maykop council in 1990, he had enjoyed an active career in the "voluntary" associations, and was head of the Federation of Trade Unions of the Agroindustrial Complex. Lednev is the "public-minded" climber archetype described in Friedgut's study of the USSR's local soviets.[10] The other prominent opposition members included two younger Komsomol activists, Vladimir Stasev and Sergey Stel'makh. Stasev was a factory worker who apparently had chosen a party career, and was pursuing the standard route into the Soviet political elite. By the time he had been elected to the Maykop council he was the secretary of his factory's Youth League cell. Stel'makh, another activist deputy, was a Komsomol functionary still in his twenties.

The above basic investigation reveals the distinct middle- to lower-level *nomenklatura* makeup of the opposition coming from within the soviets. The individuals in question occupied managerial posts at enterprises, educational, or other establishments. At the same time, those from within the working class professions tended to be actively involved in Komsomol, party, and trade union work. The pluralist or society-centered arguments for their involvement would be that they performed the interest aggregation and articulation functions expected of them in an ideal-type situation. An example of the pluralist approach to the 1990 soviets is Jeffrey Hahn's study of Yaroslavl *oblast'*. Hahn's methodology is based on Lyn Ragsdale's test of "linkage," whereby local councils are seen as providing links between the citizenry and the polity, allowing the former to participate indirectly in decision making.[11] While Hahn was hesitant to express overoptimism about the degree of linkage, he found that deputies demonstrated an awareness of the views of the workers that had elected them.[12] Steven Fish, another observer of *perestroyka*-era local politics, regarded the soviets as more broadly representative and as aggregating the interests of the society at large. He wrote: "After 1989 some soviets actually became forums for the expression of public resistance to the extant political system."[13] These scholars explained what they saw as the soviets' failure to become effective instruments of policy change by such factors as repression,[14] the lack of a legal basis for registering political parties prior to the elections,[15] and the "inexperienced" and "amateur" nature of local soviets' deputies.[16]

These approaches are vulnerable to a number of criticisms. First, as has been indicated above, the activist deputies often occupied positions of power and influence within the enterprises that nominated and elected them, whether they were managers or secretaries of party and Komsomol cells. This would suggest that they were not necessarily amateurs *tout court*, and will have at least acquired schooling in Soviet public activism, a rite of passage into the *nomenklatura*. More importantly, their professional affiliations would suggest that the direction of influence might not necessarily go in ways indicated by pluralists. Pluralist studies in fact contain evidence that there was little influence on the deputies from their social constituencies. Hahn in his study of Yaroslavl, for example, admits that deputies frequently lost touch with their constituencies after the elections and even espoused different political views along the left-right political spectrum.[17] At the very least, such evidence suggests that there was little or no input from the broader social constituencies to the agencies that ostensibly represented them.

This experience is not unheard of in Western settings. France is notorious for the predominance of "notables" in local councils. The councilors tend to be disproportionately drawn from middle-class professions "relative to their position in the wider social structure," such as the managers and the "higher intellectual professions."[18] The localities are also known for the towering role of the local mayors, exerting "domination" over their constituencies.[19] Writing about British local government some decades ago, Ken Newton suggested regarding the overwhelmingly middle-class local councilors as members of the elite and not the grassroots. This phenomenon, as some recent studies have shown, to various degrees continues to be a feature of the United Kingdom's local government, with councilors being "at some considerable social distance from the majority of their constituents," often shaping the constituents' perceptions of local agendas, rather than the other way around.[20] These patterns have been replicated in the new democracies in Central and Eastern Europe, where local government elections yielded the predominance of "men, the middle aged, well-educated, and higher income groups."[21]

The peculiar makeup of these ostensibly grassroots bodies across democracies and the superior institutional resources that come with their office and status has led some scholars to challenge the pluralist notion of grassroots "inputs" shaping local decision making, and to draw attention to the role of institutions in which these actors operate. Referring to Robert Michels's "iron law of oligarchy,"[22] Newton wrote with regard to local representatives: "There is no reason in principle why the iron law should not apply to them."[23] In other words, he suggests that local councilors should be regarded as every bit as much institutional as social actors. Perhaps a good way of looking at it would be to say that they grow into the institutions rather than spring from the grassroots.

The Soviets and Public Associations

Another important question concerns the nature of the relationship between local governing or state agencies, and the organized interests, or the voluntary associations, rather than just the broader constituencies that the deputies represented. The previous chapter has shown that in Adygeya and Bashkortostan, such nationalist groups as the Union of Slavs of Adygeya and the Tatar Public Center maintained close links with the local soviets and the latter frequently deferred to them in articulating opposition sentiments. If deputies had weak links with their constituencies, perhaps they were subject to influence by the more organized social agencies.

The question has been a subject of much debate in community power studies. Pluralist scholars regard the self-organizing voluntary associations as crucial in the "input" side of the local political process. Even if the prima facie decision makers are the institutional actors, such as Mayor Lee in Robert Dahl's New Haven, their decisions are made based on "anticipated" reactions from the associations and the wider publics.[24] Pluralist approaches are vulnerable to criticism since even the anticipation of possible reactions from the civic groups by political institutional actors does not mean that they actually exercise meaningful influence. Philip Selznick's skeptical take on the American "grassroots" is a case in point. He cautioned against confusing "the need to share the responsibilities for . . . power" with power itself,[25] and against confusing the "substantive participation, involving an actual role in the determination of policy" with "mere administrative involvement."[26]

The above and similar premises could be defended on the grounds of the unequal distribution and possession of resources by the social versus the state agencies. As I have discussed in the introductory chapter, it is possible to distinguish between three sets of resources crucial for voluntary association and social movement activism. They are control over material resources proper; over organized networks, which facilitate collective action and decision making; and over agenda setting.

All of the above three sets of resources are relevant to the question of the state agencies' *formal* jurisdiction over voluntary groups. This latter question is not usually raised in community studies in Western settings considering the facility with which groups can organize and function with the minimal involvement of the state. It is, however, highly pertinent in bureaucratized and statist political settings, such as those found in the late Soviet and post-Soviet periods. Whether groups owe their existence to the state and whether the state can influence the groups' original stated goals and activities become highly salient issues, which have not been sufficiently appreciated either in the West or in Russia. An investigation of the nature of the relationships between the soviets and the nationalist groups should therefore begin by establishing the origins of these groups and the state's influence on their activities, if any, once they had been established. The following section discusses the authority relationships between the two sets of agencies. It then examines the distribution of resources between them in order to assess the relative influence of the two in affecting movement outcomes.

Cooperation or Control?

In order to investigate the direction of influence between the public associations on the one hand, and the soviets on the other, it is important to establish formal authoritative relationships between them. As discussed in chapter 2, the soviets in the Soviet system maintained control over networks of the so-called voluntary associations, such as the Youth League branches, trade unions, voluntary militia, and so forth. The soviets were the coordinating and supervising bodies for these agencies, which permeated society as deep as neighborhood and individual household levels. This situation changed when Gorbachev allowed the formation of independent voluntary associations. The new USSR and RSFSR legislation on the local councils and public associations was to reflect the new thinking on society-state relationships. In reality, the most crucial pieces of legislation preserved the pillars of the old system.

The RSFSR July 1991 law On Local Self-Government stipulated that public associations operating in a given locale are to be registered with the respective local administrations, which were de jure subordinate to the soviets. Similar provisions were applied with respect to their press organs.[27] These provisions, however, were soon nullified in December 1991 by a RSFSR Supreme Soviet stipulation on registering public associations. In an apparent contradiction to the earlier law, the stipulation delegated this responsibility to the relevant "justice organs," or the territorial branches of the RSFSR Ministry of Justice. A December 1991 RSFSR law On Mass Media likewise took the prerogative over press registration from the soviets, delegating it to the "appropriate territorial organs of the State Inspectorate for the Protection of Freedom of the Press and Mass Media of the Ministry of Press and Information of the Russian Federation." Thus, at least de jure, the soviet administrations had jurisdiction over public associations and their press for a very short period between July and December 1991.

The soviets were also responsible for authorizing public activities of the voluntary associations. This authority stemmed from the general references to their role in ensuring "law and order" and supervision of demonstrations and other mass acts. Before holding a demonstration or some other mass act, public associations had to file a formal request with the respective local councils, which the council was then to consider, and authorize or refuse permission accordingly. It was also responsible for authorizing or selecting a suitable location in which voluntary associations' activities could be held. In so doing, it was to consider such issues as "public safety" and "security." The July 1991 RSFSR law On Local Self-Government passed this authority from the representative bodies to respective local administrations, that is, the local executive bodies, which were still de jure, however, subordinate to the soviets.[28]

The local councils' jurisdictions over public activism are not significantly different from those in Western democracies, where they are more likely to be exercised on an impartial basis. This impartiality, however, becomes problematic where strong political, social, ethnic, or other cleavages exist, which serve to divide both the elite/institutional and the social actors. The local councils played a facilitating role in the Netherlands, for example, during the peace movements' mass protest acts. Opposed by state-level actors, these movements often find sympathy on local council level. Where local communities are divided, councilors may use their institutional resources to further the interests of a given side in a conflict. In India, another decentralist state, Paul Brass notes the role of the members of local assemblies in constraining or fostering communal rioting through their control over the local police forces, which may be used as agents provocateurs.[29] This control capacity is more likely to be employed in situations of political cleavage and contest.[30] In such contexts, power contenders have the incentives to increase the scope of the contagion of conflict by getting "the audience" involved.[31]

Since formal jurisdictions are not sufficient for establishing the nature of the relationships between the two sets of agencies, we need to investigate the de facto use of the formal resources. It is also important to explore any informal links between the two sets of agencies. These questions are particularly salient considering the presence of strong ethnosocial cleavages in Russia's republics, and the potential partiality of the soviets in the exercise of their prerogatives.

The Use of Formal and Informal Links

In neither of the republics did the soviets consistently use their prerogatives to register the public associations discussed above. This appeared to stem from the legal confusion fostered by the proliferation of laws on different levels of the USSR and RSFSR, as well as by quick succession of different legislation on local self-government and that related to public associations. In Bashkortostan, a TOTs activist recalls the legal and jurisdictional ambiguity with regard to the hitherto unprecedented boom of public associations. In 1989 when TOTs was being set up, no one knew exactly how to go about registration. The activist was finally referred to a Stalin-era law on the procedures for registering public associations dating back to 1937. In Soviet years, however, this law referred to such "voluntary associations" as the DOSAAF (official automobile union) and the hunters' and fishers' associations. "The obstacle," he maintains, "was a bureaucratic one. They were not used to taking responsibility for their actions . . . especially [since] there was no precedent." Since it was unclear which agency was in charge, several bodies reviewed the registration application, including the Cabinet of Ministers and the Supreme Soviet presidium. The local TOTs branches, however, also eventually filed papers with the local soviet *ispolkomy*. In going through the registration procedures, according to the Tatar association member, TOTs "literally had to fight for every phrase, every word, and every comma."[32]

The Union of Maykop Cossacks, founded by Valentin Lednev, the trade union leader, and Anatoliy Rybakov, a USSR Supreme Soviet deputy from Adygeya, faced a similar legal ambiguity. These associations, however, had the advantage of having been founded by institutional actors. Thus, a Union activist maintains, "We just organized ourselves and announced that we created [public associations] . . . and only later we worked out documents that were required by law."[33] Eventually the charter and other founding documents were filed with the local Ministry of Justice.

The soviets did exercise their authority over mass activism. The presidia, composed of soviet deputies in charge of standing committees, the soviet chairman, and its deputy, considered the petitions filed by the respective public associations, and decided whether to sanction or deny the right to hold them. "Public safety" and "morals," and the need to avoid conflicts were cited as the main criteria for decision making. The presidia, therefore, had to familiarize themselves in advance with the slogans that were to be displayed at public gatherings, and they actually did influence their wording. The PAs had to comply or risk not holding the planned acts altogether. The nature of this influence, however, depended on the positions of those sitting on the presidia and the degree of fusion between the soviets and the public associations.

In Ufa, TOTs had sympathizers in the Ufa soviet presidium in the person of an ethnic Tatar deputy chairman of the Ufa soviet. "Everything that happened in Ufa," maintained the deputy, referring to public activities, "required registration . . . and went through me, so I dealt with it for two years."[34] The deputy, while sympathizing with the Tatar movement, nevertheless tried to exercise a moderating influence. A TOTs activist maintains, "I was personally present each time, explaining what and how, goals, slogans. . . . They [presidium members] [tried to influence] in the sense that such and such slogans are undesirable, such and such are not allowed . . . not because it was illegal, but because according to their opinion this . . . will introduce disorder."[35] In Maykop, according to the leaders of the Russian movement, the presidium exercised effective control over the city's public activities. While in Bashkortostan, there was a more clear separation between the soviets and the prominent "public" associations, in Adygeya, there was a virtual fusion of the two. The Deystvie group controlled the Maykop soviet presidium. The group's leaders like Lednev and Stasev were in turn active sponsors of the Slavic movement in Maykop. They both claim to be the "founding fathers" of the Russian opposition movement and the organizations that represented it—the Union of Maykop Cossacks and the Union of Slavs of Adygeya.

If presidium memberships overlapped with those of public associations, as was the case in the two republics, this jurisdiction and decision-making capacity raise important theoretical questions about the nature of state-society relations. In practice, it meant that individuals from public associations who filed petitions about holding mass acts were also members of the presidia who decided on these acts. One may of course argue that the deputies performed the interest aggregation and articulation functions and represented the various public groups. Yet, in most cases they only joined or indeed created these associations after becoming deputies. Many of these associations did not even exist before the 1990 elections; in fact, they only mushroomed after the elections.

Such a fusion of local government with the "social" agencies is in fact a common feature of local politics in Western settings. A quote from a local government official, interviewed in the context of Newton's study of local politics in Birmingham, is a case in point: "We are in a rather special position. You see, as well as being secretary of — Association, I also work in — Department. That means as secretary I write a letter, put it in my pocket, go into the other office, and then deal with the letter with my other hat on. Things get done quickly that way."[36] "Time and again," writes Newton, "the interviews showed a series of elaborate networks of quasi-official and semiofficial communications linking community organizations and local government departments."[37]

While local government having a facilitating role is not intrinsically undemocratic, it becomes so when state support and fusion with the voluntary associations is a sine qua non for getting anything done. In Newton's Birmingham, those associations that lacked the privilege of formal or informal links to local government were often denied assistance and even access, their lobbying letters simply binned.

The tendency of a reliance on "official" or state agencies continues to be even more pronounced in postcommunist settings than in the West. Grzegorz Ekiert and Jan Kubik found that in Poland, East Germany, Hungary, and Slovakia, activists had to rely to a much larger degree on "traditional organizations," such as the trade unions and professional associations, and to a much smaller degree on social movement organizations proper, compared to Western European countries.[38] They also conclude: "It seems that regardless of the issue at stake, protesting groups look to the state and central authorities for solutions."[39]

The fusion of local government and "voluntary" groups, however, still leaves open the question of the direction of influence between public associations and local government agencies. If resource distribution favors the state agencies, why do they associate themselves with the social actors? And how does the nature of this association ultimately affect political outcomes?

The Fostering of "Civic Life"

Interviews with deputies and PA leaders suggest a number of reasons for cooperation. They can be divided into two groups, although there is overlap between the two. One can be categorized as legitimacy, and the other is related to the purely material/logistical resources. Legitimacy was relevant for a wide range of movement issues, including the acquisition of material resources. Most importantly, it affected movement image and identity in the media and the public domain in general. Both the soviets and PAs relied on each other for the manufacture of legitimacy. It was a reciprocal relationship, albeit one in which the institutional actors enjoyed a clear advantage considering their jurisdictional prerogatives over public associations.

In 1990, by which time the old structures were rapidly losing legitimacy, the emerging public associations nevertheless had to struggle to project a "respectable" self-image. This in turn negatively affected their potential to get anything done independently of "official" support. A Tatar movement activist sums up the anxieties felt by the TOTs: "The public movement is easy to smear in dirt; it can be stigmatized as composed of street ruffians, losers, etc., but the *nomenklatura* is not so easily vulnerable . . . they are known in the republic." An activist of the Russians' association Rus' maintained, in a similar vein, that it was important for him to rely on the "notables" in the Ufa soviet to facilitate the attaining of Rus's objectives.[40]

This phenomenon has commonly been observed with social movements in the West. Unless they find "respectable" allies or assume an appropriate image, Western movements have shown vulnerability to being labeled "riffraff." As William Gamson and Andre Modigliani point out, the perception of movements as either socially integrated or not, something often influenced by the media, affects their perception by the elites, and levels of mass support they are likely to get.[41] In the late Soviet and early post-Soviet periods, the continued overbureaucratized nature of the system, which had almost no record of an independent public sphere, made such "people's tribunes" even more vulnerable to stigmatization. As a result, PA leaders often had to use their official Soviet professional affiliations, or rely on those of their allies in the soviets, to get any movement activity done.

Deputies allied with the public movements had to invoke their "official" status when addressing the key movement logistical issues—from the setting up and registering of a public association, to getting manpower and resources for mass acts, to acquiring permission for holding "roundtable discussions." This role was crucial considering the virtually complete absence of a private economy, and the degree of control over the society and material facilities by enterprises and state institutions. We shall see in the subsequent chapters that this situation did not change as late as 1999, when movement activists had to get the permission of a local head of administration in order to get anything done. A quote from a Russian movement figure, who was also a city council member, illustrates the reliance on establishment institutions for material facilities, and their reluctance to aid "people from the street":

> When I come to any factory director . . . asking to give something for Cossacks
> . . . he would say: What if the party *obkom* found out? I would say: Vacate this
> premise and give it to *gorkom* . . . and when he would be called and told, how
> come you assigned space to the Union of Slavs, he would say: Nothing like
> that, I did it for *gorkom*.[42]

Thus, the Russian activist would use his "official" party affiliation in order to get logistical support for the Cossacks' or Union of Slavs' activities. This official "roof" would in turn be used to legitimize the support by other establishment sympathizers, who would otherwise be reluctant to do so in the face of party scrutiny.

The deputies' official status also enabled them to mobilize relatively large groups of people through the networks that they controlled. Although scholars of Russia point to the atomized nature of Soviet society, it was in fact highly organized and structured, facilitating rather than impeding mobilization. The control capacity over such structured networks is crucial considering that successful movements are "networks of networks and organizations."[43] One activist's "multiorganizational field"[44] included the Deystvie group and the soviet presidium; the vast agroindustrial trade union network with its local branches, and the newly created Cossack and Union of Slav structures. Other deputies in the Deystvie group in turn had influence within the industrial giants that they represented, such as the Tochradiomash, Reductor, and Stankonormal' electronics and machinery plants. "The [soviet's political discussions]," maintained a Russian movement leader, "were quite broadly announced by deputies themselves. . . . I also got my trade union staff involved."[45] Another deputy from one of the plants, referring to the mobilization of people for rallies, maintained, "I used all the channels: the Committee on Local Self-Government, Housing, and Management, Communist cells—that is, everything that represented an organization."[46]

While the public associations clearly benefited from deputy affiliations, so did the established actors benefit from links with or labels of the social agencies. The projection of the "public" or "social" image stemmed from the need to enhance the legitimacy of the movement and the institutional actors who stood behind it. It was also aimed at representing the movement as a powerful social force with significant levels of mass support. In both republics the sponsorship of or support for nontitular nationalist organizations was a form of "counter-movement" to such titular *nomenklatura*-endorsed PAs as the Adyge nationalist organization Adyge Hase and the radical Bashkir group BNTs.

Similar to the titular *nomenklatura*, the soviet actors were vulnerable to their naming as *partkhozaktiv* by their rivals. The "movement" or "public association" label was also advantageous in that it suggested an infinite force in contrast to the finite number of deputies and deputy groups. This is why, according to movement activists, the actual numbers of participants in these bodies was kept secret. A related strategy was the proliferation of agencies whose members were in fact the same people. One movement leader, who perceived the struggle with the *obkom*-supported forces to be an unequal one, stated, "We had a minimum of three organizations" against only one—Adyge Hase. "The more labels you have, the better,"[47] echoed another Union of Slavs activist, suggesting their variable legitimacy in different circumstances.

Institutional Support: Constraining or Facilitating Role?

If institutional support was essential for the activities of public associations, the impact of this support on the movements and broader political outcomes remains to be investigated. The role of state support vis-à-vis the social agencies, namely the social movement organizations and civic groups, is a subject of much scholarly debate. Much of the social movement literature is premised on two key assumptions: (1) the essentially reactive, rather than proactive, nature of state support to change or resist changes in the existing social order, and (2) the inherently conservative nature of state institutional actors. This latter argument implies that when there is state/elite support for movements, it is usually aimed at more moderate, rather than radical, elements. The radicals become marginalized, while the moderates are co-opted by the state/elite actors. This could lead to several outcomes. Co-optation could lead to a failure to achieve movement goals because of "strategic rigidity,"[48] or even to the demise of the movement itself.[49] Alternatively, the state could have an overall moderating effect on the movement, increasing levels of mass support by the otherwise conservative constituencies, rather than just the radical or lunatic fringe.

As I have discussed in the introductory chapter, the above-mentioned approaches are vulnerable to criticism because of their implicit rigidifying of the concepts of the "elite" and the "state." They assume that there exists an "established structure of polity membership,"[50] and that the state is an "inherently conservative institution, committed to the maintenance of social order."[51] These approaches underestimate the potential for elite divisions or for situations of radical social change where elite and polity memberships fluctuate. The very premise of challenges to the social order and rules of polity membership from below is also questionable. Rules for entry into the polity are often changed from above, creating a potential for excluding those already high up in the political system. The rigidifying of the concept of the state is also inappropriate.

This is particularly true for federal or decentralist systems. In federal states, nationalist challenges threatening the existence of the polity itself and not just its elite membership often take an institutional dimension and coincide with a federation's subunits. Likewise, in polities with strong elected municipalities, the mayors have often been key political players fostering political cleavages between a given locality and the larger polity.

However, even if we accept the possibility of proactive state/elite support originating within state institutions, the question remains as to the broad impact of such support on the course of the movement. If we accept the premise of the generally conservative nature of the elite or political institutional actors, we would expect them to have a moderating effect on the movement as a whole even if these actors had been active in fostering the movement. However, it is also important to disaggregate the proactive and movement-facilitating "elite" itself, since various elements thereof may have variable preferences and resources to affect movement outcomes.

The preceding empirical sections have identified the soviets as proactive and facilitating agencies in the nontitular opposition movements, which included the public associations and the wider publics. The following sections disaggregate the various movement actors, identify their preferences, and assess their impact on the movements' history and goal achievement.

Institutional versus Social Movement Preferences

While the various public associations and soviet actors generally agreed on movement goals, their preferences differed when it came to deciding on strategy, tactics, and issue framing. It was common for the activist deputies to accuse council chairmen, who otherwise sided with the movement, of excessive wavering and backtracking. Public associations separate from the deputy corps or activists within them in turn accused the deputies of "selling out" on their more radical demands and positions. Both the public associations and deputies recognized that the position of the key local "notable," that is, the council chairman, was ultimately very important, if not decisive. The public associations also recognized that the positions of the activist deputy corps likewise had a major impact on policy outcomes, considering their influence with the Supreme Soviets as "official" figures.

In both Adygeya and Bashkortostan, the council chairmen in the capital cities set the tone for the movement, and attempted to moderate the demands of the opposition. These figures, who had already achieved positions of power and influence within the Soviet institutional hierarchies, were more prone to cooptation than those in the lower echelons. At the same time, while they could not be removed from office by the higher bodies, they were more vulnerable to sanctions from them than the average deputies. The chairmen often continued to combine their posts with those of local party leadership up until August 1991.

Despite efforts to democratize both the soviet and party systems, these hierar-chies still preserved centralist elements.

Thus, against the background of social opposition to the Supreme Soviet, the chairmen of local soviets would be accused by the Supreme Soviets' presidia of not conducting enough "explanatory work" with the population and were held responsible for the social processes in their respective locales. Unlike the aver-age deputies, these figures held regular meetings with the republic-level leaders; they could use their stature to pressure republic leadership, but they could also be vulnerable to greater compromises. The positions of Lev Simatov and Mik-hail Zaytsev, the chairmen of the Maykop and Ufa soviets, respectively, illus-trate this point.

In Adygeya, Simatov took the more moderate and wavering position, agree-ing to support Deystvie and then making compromises with the Adyge leader-ship. This position was evident in the soviet's more general line towards the higher Adyge bodies, and in the specific stance with regard to sovereignty and parity arrangements. During the August coup, when the activist deputies within the council took an uncompromising position, challenging the wait-and-see posi-tion of the presidium, Simatov attempted to steer the council to take a less con-frontational stance. Deystvie insisted on a full "extraordinary" session of the soviet; Simatov opted for the meeting of the "small soviet," involving just a handful of deputies instead. The "extraordinary" session, on which Deystvie insisted, had a much stronger public resonance, and its criticisms of the Supreme Soviet *nomenklatura* were widely publicized.

When parity came up on the agenda, Simatov assumed an even more am-biguous position. One activist deputy, alluding to Simatov's negative role in goal achievement, maintained, "He constantly took initiative in what he said . . . that is, things that had not been discussed, agreed upon, he . . . presented . . . as though it had already been decided; as a result, it was impossible to protest it."[52] On the one hand, Simatov would travel to Moscow to determine the constitu-tionality of the parity option, raising the profile of the no-parity movement. At the same time, Simatov urged the Slavic community to opt for some form of parity, perhaps short of institutionalizing it. To this effect he endorsed a special appeal of the "working group on the elections in Adygeya," signed both by prominent Adyge and Russians.

The head of the other Russian soviet, the Maykop *rayon* soviet, Krokhmal', was likewise accused by the movement of excessive compromises. According to one deputy, "he did not moderate the conflicts as they emerged, and at the same time did not make them more intense."[53]

In Bashkortostan, Zaytsev assumed a similarly ambiguous position. Zay-tsev's signature appeared on statements challenging the proposed language law, and, according to him, he consistently opposed the language provisions privileg-ing the Bashkirs. As soviet chairman, he was also mandated to ratify the deci-sions passed by the majority of the council. However, in many cases, he skill-fully handled agenda setting and the floor, often preventing the more radical issues from being placed on the agenda altogether; in others, he failed to attach his signature to the soviet's protest statements under various pretexts. He urged the body not to get distracted with "idle politicking" and to deal with "real" day-to-day issues instead. Thus, at one of the sessions, when a group of deputies harshly criticized Bashkir nationalism and the radical Bashkir nationalist group BNTs's capture of the TV center, proposing that the city soviet get involved with the issue, Zaytsev said,

> Think about the consequences. . . . We are today getting dragged into politics, must we now begin to analyze, to probe. . . . Is it our business, to get involved with all of this today, to analyze everything? Well, see for yourself, whether we really want to exacerbate the situation even further. . . . Let's just work. . . . We've had enough of heightening of emotions![54]

At the same session, the deputy Timur Sablin proposed to adopt and publicize a statement critical of the requirement for the Bashkir president to be fluent in Bashkir, thus "placing 80 percent of the population who do not know Bashkir, in the position of being able to elect, but not to occupy this post." The statement criticized the requirement as "contradicting the Universal Declaration of Human Rights."[55] Zaytsev responded,

> Comrades, today the deputy corps of our city is viewed from two sides: positive and negative. Both the city residents and those in the higher power echelons have a complex view. I think that yet another appeal, even if it is made on behalf of a group of deputies, has to be well thought through and aimed first and foremost at stabilization, and not at the heightening of some other tensions today in the city. I think that the provisions of this appeal will exacerbate the situation in the city and the republic. Sometimes silence and a calm perception of some nuances can bring more good. . . . As chairman I strongly call upon you to decide whether such a document needs to be produced at all. . . . Comrades, it is very easy to play with fire, but it is very hard to extinguish it later.[56]

While admitting that deputies have the right to express their views in *VU*, Zaytsev urged them not to use the soviet label, or present them as expressing the position of the soviet at large: "Well, sign if you want, as a group of deputies. I am not going to sign such a document."[57]

In the Maykop soviet, Deystvie, in turn, was less radical than the activists in the Union of Slavs. Many Union of Slavs activists were on principle opposed to any form of institutionalization of Adyge overrepresentation in either executive or legislative structures. The deputy Lednev, in contrast, advocated parity in executive bodies, and was ready for dialogue with Adygeya's leader Aslan Djharimov on this issue. He argued that cabinet parity, ensuring an even distribution of key posts between the Adyge on the one hand, and the non-Adyge on the other, would prevent the Adyge leadership from abusing the appointments by giving most of the senior posts to the ethnic Adyge, while reserving the minor ones for the Russians. Ultimately, the Union of Slavs activists, including

Lednev, blamed Simatov, Krokhmal', and other "prefects" for giving carte blanche to Djharimov to introduce the discriminatory arrangements.

Issue Frames

The variable positions of the different actors were reflected in their preferences for the interpretation of and presentation of the various political issues. The deputies and soviets' chairmen in particular appreciated the potential public impact and resonance of official statements, hence the careful choice of wording. An examination of the political statements of public associations, on the one hand, and those made on behalf of the soviets on the other, reveals significant differences. Those made on behalf of the soviets in turn reflected a tug and pull of the opinions of the various deputies on the one hand, and the council chairman and other influentials within the soviets on the other.

In Bashkortostan, both these broad sets of actors opposed the nationalist programs of the Supreme Soviet. However, TOTs ethnified the discourse, while the Ufa soviet downplayed nationalism and stressed the *nomenklatura* credentials of the Bashkir elite instead, the potential expenses, and the waste involved in the sovereignty project, rather than its emotional or symbolic nationalist significance. The Bashkir Supreme Soviet's nationalism was portrayed as a sabotage of Russia's progressive liberal reforms by the conservative *nomenklatura* and the "partocracy." Its "lack of competence," the Ufa deputies argued, fueled ethnic hostilities and served to sabotage the compliance with the laws of the RSFSR aimed at the furthering of economic and political reforms.[58]

In an open address to Boris Yel'tsin, a group of Ufa soviet deputies wrote: "Anti-*perestroyka* forces tear at the state like a rugged blanket; in reality, the concern is not for the well-being of the people, but for that segment of the population which is about to go out of business."[59] Market forces, they argued, would make the elites curb the number of ministries and the size of the bureaucracy; hence their desire to obtain republic status. "All this, especially in the market conditions," the letter warned in a businesslike fashion, "could lie as a heavy burden on the shoulders of the taxpayer." Only in the end did the letter turn to ethnicity, warning that Bashkortostan is home to dozens of nationalities, and that Union status for just one nation could threaten "another Karabakh."

TOTs, instead, opted for the opposite, with pure economics acquiring ethnic significance, and ethnicity stressed above everything else. "Certain forces in the republic," maintained a TOTs spokesman, "are bound to use the profits from oil for the development of the regions with predominance of eastern Bashkirs." As a solution TOTs proposed a redistribution of revenues to the Tatar areas as well, so as to check the "eastern Bashkir chauvinism" of the republic's elites, and the imposition of "control over the purchase of lands in the traditionally Tatar areas."[60] TOTs advanced these demands as a conscious strategy for achieving greater public resonance by stressing the ethnic dimension of the issue. Similarly, when the ethnic Tatar Prime Minister Marat Mirgazyamov was forced to resign, a Tatar activist privately urged him to expose publicly the alleged anti-Tatar discrimination that led to his resignation, rather than other factors, but Mirgaziamov refused.[61]

In the sovereignty discourse, which represented a complex of ethnic, legal, political, and economic issues, the Ufa soviet tackled the legal, economic, and constitutional aspects, while downplaying nationalism. It welcomed sovereignty since it would allow greater economic freedom, give the republic greater rights over its natural and other resources, and hence be beneficial for all in the republic. The kind of sovereignty proposed by the Supreme Soviet, however, was condemned as threatening Bashkortostan's exit from Russia's "constitutional space." Possible exit from Russia was also presented as opposition to President Yel'tsin and his reforms.[62] TOTs welcomed sovereignty as such, because of its sympathy for Tatarstan and its decentralist efforts. Yet, its main public critique of Bashkortostan's handling of the issue, unlike that of the Ufa soviet, centered less on the legal, economic, and constitutional aspects and more on the ethnic ones. TOTs and Rus' focused on such symbolic issues as the draft constitution's preamble granting sovereignty to just one nation, the Bashkirs.[63]

The more moderate frames of the soviet, however, likewise represented a significant watering down of the positions of the more activist and radical deputies within the Ufa soviet. These were carefully debated behind closed doors, word by word, and in all likelihood had the moderating stamp of the council chairman.

When Bashkortostan tried to introduce the post of president with the requirement of fluency in Bashkir, the deputy Timur Sablin proposed to adopt and publish a special resolution on the matter. The resolution tackled the language issue and its possible consequences for the ethnic situation in the republic, and, moreover, linked the language law with the recent extremist capture of the TV center by the Bashkir nationalist group BNTs, even though there was no direct evidence of the Supreme Soviet's involvement in the act.

The statement expressed "alarm" at the recent developments in an entity "hitherto free of interethnic conflicts and political extremism," possibly leading to "unpredictable consequences." "The proposed law," the draft read, "serves to exclude 80 percent of the non-Bashkir-speaking population from the right to run for the presidency, and is discriminatory."[64] The soviet's chairman Zaytsev maintained in response,

> In Ufa, today, there are only 14 or 17 percent Bashkirs. Therefore, does it make sense for us to juxtapose such a statement to this nationality? . . . Each word, each letter, each comma, has to be very precise, especially in such circumstances. . . . Therefore, I think that such a document . . . must again be reviewed in the most thorough way possible. You can't adopt it in its current form.[65]

Zaytsev urged the decoupling of the presidency issue from BNTs's extremism and Bashkir nationalism: "Comrades, I urge you, Timur Vital'evich [Sablin], I had a conversation with you; you know my position. . . . I don't know who needs this appeal, I am against it." Timur Sablin responds, "Well, as regards the language issue, perhaps we should remove it so as not to stir the public. . . . The goal is to announce, comrades, that in Ufa we have one law for every nation, for every person."[66]

As a result, the document that came to light and was published in *VU* was significantly different from the original version. It began by pointing out that the law on the presidency failed to mention Bashkortostan as part of the Russian Federation. It then criticized as unfair the requirement of having over 100,000 signatures, equal to that required for the federal presidency, thus underprivileging public associations, which would have trouble achieving the result. It also pointed out that under the proposed law, only political parties or trade unions, and not the smaller public associations, had the right to nominate presidential candidates. Only at the end of the document was the language issue addressed.[67] The revised document's main concern was democracy, and not nationalism.

Zaytsev urged the same democratic frame to be adopted for the opposition movement at large, hence his efforts to bring together the various nationalist groups and come up with joint statements of democratic, rather than narrow, nationalist orientation. A TOTs leader maintained that the Ufa soviet "always tried to attract Bashkirs . . . well, as 'democratic forces,' so that they could also join in."[68] These efforts, which usually took the form of "roundtable discussions," "often turned into heated arguments [*perepalki*], first and foremost between TOTs and the Bashkirs, and secondly, between all the rest and the Bashkirs."[69] They were, however, moderated by city officials. Says a city functionary, "We all gathered together in my office, and if [a] TOTs [member] behaved from a position, well, from my point of view, not a very correct one, nationalist . . . I simply perhaps tried to convince him that one shouldn't act like this, one needs to somehow form a united front."[70] The influence of such a strategy was felt in the statements made jointly by the soviet, the democratic groups, and the nationalist ones like TOTs. They stressed "democracy," the need for referenda in deciding major political issues, as respecting the "principle of true people's power," and the involvement of public associations in the otherwise closed decision-making process of the Supreme Soviet.[71]

In Adygeya, the peculiar ethnic composition of the republic determined a less ethnocentric frame for the non-Adyge opposition. The fact that the Slavic groups formed a large proportion of the entity's population encouraged the movement to adopt a more democratic and liberal discourse. Here too, however, the establishment actors exercised greater moderation compared to movement figures not associated with establishment institutions, downplaying rather than stressing ethnic differences and showing a greater willingness to compromise with the republic regime. They urged the Bashkir leadership to respect the "sovereignty of the individual,"[72] and to adopt electoral principles, based on "intellectual, business, professional moral and other qualities."[73] While many Union of Slavs activists were opposed to parity arrangements, Lednev was prepared to accept parity as long as ethnicity would not be stressed as the main criterion for all office appointments. "Parity is possible," maintained Lednev, "based solely on a moral basis, on mutual trust and national accord, but by no means on the juxtaposition of one nation to the other."[74]

Conclusion

The preceding analysis implies that the "palace guard," that is, the middle- to lower-level *nomenklatura*, was behind much of the nontitular activism in the early 1990s. They had the incentives for mobilization, considering the implications of the republic nationalizing projects on political elite mobility. However, their incentives alone were not sufficient preconditions for effective mobilization and goal achievement. Despite Gorbachev's decentralization of the institutional hierarchy, the city soviets were in a comparatively weak position vis-à-vis the higher *oblast'* and republic bodies. Yet, they had a significant advantage in terms of their proximity to and indeed control over the "grassroots." Schattschneider notes: "It is the *loser* who calls in outside help."[75] It is not incidental, then, that mobilization originated within these institutions. They possessed most of the resources identified by social movement literature as crucial for mobilization: from their "horizontal" control over local social networks, to that over instruments of local public opinion framing, to that over local material resources. This control allowed for the transformation of what could have been limited to simple lobbying of the higher structures, into mass-based activism involving the broader social agencies. These premises challenge much of the scholarship on the local soviets, which either has dismissed them as useless "debating chambers" with no clout,[76] or, based on pluralist assumptions, has assumed a bottom-up approach to political outcomes.[77] The foregoing investigation has shown the soviets to be powerful and activist agencies shaping much of the "grassroots" activism.

Evidence presented above also challenges the society-centered premises of much of the Western social movement literature. Rather than being "reactive" agencies bent on preserving the social order, political institutional actors actively fostered movement activism and affected its goal achievement. To a certain extent, however, evidence from Adygeya and Bashkortostan supports the contention of some social movement scholars to the effect of the generally constraining nature of institutional or elite support.[78] The lower-level soviet deputies and particularly the soviets' chairmen were still subject to co-optation or reprisals by the higher agencies, although Gorbachev's reforms fostered a degree of "institutional segmentation" and undermined the traditional centralist hierarchies. The deputies' experience of climbing the Soviet career ladder also encouraged a preference for consensus-seeking strategies and frames, which stressed interethnic cooperation to achieve mutual objectives and such Soviet-style action frames as "roundtable discussions."

The above findings also have broader implications for our understanding of the ethnopolitical developments in Russia and the post-Soviet space in general. They explain why in Russia the Ossetiyan-Ingush conflict remained a deviant case, rather than the rule. If the state has had an overwhelming influence on society, and the state has tended to have a constraining impact on social activism, then this would explain the generally peaceful nature of ethnopolitical developments even where strong elite cleavages were present and the elite mobilized the masses for social protest and even where the radical nationalists preferred militant tactics. Since the position of political institutional actors tended to predominate, the result was that protest was bound to be limited to moderate activism. The following chapter introduces the third case, the Ingush movement in North Ossetiya and Ingushetiya, in an effort to explain the violent outcome of that movement.

Notes

1. *Adygeyskaya Pravda (AP)* 8, 10, 21, 23 March; 24, 25 April; 19 June 1990.
2. *Sovetskaya Bashkiriya (SB)*, 12, 22 March; 22, 25 April; 1, 11 May 1990.
3. Darrell Slider, "Elections to Russia's Regional Assemblies," *Post-Soviet Affairs* 12, no. 3 (1996): 258.
4. Jeffrey W. Hahn, "The Development of Local Legislatures in Russia: The Case of Yaroslavl," in *Democratization in Russia: The Development of Legislative Institutions*, ed. Jeffrey W. Hahn (London: Sharpe, 1996), 166.
5. Jeffrey W. Hahn, "Local Politics and Political Power in Russia: The Case of Yaroslavl," *Soviet Economy* 7, no. 4 (1991): 327.
6. James Hughes, "Sub-National Elites and Post-Communist Transformation in Russia: A Reply to Kryshtanovskaya and White," *Europe-Asia Studies* 49, no. 6 (1997): 1019.
7. Slider, "Elections."
8. Theodore H. Friedgut, "Community Structure, Political Participation, Soviet Local Government: The Case of Kutaisi," in *Soviet Politics and Society in the 1970s*, ed. Henry W. Morton and Rudolf L. Tokes (New York: Free Press, 1974), 261-96.
9. Anthony Oberschall, *Social Conflict and Social Movements* (Englewood Cliffs, N.J.: Prentice Hall, 1973).
10. Friedgut, "Community Structure."
11. Hahn, "Development of Local Legislatures," 161.
12. Jeffrey W. Hahn, "Conclusions: Common Features of Post-Soviet Local Politics," in *Local Power and Post-Soviet Politics*, ed. Theodore H. Friedgut and Jeffrey W. Hahn (London: Sharpe, 1994), 270-80; Jeffrey W. Hahn, "How Democratic are Local Russian Deputies?" in *In Search of Pluralism: Soviet and Post-Soviet Politics*, ed. Carol R. Saivetz and Anthony Jones (Boulder, Colo.: Westview, 1994), 62-85; Jeffrey W. Hahn, "Reforming Post-Soviet Russia: The Attitudes of Local Politicians," in *Local Power*, 208-38.
13. M. Steven Fish, *Democracy from Scratch: Opposition and Regime in the New Russian Revolution* (Princeton, N.J.: Princeton University Press, 1995), 26.
14. Fish, *Democracy from Scratch*, 80-199.
15. Hahn, "Development of Local Legislatures," 167.
16. Hahn, "Development of Local Legislatures," 190.
17. Hahn, "Local Politics."

18. Richard Balme, "Councilors, Issue Agendas and Political Action in Two French Towns," in *Local Politics and Participation in Britain and France*, ed. Albert Mabileau et al. (Cambridge: Cambridge University Press, 1989), 136.

19. Albert Mabileau, "Local Government in Britain and Local Politics and Administration in France," in *Local Politics and Participation*, 28.

20. George Moyser and Geraint Parry, "Councilors, Citizens and Agendas: Aspects of Local Decision-Making in Britain," in *Local Politics*, 159, 169. For a discussion of the social composition of local councils in the United Kingdom and other Western democracies, see also John Meadcroft, "Political Recruitment and Local Representation: The Case of Liberal Democrat Councilors," *Local Government Studies* 27, no. 1 (2001): 19-36.

21. Audun Offerdal et al., "Elites and Parties," in *Local Democracy and the Processes of Transformation in East-Central Europe*, ed. Harald Baldersheim et al. (Boulder, Colo.: Westview, 1996), 109.

22. Robert Michels, *Political Parties: A Sociological Study of the Oligarchical Tendencies of Modern Democracy*, 2d ed. (New York: Free Press, 1966).

23. Kenneth Newton, *Second City Politics: Democratic Processes and Decision-Making in Birmingham* (Oxford: Clarendon, 1976), 171.

24. Robert Dahl, *Who Governs? Democracy and Power in an American City* (New Haven, Conn.: Yale University Press, 1966).

25. Philip Selznick, *TVA and the Grass Roots: A Study in the Sociology of Formal Organization* (New York: Harper & Row, 1966), 219.

26. Selznick, *TVA and the Grass Roots*, 220.

27. An earlier 9 October 1990 USSR law On Public Associations left these matters to the "state organs" of the union and autonomous republics.

28. For provisions regarding the jurisdiction of city administrations over meetings and other mass acts, see, for example, art. 76.5.

29. Paul R. Brass, *Theft of an Idol: Text and Context in the Representation of Collective Violence* (Princeton, N.J.: Princeton University Press, 1997), 56.

30. Brass, *Theft of an Idol*, 27.

31. E. E. Schattschneider, *The Semi-Sovereign People: A Realist's View of Democracy in America* (New York: Holt, Rinehart & Winston, 1960), 18.

32. Interview by author, tape recording, Ufa, 7 June 1999.

33. Interview by author, tape recording, Moscow, 24 May 1999.

34. Interview by author, tape recording, Ufa, 8 June 1999.

35. Interview by author, tape recording, Ufa, 7 June 1999.

36. Newton, *Second City Politics*, 66.

37. Newton, *Second City Politics*, 66.

38. Grzegorz Ekiert and Jan Kubik, "Contentious Politics in New Democracies: East Germany, Hungary, Poland, and Slovakia, 1989-93," *World Politics* 50, no. 4, (1998): 559.

39. Ekiert and Kubik, "Contentious Politics," 561.

40. Interview by author, tape recording, Moscow, 25 May 1999.

41. William A. Gamson and Andre Modigliani, "Media Discourse and Public Opinion on Nuclear Power: A Constructionist Approach," *American Journal of Sociology* 95, no. 1 (1989): 1-37.

42. Interview by author, tape recording, Moscow, 24 May 1999.

43. Bert Klandermans, "The Social Construction of Protest and Multiorganizational Fields," in *Frontiers in Social Movement Theory*, ed. Aldon D. Morris and Carol McClurg Mueller (New Haven, Conn.: Yale University Press, 1992), 77-103.

44. Klandermans, "Social Construction of Protest."

45. Interview by author, tape recording, Moscow, 25 May 1999.

46. Interview by author, tape recording, Maykop, 12 August 1999.

47. Interview by author, tape recording, Maykop, 12 August 1999.

48. Michael Schwartz and Shuva Paul, "Resource Mobilization vs. the Mobilization of People: Why Consensus Movements Cannot Be Instruments of Social Change," in *Frontiers*, 205-23.

49. Doug McAdam, *Political Process and the Development of Black Insurgency, 1930-1970* (Chicago: University of Chicago Press, 1982), 27.

50. McAdam, *Political Process*, 26.

51. Craig J. Jenkins and Craig M. Eckert, "Channeling Black Insurgency: Elite Patronage and Professional Social Movement Organization in the Development of the Black Movement," *American Sociological Review* 51 (1986): 812-29.

52. Interview by author, tape recording, Maykop, 12 August 1999.

53. Interview by author, tape recording, Moscow, 24 May 1999.

54. Stenographic records, XII session, 14 October 1991.

55. Stenographic records, XII session.

56. Stenographic records, XII session.

57. Stenographic records, XII session.

58. Appeal of a group of deputies (in Russian), *VU*, 19 July 1991, 2.

59. "Komu nujhen soyuznyy status?" *VU*, 14 August 1990, 1.

60. "Dokumenty plenuma Tatarskogo obshchestvennogo tsentra O shestom vneocherednom vsebashkirskom kurultae," *VU*, 13 February 1992, 2.

61. Interview by author with Tatar activist, tape recording, Ufa, 7 June 1999.

62. "Decision on the draft declarations of state sovereignty of Bashkortostan" (in Russian), *VU*, 23 August 1990, 1.

63. Appeal to people's deputies of the Republic of Bashkortostan by Kerim Yaushev, chairman of TOTs, and Alexandr Arinin, chairman of the Duma of the public association Rus' (in Russian), *VU*, 11 June 1992, 1.

64. Stenographic records, XII session.

65. Stenographic records, XII session.

66. Stenographic records, XII session.

67. "Reshenie Ufimskogo gorodskogo soveta narodnykh deputatov O proektakh zakonov O prezidente BSSR i O vyborakh prezidenta BSSR," *VU*, 29 October 1991, 1.

68. Interview by author, tape recording, Ufa, 18 June 1999.

69. Interview by author, tape recording, Ufa, 7 June 1999.

70. Interview by author, tape recording, Ufa, 18 June 1999.

71. Appeal to the deputies of the Supreme Soviet of BSSR, signed by a group of Ufa soviet deputies, the Bashkir Association of Electors and Deputies, the Bashkir Branch of the Democratic Party of Russia, TOTs, and the Ufa Historical-Patriotic Society, among other organizations (in Russian), *VU*, 8 October 1990, 1.

72. V. Karataev, "Lobbi dlya parlamenta," *MN*, 18 October 1991, 1.

73. K. Sal'nikov, "Chto i kto stoit za paritetom," *MN*, 1 November 1991, 1.

74. "V poiskakh vykhoda iz tupika," *MN*, 6 November 1991, 1.

75. Schattschneider, *Semi-Sovereign People*, 18.

76. For example see Mary McAuley, "Politics, Economics, and Elite Realignment in Russia: A Regional Perspective," *Soviet Economy* 8, no. 1 (1992): 46-88.

77. Hahn, "Local Politics."

78. Jenkins and Eckert, "Channeling Black Insurgency"; Schwartz and Paul, "Resource Mobilization."

Chapter 5

The Soviets and Ethnic Conflict: The Deviant Case of North Ossetiya

The Ossetiyan-Ingush conflict of 1992 is the only case of large-scale interethnic (as opposed to secessionist) violence on the territory of the Russian Federation. Little has been written about this conflict: Russian sources have largely been limited to journalistic accounts, while Western scholarship is virtually nonexistent. The conflict, which claimed over 600 lives and displaced thousands of people, was overshadowed by developments in neighboring Chechnya and the "parade of sovereignties" elsewhere at the time.

Lack of scholarly exploration of the case can also be explained by its "messiness," which does not easily lend itself to parsimonious explanations. The conflict was over a territory with a predominantly Ingush population in North Ossetiya, the Prigorodnyy *rayon*. It was the culmination of a mass Ingush movement for their rehabilitation after deportation under Stalin. They were allowed to return to their lands in 1956, but were subject to political discrimination by the Ossetiyans, who now had administrative control over the formerly Ingush areas. The Ingush group also had an administrative entity of their own, but it was part of the larger Chechen-Ingush republic, where they were likewise politically underrepresented.

The parties to the conflict that erupted in 1992 were the North Ossetiyan republic, the Ingush in North Ossetiya's Prigorodnyy *rayon*, and the Ingush in Checheno-Ingushetiya. The Russian federal center may also be considered a party to the conflict. The Yel'tsin administration supported a controversial law which legitimized conflicting territorial claims on Prigorodnyy. It also contributed to the militarization of Ossetiyan authorities and, according to several independent and authoritative accounts, backed them in the conflict.[1]

It is thus a "unique" case of ethnic conflict and violence involving several institutional actors, and, as such, is unlike the other republics and their nontitular movements. However, the unique complexity of the case need not preclude comparative analysis. The conflict is interesting to the extent that it involves a nationalizing titular group, the Ossetiyans, and the republic's nontitular Ingush minority, although the Ingush in Ingushetiya played an important mobilizing role in the movement.

The case differs from the other republics along a number of dimensions other than violence, the degree of Ingush grievances being just one of them. But if similar causal mechanisms are observed in this "most different" case, it will be possible to make further generalizations about the other cases. At the same time, differences among the independent variables would allow for explanations of different outcomes in this and other cases. The differences on the dependent variable are easily identifiable: the intensity of the movement, which had greater mass-based support than did nontitular movements in Adygeya and Bashkortostan; the exclusive Ingush ethnic, rather than broadly nontitular, nature of the movement; and the violent outcome.

Since my principal hypotheses concern the role of local governing bodies, the purpose of this chapter is to identify differences in this independent variable. To what extent were the local soviets involved in the movement? How different was their composition from the other republics? How different was their institutional setup? How did they interact with independent nationalist groups? What resources did they furnish to the movement actors? And what was their contribution to the nature of the movement's issue framing and agenda setting? I will attempt to address these issues after first providing background information about the case. The investigation covers the two-year period leading up to the conflict (1990-1992).

Historical Background

North Ossetiya is a small, highly urbanized republic of only 8,000 square kilometers. In the south, it is bordered by Georgia's South Ossetiya and Russia's republics of Kabardino-Balkariya, Ingushetiya, and Chechnya, and by Stavropol' *kray* in the north. Its 664,200 population consists of 53 percent largely Orthodox Christian Ossetiyans, 29.9 percent Russians, and 5.2 percent Ingush.[2] The remaining population is largely comprised of Armenians, Georgians, Ukrainians, Kumyks, and other smaller groups.[3] Located in one of Russia's most unstable areas, it absorbed a substantial number of refugees from South Ossetiya, and subsequently from breakaway Chechnya, becoming Russia's most densely populated entity. In 1992, a violent conflict broke out in North Ossetiya between the titular Ossetiyans and the Ingush minority, erupting against the background of Chechnya's declaration of independence from Russia, Russia's adoption of the controversial law On the Rehabilitation of Repressed Peoples, Ossetiya's nationalization program, and the Ingush irredentist claims to Vladikavkaz and the Prigorodnyy *rayon*.

Ossetiyans were one of the first groups in the North Caucasus to accept Russian rule. This voluntary union stemmed from their Orthodox Christian identity in an overwhelmingly Muslim territory. Russia's hold over this strategically important area facilitated further conquests in the North Caucasus, which, until the mid-nineteenth century, was detached from the Christian areas—Georgia and Armenia—which Russia already controlled. The Ossetiyans, who were the only North Caucasus group to have opposed Shamil in the nineteenth century,[4] traditionally enjoyed a privileged position with the Russian rulers in the North Caucasus. Like the Christian Georgians, they benefited from the establishment of Russian lyceums and other places of learning, and occupied important posts in the tsarist administration in the North Caucasus.

The influx of Russians into the area dates back to the eighteenth century. A number of Cossack fortresses were established in Ossetiya to guard the strategically important Georgian Military Highway, linking Russia with Georgia and the rest of the Transcaucasus. Their numbers continued to rise throughout the following century. One such fort, Vladikavkaz, the future capital of North Ossetiya, was established on the Terek River in 1784. The fort was located on the border between the settlements of the Ossetiyans (left bank) and the other indigenous group, the Ingush (right bank). These settlements were recognized in the Russian administration's demarcation of the area, which lasted until 1860.[5]

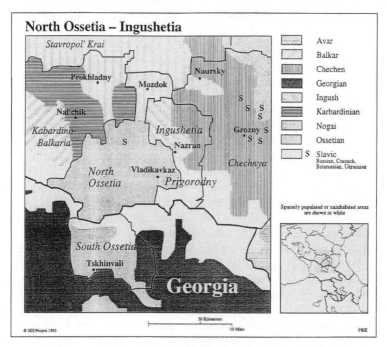

Figure 5.1. Map of North Ossetiya and Ingushetiya
Source: Fiona Hill, *Russia's "Tinderbox": Conflict in the North Caucasus and Its Implications for the Future of the Russian Federation* (Cambridge, Mass.: Harvard University, John F. Kennedy School of Government, Strengthening Democratic Institutions Project, 1995).

A mountainous group, the Ingush had from the sixteenth century onwards begun a process of migration to the fertile plains of the Tarskaya valley.[6] Here in the mountain foothills they founded the village of Angusht from which the word "Ingush" originated. Angusht became known as Tarskoe *selo* (village) in North Ossetiya's Prigorodnyy *rayon*. The Ingush used this fact during the Ossetiyan-Ingush conflict in 1992 to justify their claim over the disputed region.

By the eighteenth century, the Ingush had established a number of other settlements along the right bank of the Terek River in the Tarskaya valley. The Ingush initially accepted Russian rule voluntarily in 1810, participating in the defense and patrolling of the Military Highway in exchange for the right to use lands along the Terek's right bank. After the Caucasus wars in the 1860s, the Ingush were resettled in the mountains and their lands were given to the Cossacks, substantially complicating relations between the two groups.[7]

The Russian Civil War struggles over the North Caucasus further exacerbated the situation. Owing to the Cossacks' support of the Whites in 1920-1922, the lands along the Terek's right bank reverted to Ingush control. This decision was based on the Ingush's purported support for the Bolsheviks in the Civil War. The displaced Cossacks were resettled in other areas of the North Caucasus.[8] In 1922, together with Ossetiya, the areas of Ingush settlement were made part of the short-lived Mountainous Republic, which united the Chechens, Ingush, Ossetiyans, Karachays, Balkars, and Kabardines. Two years later, it splintered into a number of ethnically defined republics. The last of these to separate, the North Ossetiyan and Ingush Autonomous *oblasti*, were established in July 1924.

Until 1934, the capital city, Vladikavkaz, served as an administrative center for both North Ossetiya and the Ingush autonomous *oblasti*.[9] The city was effectively divided into two ethnic autonomies, as "two peoples, not one, clung on [to the city], who, on the basis of this, always had suspicions that one is trying to squeeze out the other one and will establish control in this city."[10] This is why, according to the Soviet administrators, "The issue of ethnic peace between these two nationalities . . . [was] extremely important."[11]

Between 1921 and 1934, the Ingush and the Ossetiyans maintained their own party and state organizations along the right and left banks of the Terek, respectively; they also maintained separate jurisdictions over different administrative buildings and enterprises.[12] The Ingush autonomy within Vladikavkaz, for example, possessed formal jurisdiction over eleven industrial enterprises.[13] When Ingushetiya was united with Chechnya to form a Chechen-Ingush Autonomous Republic, Groznyy became the capital of the new republic, and Vladikavkaz remained part of North Ossetiya. The largely Ingush-populated areas outside of Vladikavkaz, in Prigorodnyy *rayon*, remained part of Checheno-Ingushetiya until 1943. The Ingush have since regarded the loss of control over Vladikavkaz as a major setback; they now lacked a capital of their own with the required infrastructure, industrial, and cultural facilities.[14] Indeed, within the new Checheno-Ingush entity, most of the enterprises, including the oil-extracting, oil-processing, gas, and machine-building enterprises, as well as the cultural facilities, were located in Chechen territory, including and in particular the largely Chechen- and Russian-populated city of Groznyy.[15]

In 1943, Checheno-Ingushetiya was abolished. The two titular groups were deported en masse to Central Asia, sharing the fate of the Volga Germans, Crimean Tatars, Karachays, Balkars, Kalmyks, and the Meskhetian Turks.[16] The decision followed Stalin's allegations of their collaboration with the Nazis during the German occupation of, or proximity to, these respective areas.[17] With regard to the Chechens and Ingush, the decision was motivated more by the already present anti-Soviet movement in the area than by a substantial record of collaboration. On the eve of the German invasion, in 1940, the Chechens and Ingush mounted a rebellion against Soviet rule, establishing a Temporary People's Revolutionary Government of Checheno-Ingushetiya. In June 1942, the rebels urged local populations to welcome the approaching Germans as long as they recognized the independence of the Caucasus. The Germans, however, while sending recruiting missions to the area, never reached Checheno-Ingushetiya, a factor which did not prevent Stalin from accusing the Chechens and the Ingush of treachery.[18] Following deportations, the territory of Checheno-Ingushetiya was divided between North Ossetiya, Stavropol' *kray*, and Georgia. The formerly Ingush-populated Prigorodnyy *rayon* was transferred to North Ossetiya and largely resettled by ethnic Ossetiyans. For many years, the official press made no mention of the deported peoples. Their names were also wiped out from statistics books and maps, in what Robert Conquest, paraphrasing George Orwell, referred to as the emergence of "unnations."[19] The deported people were not allowed to return until Khrushchev reestablished the Chechen-Ingush autonomy in 1957. The Prigorodnyy *rayon*, however, remained administratively part of North Ossetiya.[20]

Even after their rehabilitation, the Ingush were underprivileged, particularly in North Ossetiya, but also in Checheno-Ingushetiya, where they comprised minority populations, third in size after the ethnic Russians. Although the Ingush were officially allowed to return to Prigorodnyy *rayon* after 1956, the Ossetiyan authorities threw up numerous obstacles to their resettlement. In particular, they tried to restrict their *propiska* (acquisition of residence permits), and discouraged the sale of land to them.

A secret Ossetiyan Council of Ministers directive gave this policy official sanction by explicitly prohibiting the sale and rent of homes and land to the Ingush.[21] The directive was reinforced after 1982, the year in which the Ingush were scapegoated for the murder of an Ossetiyan taxi driver in North Ossetiya; a "special regime" was introduced for house purchase in Prigorodnyy, leading to further anti-Ingush discrimination.[22]

From 1956 onwards the North Ossetiyan authorities also encouraged the migration of Ossetiyans from South Ossetiya into Prigorodnyy *rayon* in order to change the republic's ethnic balance.[23] The Ingush return and purchase of land continued nevertheless, with scores of Ingush residing in the area unofficially. In 1989, 33,000, or 6 percent of the Ingush population, lived in North Ossetiya, while 164,000, or 13 percent of the republic's population, lived in Checheno-

Ingushetiya, out of the USSR's total Ingush population of 215,000.[24] The vast majority of the Ingush population of North Ossetiya was concentrated in Prigorodnyy *rayon*, where in some towns (Chermen, Dachnoe, Kurtat, Mayskoe, and Tarskoe) the percentage of the Ingush ranged from 50 to 80 percent.[25]

The semilegal existence of many of the Ingush in Prigorodnyy exacerbated the severe unemployment and related problems in the area. While the Ossetiyan authorities pointed to the economic success and mobility of the Ingush in North Ossetiya, politically the Ingush remained underrepresented in the republic, also true in neighboring Checheno-Ingushetiya. Valery Tishkov writes that in 1992 there were only seven Ingush deputies in the North Ossetiyan Supreme Soviet, and none in the republic presidium or the government.

Despite their sizeable presence in the Prigorodnyy district, out of the fifty-three top party, soviet, and managerial posts only five were occupied by ethnic Ingush. In Checheno-Ingushetiya the Ingush occupied only four out of seventy-three posts in the republic's CPSU Central Committee, four out of the fifty-six government posts, and only three out of the twenty-one government and committee chairs.[26]

In 1990, North Ossetiya declared sovereignty, stressing the "inviolability of its borders." In April of the same year, the RSFSR Supreme Soviet adopted the controversial law On the Rehabilitation of Repressed Peoples, implicitly challenging that very "inviolability." The law provided for the restoration of "territorial integrity" and "territorial rehabilitation" for the deported and repressed peoples.[27] As such, it could be interpreted as justifying the Cossacks' claim to the areas claimed by the Ingush and vice versa.

These events, combined with events in neighboring Checheno-Ingushetiya, served to exacerbate relations between the Ossetiyans and the Ingush on the one hand, and the Ingush and the Cossacks on the other. North Ossetiya's nationalizing policies are discussed further below. The following is an outline of political developments in the Chechen-Ingush republic. In September 1991, the All-National Congress of Chechen People came to power after a nationalist coup disbanded the Supreme Soviet of Checheno-Ingushetiya. The Congress, headed by Djhokhar Dudaev, established the Temporary High Council of Checheno-Ingushetiya, and proceeded to proclaim a separate Chechen republic. This decision, taken without Ingush participation, meant that Ingushetiya became a separate entity by default.

The republic thus found itself virtually without official power structures, the soviets in the three predominantly Ingush *rayony* (Nazran', Malgobek, and Sunjha) acting as interim government organs. The split of the republic exacerbated the Ingush territorial claims to the Prigorodnyy district. Not only did the Ingush find themselves without government structures, but, without Groznyy, they also lacked a developed administrative center. Nazran', which became the capital of the new republic, was a small town with undeveloped infrastructure. In contrast, the Prigorodnyy *rayon* and the right-bank side of Vladikavkaz, to which the Ingush movement laid claim, concentrated much of North Ossetiya's industrial and administrative facilities, and educational and other academic establishments.

North Ossetiya's Nationalizing Policies

The above factors, as well as North Ossetiya's nationalizing policies, contributed to the exacerbation of Ossetiyan-Ingush tensions leading up to the conflict. What is puzzling is that no other nontitular movement emerged to contest these policies. North Ossetiya was the first republic to declare its sovereignty. The most important clause of the declaration was related to territorial integrity, which was a response to Ingush territorial demands. North Ossetiya otherwise followed the usual path by declaring sovereignty and making efforts to ensure the titular group's predominance in local political structures. Although a new constitution would not be adopted until a later date, in 1991 the Supreme Soviet was already defining the boundaries of the document as one based on the "national traditions of the Ossetiyan people."[28] The de facto Ossetization of political and other appointments at the expense of nontitular groups, and not just the Ingush, was evident very early in the sovereignization process. The 1990 elections to the Ossetiyan Supreme Soviet had already yielded a massive overrepresentation of the titular group, with Ossetiyans comprising 70 percent; Russians, 24 percent; and other groups, 6 percent of the deputy corps. This was despite the proportional distribution of the above groups in the republic at large being 53, 30, and 17 percent, respectively.[29] Subsequent elections held in 1995 underscore the trend of increasing nativization, with elections yielding 86 percent Ossetiyans, 10 percent Russians, and 4 percent categorized as "others."[30] Significantly, the capital of Vladikavkaz, with its sizeable Russian presence (37 percent of the population), yielded only one Russian deputy, the mayor M. Shatalov.[31]

As in Adygeya and Bashkortostan, these policies were accompanied by strong nationalist discourse. The Ingush claims to Prigorodnyy and the conflict in South Ossetiya fostered a doomsday rhetoric about a threat to the survival of the Ossetiyan nation, its ongoing or potential national and cultural extinction, and indeed "genocide" at the hands of Georgians, Ingush, and other groups. The official proceedings of the Extraordinary Congress of the Ossetiyan People, organized by the Ossetiyan Supreme Soviet, reveal the nationalist rhetoric of the moment. The proceedings read: "In this period, difficult for our Fatherland, we have gathered to eliminate the imminent threat to . . . Ossetiya."[32] The Congress called for the "social protection of the Ossetiyan people" in the face of the challenge to the "destiny of the nation" and the threat of its "physical extinction and spiritual degradation."[33] It also urged the adoption of "extraordinary measures for the defense of and national rebirth of the Ossetiyan people."[34] The conflict in South Ossetiya, which fostered the titular elite's debate about a potential unification of the two entities, was likewise couched in terms suggesting a possible establishment of an ethnocracy.

These nationalizing trends were broadly similar to those in the other two cases, and, as in Adygeya and Bashkortostan, affected the mobility of the non-titular groups based on ascriptive criteria. The Ingush, however, were the only nontitular group to contest these policies, although they linked them with the territorial question. The Ingush movement, as in the other two republics, united a variety of actors—the nationalist groups, local soviet deputies, and Ingush intelligentsia in North Ossetiya, Checheno-Ingushetiya, and Moscow. Conspicuous for its absence was any involvement from broader nontitular forces. Indeed, unlike in Adygeya and Bashkortostan, no significant Russian or Slavic public associations emerged to contest Ossetiya's nationalizing policies. The capital city soviet was likewise conspicuously absent from the movement. So were the soviets in the other predominantly Russian and Cossack regions.

In short, there was no Russian, or indeed, broadly nontitular movement, to speak of, though we have established the case for objective grievances of the nontitular population as a whole. In contrast, the Ingush movement was a lot more intense, sustained, and mass-based than the nontitular movements in the other two cases, and the Ossetiyan-Ingush confrontation had a violent outcome.

The Ossetiyan-Ingush Conflict

The violence that took place in November 1992 is attributed to a variety of factors including the role of the federal center. In 1991, Ossetiyan anti-Ingush discrimination in Prigorodnyy and claims of the Ingush soviets to the *rayon* and the right-bank side of Vladikavkaz, as well as their threats to march on North Ossetiya to recapture their homes, led to the deterioration of the situation in Prigorodnyy. The Ingush claims were in turn used by North Ossetiya as a justification for further anti-Ingush measures. In April, clashes between Ossetiyans and the Ingush led to North Ossetiya's establishment of a curfew in the *rayon*, legitimizing still more anti-Ingush discrimination with regard to housing permits. An "extraordinary" Ossetiyan Supreme Soviet session held on 29 April featured strong anti-Ingush rhetoric, provoking the Ingush deputies to walk out. By the end of the year, the republic succeeded in establishing its own military formations, the "republican guard," with the declared aim of fending off the Ingush irredentist claims.

In May 1992, the Ossetiyan Supreme Soviet decreed the production of military equipment in North Ossetiya's enterprises in order to equip the "republican guard." It also secured the deliveries of military hardware for its OMON (special police forces) from Moscow, which led to claims by Ingush and independent observers that a campaign of ethnic cleansing involving both the federal center and North Ossetiya was being planned. At the same time, the Ingush in Prigorodnyy's towns and those in the Chechen-Ingush republic were also establishing their own military formations and stockpiling weapons. The three Ingush soviets in Ingushetiya and deputies from the Prigorodnyy *rayon* organized the guards and subordinated them to the local Internal Affairs forces. These were in turn subordinated to the soviets, which served to legitimize the Ossetiyan OMON's raids of Prigorodnyy, triggering further hostilities. In October an Ingush girl was accidentally run over by an Ossetiyan armored vehicle in the Prigorodnyy *rayon* in what some saw as a deliberate provocation. On 31 October the Ossetiyan military formations, backed by the Russian Internal Affairs forces, clashed with those of the Ingush in Prigorodnyy. The hostilities lasted until 5 November, claiming hundreds of lives on both sides and resulting in the expulsion of thousands of Ingush from the *rayon*.[35]

Most accounts of the conflict have focused on the violent exchanges and events immediately preceding them, such as the accident involving the Ingush girl. In other words, the Ossetiyan-Ingush case was interesting to scholars from the point of view of explaining violence. Yet violence is just one possible outcome of movement dynamics, or, according to some scholars, one of a movement's many "repertoires" of collective action. There are few scholarly analyses of the Ingush movement, its most important actors, resource bases, strategies, and so forth, factors identified in the introductory chapter as essential for explaining movement dynamics. Here is an opportunity to test further the hypotheses about the role of local governing bodies, if any, in this "most different" case. The following sections investigate the role of the local soviets along dimensions identified in the analysis of Adygeya and Bashkortostan, that is, their composition, relationships with public associations and local societies, the resources they controlled, and the nature of their agenda setting.

The Soviets

The Ingush local soviets, elected in 1990, were present as actors before and during the Ossetiyan-Ingush conflict. To what extent was their composition different from the soviets examined in Adygeya and Bashkortostan? The soviets that became identified with the Ingush nationalist movement were the Nazran', Malgobek, and Sunjha *rayon* soviets in Checheno-Ingushetiya. Although a complete list of deputies in the three Ingush *rayony* is not available, published candidate lists and deputies' biographies give some indication of the makeup of these lower bodies.[36] They leaned towards rural *nomenklatura* and managers, such as directors of collective farms and enterprises. Party, Komosomol, trade union, and "voluntary association" leaders and activists were also well represented. Of the 177 registered candidates for the Nazran' *rayon* soviet, eighty, or almost half, occupied manager, director, or chairman posts in enterprises, schools, local soviets, or the local party hierarchy.[37] Rural professionals and intelligentsia, such as engineers, teachers, and middle-level managers were also well represented. The composition of the lower soviets therefore did not differ significantly from their counterparts in the other two republics.

The three soviets were also overwhelmingly Ingush. This reflected what Tishkov described as an unwritten consensus in the republic whereby, while being underrepresented in the Chechen-Ingush republic bodies, the Ingush were allowed to enjoy political predominance in the three Ingush areas of Checheno-Ingushetiya.[38]

The one identifiable difference with Adygeya and Bashkortostan is the orientation of candidate platforms, and it is therefore worth discussing at some length. Candidates' lists of social, economic, and other concerns in some cases also included a reference to the Ingush issue. Moreover, those who did address the Ingush question often pledged to work for the restoration of the Ingush autonomy in its "historical" borders, with the capital in North Ossetiya's right-bank side of Vladikavkaz. However, most candidate deputies for the *rayon* and city soviets avoided the issue altogether, focusing on specific practical measures that they would undertake in a given locality. Thus, a doctor pledged to improve medical transport, and relieve the deficit of medication for patients in his constituency;[39] a department store head pledged to meet the demands of rural and urban dwellers in terms of consumer supply;[40] and a deputy head of a transport enterprise pledged to work for "the well-being and the development of greenery in the microdistrict number three on Moskovskaya Street, the development of sport and cultural activities among the district's youth."[41] I was able to identify only one deputy candidate for the *rayon* soviet who placed the Ingush issue as his number one priority.[42]

It was the candidates for the RSFSR and the USSR Supreme Soviets who most explicitly addressed the Ingush question. There appears to have been an assumed difference in perceptions of the prospective responsibilities of those in the RSFSR and union bodies on the one hand, and those in the regional and local soviets on the other. The RSFSR and USSR candidates and deputies saw themselves primarily as lobbyists for legislation that would address the consequences of Stalin's repressions against the Ingush, and Ingushetiya's political and territorial status.

Those who had a record of involvement with the Ingush movement took great pains to emphasize it in their biographies. The platform of Bembulat Bogatyryov, who was to become a key spokesman of the Ingush in Moscow, read: "As a member of the organizational committee, elected at the second congress of the Ingush people, he . . . incessantly works to restore the Ingush autonomy as part of Russia."[43] The platform of Ibragim Kostoev, another prominent Ingush activist, likewise pledged to work within the constitutional space in order to address the evils of ethnic cleansing under Stalin.

This contrasts with the lower-level deputies, whose credentials and career paths were those of the typical mid- or low-level party and administrative *nomenklatura*. The openness with which the RSFSR and USSR deputies addressed the Ingush questions in early 1990 suggests no taboo at the time in voicing the Ingush nationalist grievances. It is evidence that prospective candidates for the lower bodies stressed the day-to-day administrative concerns of their constituencies as their main functions, that is, those expected from them as local deputies.

The impression one gets from an examination of the local soviet deputies' corps is confirmed in interviews with Ingush movement activists of different political orientations. They dismissed the soviets and their deputies as composed of *nomenklatura* officials with no prior involvement in the Ingush movement. Some were even actively involved in persecuting Ingush nationalists during the Soviet period. Abdulkhamid Aushev, the chairman of Nazran' *rayon* soviet, who in the 1990s became a supporter of the Ingush nationalist group Niyskho (Justice), is alleged, in the 1970s, to have condemned Ingush activists as "rogues" and as engaged in the pursuit of "vestiges of the past," or *perejhitki proshlogo*, a Soviet label for nationalism.[44]

In spite of such a presence, the soviets actively cooperated with and supported the radical and militant fringes of the movement over 1990-1992. In this sense, they differed from their counterparts in Adygeya and Bashkortostan. At this point it is important to discuss the various strands of the movement and the two key public organizations representing it, the moderate Organizational Committee (OC) and the radical Niyskho.

Public Associations: The Radicals and the Moderates

The presses of the respective soviets and the two movements allow for an identification of distinctions in the ultimate aims, policies, tactics, and strategies of the public associations. These were hotly debated in the pages of the newspapers of the two nationalist groups, *Daymokh* and *Ingushkoe slovo* (*IS*). In fact, at one point *IS* lamented that splits within the Ingush movement had led to a situation where over 70 percent of the newspaper was dedicated to sorting out differences between the two rival groups, rather than addressing the question of the Ingush statehood proper. Both movements fought for control over the local soviets as a means of legitimizing the respective policy lines.[45]

The main differences between the various actors centered on strategies, tactics, and issue framing, and the timing of policies, rather than the ultimate goals. Niyskho, the OC, and Ingush public opinion agreed on the need for the restoration of Ingush autonomy with the capital in the right-bank side of Vladikavkaz, with the eventual return of land in the Prigorodnyy *rayon* to the Ingush. There were clear differences, however, as to the strategies for achieving this goal.

In March 1991, Niyskho and the Ingush deputies allied with it favored the declaration of Ingush autonomy without waiting for the territorial border issue to be resolved. The OC cautioned against this as potentially destabilizing. For the same reason the OC was against Chechnya's declaration of sovereignty and the resulting split from Checheno-Ingushetiya. Niyskho favored sovereignty as the quickest means of achieving Ingush statehood and in November of the same year, it urged the establishment of the Ingush republic without recourse to public endorsement. The OC insisted on a referendum as a means of obtaining a mandate and legitimacy backed by both the Ingush and non-Ingush populations. In October 1992, when Ingushetiya became a separate republic, the OC once again cautioned against haste and came out against the holding of elections to the Ingush Popular Assembly (Narodnyy sovet); Niyskho favored elections before the borders of the new entity were delineated. The difference in positions was an important one: Niyskho's position implied that the disputed areas would be included in the electoral districts despite North Ossetiya's continued claim to them. Issa Kodzoev, Niyskho's head, had previously explicitly stated that "the inhabitants of Prigorodnyy *rayon* . . . can also take part in the elections of the parliament of the Ingush republic."[46] It was ultimately destabilizing as it implied a unilateral change of jurisdictions over the disputed territory and, as the OC had feared, led to an increase in anti-Ingush militancy by the Ossetiyan authorities and the wider public.

Finally, while the OC favored quiet lobby and pressure tactics in Moscow and Groznyy, Niyskho opted for a demonstrative show of force. In September 1991, it proclaimed the establishment of the Ingush national guards and urged the public to enlist voluntarily, a measure endorsed by the Ispolkom, the Executive Committee of Ingush Deputies of all Levels. In April 1991, Niyskho announced a "peaceful march" to recapture the Ingush homes in Prigorodnyy; the OC was harshly critical of the measure since it provided North Ossetiya's president Askharbek Galazov with the means of fanning waves of anti-Ingush hysteria in North Ossetiya. In October 1992, Niyskho called for the establishment of "self-defense" units ostensibly for the defense of Ingush homes in Prigorodnyy against the Ossetiyans, a measure likewise criticized by the OC.

The different strategies were also reflected in the choice of movement frames. Disagreements between the two wings ranged from the definition of the boundaries of the Ingush movement, to the labeling of its objectives, to the definition of the precise movement issues. The OC, which lobbied in Moscow, and was associated with Russia's first-wave democrats, urged for a more inclusive umbrella for the movement. The OC was apprehensive of Niyskho's labeling of its key political organ as that composed of "deputies of all levels of Ingush nationality." Although the OC strove to further the Ingush territorial objectives, it perceived the ethnocentrism of such labeling as damaging to potential support by the other ethnic groups living in North Ossetiya and Ingushetiya. Niyskho, in contrast, stressed its own popular credentials as the only organ speaking on behalf of the "Ingush people."[47]

The Soviets and Extremism in the Ingush Movement

In terms of their involvement with the radicals, the position of local soviets and individual Ingush deputies in North Ossetiya and Ingushetiya is puzzling. The radicals' key political organization and political forum had the soviets' label attached to it, namely the Ispolkom. The soviets of the three Ingush *rayony* in Checheno-Ingushetiya (Nazran', Malgobek, and Sunjha), their chairmen, and local deputies from North Ossetiya's Prigorodnyy *rayon*, appeared also to have been active players in the movement. Signatures of those who made up the above organs graced the radicals' major nationalist pronouncements, and they also made nationalist statements and demands in their own right.

Such efforts, however, were at odds with perceptions and evidence of the actual power and political orientation of the soviets at the time. When interviewed, the Ingush activists, both the radicals and the moderates, assert that the soviets were powerless agencies with little or no potential to influence local political developments. Moreover, as mentioned above, they claim that council chairmen and deputies who cooperated with the movement had no prior record of involvement with it. Finally, the soviets' involvement was at odds with assertions of scholars, activists, and policy makers about the general "power vacuum" and "chaos" which ensued after Ingushetiya became separate from Chechnya. The implication was that Ingushetiya lost the government bodies based in Chechnya, for which the weak lower-level soviets, composed of part-time deputies, could not compensate. Then why cooperate with these bodies? And why did these bodies find it advantageous to cooperate with the nationalists, particularly the radicals?

An investigation of press accounts of the movement and interviews with activists suggests several reasons for cooperation. While these are largely similar to those discussed in the cases of Adygeya and Bashkortostan, they also stem from the peculiar institutional circumstances in which the republic found itself after its separation from Chechnya.

The main reason for cooperation with the soviets was the facility with which they could claim to be legitimate organs—both as "grassroots" and "official" agencies—depending on who they were dealing with and the circumstances of such labeling. In other words, it changed depending on whether the Ingush activists dealt with the power structures in Moscow, or whether they were trying to sell a given line to the Ingush population. Despite the weakness of the local soviets, the legitimacy factor was particularly important in the case of the Ingush movement. The circumstances of the "power vacuum," whereby Ingushetiya lost the main state bodies, made the soviets the only "official" agencies and as such facilitated their lobbying efforts in Moscow. At the same time, as popularly elected bodies, they were well placed to legitimize a given line as "truly representative" of Ingush mass opinion, whatever the actual extent of Ingush mass support for the radicals. A former Niyskho activist recalled how in its struggles against the rival OC, Niyskho maintained: "You are not a legitimate organ. . . . In terms of authority, we have the *rayon* soviets."[48] Another example, with respect to what was representative of the association of the soviets and deputies with "the people," a statement of the Niyskho-controlled Ispolkom reads:

> The Ispolkom is the only organ empowered to speak on behalf of the Ingush people, since it is elected by the deputies of all levels. One who offers obstacles to the Ispolkom is an enemy to our popular cause, the enemy of the Ingush people. The mandates of the Ispolkom of Peoples' Deputies of Ingushetiya have been approved by the three *rayon* soviets, and hence, by all power structures of Ingushetiya. The Ispolkom . . . is the core [*ochag*] around which the Ingush people have to unite for the sake of their future.[49]

The second reason for cooperation was the resources that the soviets possessed. The soviets may not have directly funded the activities of Niyskho, but they had jurisdiction and control over material assets in their respective territories. These were used for important movement activities, but also, according to

Niyskho's rivals, for corruption. An Ingush activist maintains: "There was a material side [to the soviets' involvement with Niyskho]. Niyskho's members, through the soviets, built houses for themselves, could obtain cars, or could ensure that funds were transferred to their structures."[50] While allegations of corruption by the rival group may have been unfounded there is ample evidence that the soviets published their own newspapers and controlled public transportation and other facilities which were used for movement work. In the summer of 1990, for example, an Ingush delegation traveled to Moscow for lobbying purposes. The trip, involving 380 local Ingush deputies, was widely publicized in the soviets' press. The soviets' official newspaper *Put' Lenina* reported it as something of a pilgrimage:

> Some of the deputies took air and rail transport. We traveled on seven *ikarusy* [public buses]. . . . The road was long and hard, but the deputies strongly withstood all the difficulties of the journey. . . . Everybody along the route knew that the whole of the Ingush deputy corps was heading towards the capital. The republics and *oblasti* received us according to all the rules of civic ethics. No obstacles were levelled anywhere along the route.[51]

Not only was the above "pilgrimage" made on public buses, controlled by municipalities, it was also guarded by the local automobile inspection forces: "We were accompanied by GAI [state automobile inspection] cars, headed by the chief of GAI of Sunjhenskiy ROVD [*rayon* department of internal affairs], Militia Captain A. Bazgiev, as well as by ambulances."[52]

The soviets also possessed jurisdiction over local police forces, and the above quote is just one example of how they were used. This control was important in two respects. The most obvious incidence of this control was during the violence when the soviets acted as rallying points for the organization of Ingush self-defense units.

A second, equally if not more important, aspect of this control was during the two years prior to the conflict when it was used by Niyskho as a public relations strategy. Jurisdiction over the police was used as muscle flexing, not only against the Ossetiyans, as a means of portraying the movement as capable of a restoration of Ingush "statehood" by violent means and of giving "adequate" response to the Ossetiyans' vastly superior resources, but also against the rivals within the Ingush movement itself, to portray the pro-Niyskho radical wing as more powerful against the "destructive forces" in the rival OC. A notable example was Ispolkom's proclamation of the formation of the National Guard. The announcement was published in Malgobek *rayon* soviet's press organ *Leninskoe znamya*. The appeal read:

> The key aim is to ensure, together with the *rayispolkom*'s internal affairs departments, the stable functioning of all power and administrative structures, shielding them from all sorts of blackmail, disinformation, and pressure from destructive elements who dislike the constructive, democratic transformations carried out by the Executive Committee of People's Deputies of Ingushetiya of

all Levels, in the course of the preparation for and the holding of universal direct elections to the highest organs of people's power in the republic. . . . In the future . . . the National Guard will start fulfilling the tasks of a full program of military preparation. . . . Annually, a recruitment of volunteers will take place through town, village soviets, and *rayon* military commissariats.[53]

The soviets also made other martial statements with high mobilizational appeal, such as the "peaceful marches" to recapture Ingush homes in Ossetiya's Prigorodnyy *rayon*, and cavalry rides into the republic. Individual Ingush activists recognized such statements as mere bluff tactics, as indeed did the Ossetiyan authorities. Yet, they served to further justify Ossetiyan official anti-Ingush propaganda and the republic's efforts to portray the movement and indeed the group as a whole as bent on violence. They also facilitated the rallying of other groups, such as the Russians and Cossacks, behind its anti-Ingush hysteria. As the OC remarked:

Our opponents were aided by the chairman of the Nazran' *rayon ispolkom* M. Lyanov, who threatened a cavalry attack, composed of five thousand Ingush riders. And even though the leadership of North Ossetiya clearly understood that it was a bluff (at the very least because even in the whole of the North Caucasus one cannot find five (!) thousand horses, it provided another basis for the fueling of anti-Ingush sentiment in society, and for the further militarization of the republic.[54]

A final advantage derived from cooperation with the soviets was their influence over local social networks. This influence overlapped with that already possessed by Niyskho, providing overall advantages to the radicals in terms of mass-based support. At this point, it is important to discuss the social organization of the Ingush. As with a number of the other North Caucasus groups, such as the Chechens, the Ingush social organization is based on clans or *teypy*. The *teypy* are cohesive extended kinship networks of the kind that social movement scholars like Anthony Oberschall, Bert Klandermans, and Doug McAdam consider crucial raw materials for rapid mass-based mobilization.[55] Some scholars of the conflict have noted that *teypy* differences were one of the key cleavages dividing Niyskho and the OC. While the OC based its support on the Ingush community in Groznyy, Niyskho relied on *teypy* within Ingushetiya itself.[56] Niyskho thus possessed a double advantage: its activists were based in the localities within Ingushetiya itself and rooted in its social networks, enjoying the support of the local power organs, which likewise enjoyed regular interactions at the grassroots levels. The OC, by contrast, was based and socially rooted in Chechnya's capital, while its activists concentrated on lobbying higher-power organs in either Chechnya or Moscow.

The combination of social and power networks that Niyskho could rely on made up for an easily mobilizable "multiorganizational field."[57] The cohesiveness of the social networks in and of itself facilitated nationalist agenda setting, but was also reinforced by the cooperation of power organs with control over the local populations. While the public association influenced local networks by virtue of its rootedness within them, the soviets did so through their press organs, possession of mobilizational resources, such as transport, meeting spaces, and so forth. One way of looking at it is that the soviets provided mobilizational infrastructures on top of the existing social networks much like the churches in the American South did for the cohesive African American communities during the Civil Rights movement.[58]

One gets a strong sense from reading the presses of the two Ingush movement wings that it is this work with, and influence over, the "grassroots," which made up the key differences between the radicals and the moderates. The OC lamented: "We are rightly criticized that we seldom go to the villages, do not sufficiently communicate with the population of Ingushetiya, do not inform the people well about events that are taking place and about our work, and when we do, it is with delays."[59] In another statement against Niyskho's allegations against the OC, the latter retorted:

> A common allegation against the Organizational Committee made by the "democrats" from Niyskho is its separation [*otorvannost'*] from the masses. . . . I do admit that [our] meetings [with the local population] could be held more often. However, one thing is clear: the OC was elected specifically to work with power structures in order to address lawfully the Ingush problem.[60]

What is significant is that the OC often attributed its failure to reach to the grassroots to the obstruction of the local soviets. In 1991, when the OC held a congress alternative to the "extraordinary congress" organized by Niyskho, the heads of the three local soviets "directly or indirectly set obstacles to the holding of the congress, obstructing the process of the election of delegates to it."[61] In August 1992, Niyskho's Extraordinary Session of the Ingush People involving local deputies issued a mandate to "forbid the informal organizations and structures from holding unsanctioned meetings, *skhody*, and marches, before the end of the elections to the parliament of the Ingush republic."[62] The measure was clearly aimed at suppressing the OC, which considered potential elections to the parliament as destabilizing.

Institutional Differences Accounting for Variable Soviets' Roles

The soviets' support in North Ossetiya for the radical line and their contribution to militant issue framing contrasts with their restraining role in Adygeya and Bashkortostan. The makeup of these bodies does not lend itself to facile conclusions about the aggregation and articulation of variable movement preferences in any of the three cases. Indeed, as I have noted, in all three cases the local soviets had a distinctly lower- to middle-level *nomenklatura* makeup. The chairmen of the three Ingush *rayon* soviets were standard party *apparatchiki* with no record of nationalist movement involvement, much like those in Adygeya and Bashkortostan; some of them even actively fought against "vestiges of the past" during the Soviet period. In contrast to Adygeya and Bashkortostan, these chairmen and the deputies that made up Niyskho's Executive Committee of Deputies of all Levels endorsed a radical and militant line. There is no evidence that Ingush mass opinion favored extremist tactics, although the Ossetiyan press used the soviets' statements to present it as such. The fact that the movement itself was split between the radicals and the moderates reveals the complexity of the Ingush perception of the issue and the differences in preferences for achieving their goals. It is thus not appropriate to suggest that the Ingush *nomenklatura* in the soviets spoke on behalf of the Ingush mainstream opinion.

In the Ingush case, there were clear institutional differences along a number of dimensions, and I argue that they significantly contributed to the radicalization of the Ingush movement and the Ossetiyan "countermovement." Following Chechnya's declaration of independence, the Ingush soviets in the former Checheno-Ingushetiya became effectively self-governing bodies with no agencies above them. It took the Russian government in Moscow more than a year to set up new government structures in the republic. As I have demonstrated, words like "chaos," "power vacuum," and "lawlessness" were used to describe the situation that ensued, even by the Russian government functionaries involved, most notably Valery Tishkov. While local soviets in Adygeya and Bashkortostan were still part of the old structures of democratic centralism, however loose, the Ingush local soviets lost all political agencies above them, republic and federal alike. Even the police forces, while formally subordinate to the federal Ministry of Interior, became de facto controlled by the local soviets.

These institutional factors eliminated all constraints for political maneuver of the kind discussed in Adygeya, such as threats of sanctions against council chairmen and their co-optation by higher bodies. Another consequence of these institutional differences was that Ingushetiya was finally in the process of obtaining republic structures together with all the trappings of republic power and status. Those in the main government organs that existed at the time, namely in the soviets, were well placed politically to advance in the new power structures. They had the incentives to support Niyskho, which urged quick Ingush statehood without the nuanced wait-and-see position that the rival OC took.

Explaining Nonmovements

A final point to be addressed is the lack of a broader nontitular movement in North Ossetiya and the failure of the other nontitulars within the republic to show support for the Ingush movement. The Ingush were in fact not the only group with territorial claims and ethnic grievances within North Ossetiya. As in Adygeya and Bashkortostan, the capital city, Vladikavkaz, had a sizeable population of ethnic Russians and other nontitulars. Yet, there appeared to be no city-based nontitular movement on the scale observed in the other two republics. North Ossetiya also had another disputed territory, the Mozdok *rayon*, which

borders on Stavropol' *kray* and has a sizeable Cossack population. Before Stalin's deportations of the Chechens and the Ingush, the territory was administratively part of Checheno-Ingushetiya. After the two groups were deported, Mozdok was ceded to North Ossetiya's jurisdiction.[63] Coinciding with developments
in Ingushetiya, there were stirrings in the Mozdok *rayon* about a possible cession of the area to the largely Russian *kray*. These received scant publicity, and
were quickly hushed up as prompted by economic, rather than ethnic, concerns,
and those who advocated separation were branded as extremists. In other words,
there may have been strong ethnic grievances, even if there was no movement as
such. Mozdok remained part of North Ossetiya. An examination of the local
soviet newspapers suggests that not only did the local soviets and their chairmen
in Vladikavkaz and Mozdok fail to articulate nontitular grievances; they actively
suppressed nontitular political activism in their localities. They also cooperated
with the Ossetiyan authorities against the Ingush movement and supported anti-
Ingush measures such as the limiting of the Ingush residence permits.[64] The
Vladikavkaz soviet appeared to have been a particularly apolitical body and its
conflicts with the Ossetiyan Supreme Soviet centered on such trivial matters as
the jurisdiction over public monuments in the republic's capital.

   In Mozdok, the *rayon* soviet chairman waged a public relations campaign
against the head of a local public association, the Mozdok chapter of the Democratic Party of Russia (DPR), which advocated nontitular rights. The soviet's official daily, *Mozdokskiy vestnik*, harangued the chairman of the local branch of
the DPR, the key advocate of secession, as a "power hungry" "former apparatchik," a "where-the-wind-blows Communist," and ridiculed his efforts on behalf
of ethnic Russians' rights.[65] At the same time, it presented the nontitulars' aspi-
rations to join Stavropol' *kray* as motivated by economic, rather than ethnic,
concerns.[66] The soviet's deputies made strenuous efforts to remove the issue of
secession or a plebiscite from the public agenda altogether. A local critic of the
Mozdok soviet reported: "The deputies of the *rayon* soviet obstruct the issue. . . .
The question was not included on the recent session's agenda; the spring session
avoided it altogether." "The majority [of the deputies]," the article went on, "are
staunchly against this issue, arguing that it could lead to referenda at the smallest
village levels." The article concluded: "Having thus eliminated even the mere
legal possibility of giving the Mozdok constituencies the right to express their
views on the problem which concerns them, the deputies caused damage to
themselves: the opposition . . . now has an advantage in demanding the resignation of the deputies of the current soviet."[67]

   In Adygeya and Bashkortostan, the local soviets used possible territorial
splits of the republics as bargaining chips in their struggles with the titular-
controlled Supreme Soviets, although they did exercise an overall moderating
role on the movements. The main difference between the cases is the failure to
make the sentiments for greater rights or cession to Stavropol' into *public* issues
and to mobilize the deputies' constituencies behind nontitular agenda. A further
contrast with the Mozdok case is that, while the Mozdok soviets strenuously
avoided such vehicles for the mobilization and politicization of the mass publics

as plebiscites, referenda, and so forth, those in Adygeya and Bashkortostan frequently resorted to such measures. The local soviets in North Ossetiya also cooperated with the Ossetiyan authorities in their anti-Ingush campaign. During the Ossetiyan-Ingush conflict, the Mozdok and Vladikavkaz soviets, as indeed the other Russian soviets, served as focal points for the organization of Ossetiya's "self-defense" units on the ground.

The "nonmovements" are attributable to two factors relevant to this investigation. One is the failure of those who controlled key instruments of Ingush public agenda setting to devise a more inclusive frame for the Ingush movement, the result being the predominance of the radical line and the alienation of potential supporters from amongst other groups. This was largely due to the facilitating role of the Ingush local soviets. The Ossetiyan authorities used the publicity given to the Ingush radical wing by the soviets to rally the other nontitular groups, most notably the Cossacks, behind its anti-Ingush campaigns.

Such a framing contrasted with that in Adygeya and Bashkortostan, where the soviets marginalized the radical nationalists and tried to devise more inclusive democratic issue frames. The second reason for the "nonmovements" is that even where there was grassroots nontitular activism, it was consistently suppressed by the local soviets. The Mozdok case supports the contention that the position of the local soviet was crucial in the degree of grassroots nontitular activism.

Conclusion

The Ingush case differed from nontitular movements in Adygeya and Bashkortostan in that the soviets chose to cooperate with the radical fringe of the Ingush movement. While on the face of it this could have stemmed from the nationalist mandates they obtained from the Ingush population, deputy compositions and platforms suggest otherwise. Rather, the difference stemmed from the variable institutional dimension.

Such a comparative angle indicates that the structures of democratic centralism, however loose, and the *nomenklatura* makeup of the local soviets, account for the generally peaceful ethnosocial outcomes across Russia's republics. It indicates that the position the local soviets took was important in affecting movement outcomes. In the case of the Ingush movement, the soviets chose to endorse its militant fringe. They actively publicized Niyskho's martial statements, rallied people for "marches," threatened to use the local police forces to capture lands that they had claims to, and endorsed other measures, which were used by the Ossetiyans to legitimize further anti-Ingush policies.

The perception of the local soviets as both "official" state and "grassroots" agencies facilitated their efforts. The former aided their lobbying activities and added bureaucratic legitimacy to them, while the latter allowed the selling of a given line as enjoying social support. The Ingush radicals, relying on the local bodies, served to alienate potential supporters from amongst other nontitular groups. This partially, though not fully, explains the lack of other nontitular activism. Instead, as the Mozdok case demonstrates, even where grassroots nontitular activism existed, it was suppressed by the local soviets.

Postscript to the Ingush Movement

The conflict ended with the displacement of virtually all of Prigorodnyy's Ingush population to Ingushetiya and other republics. More than a decade after the conflict, the issue of the forced migration remains unresolved. Many families were blacklisted for their alleged involvement in the massacre, and have been prohibited from resettling by the multilateral community commissions which scrutinize the families. Those that did return often found their homes destroyed or occupied. Prigorodnyy continues to be an unstable area with frequent occurrences of terrorist acts, arson, and other expressions of Ossetiyan-Ingush hostility. Until recently, the local governing bodies in the republic have been notorious for furthering the official Ossetiyan line on limiting the return of the Ingush to the republic and limiting residence permits, although the situation was expected to improve with the election of a new president, Alexandr Dzasokhov.

In the meantime, neighboring Ingushetiya gradually acquired its own power structures, such as the parliament and the chief executive. The election, in 1993, of president Ruslan Aushev, an army general with no prior involvement in the movement, was received with relief by a public by now disillusioned with both Niyskho and the OC, which facilitated Aushev's consolidation of power locally. He banned all opposition groups in the republic, and eliminated local self-government in Ingushetiya. Aushev's opposition to the Kremlin earned him the wrath of the federal center and he resigned in December 2001. Elections in April 2002 brought victory to General Murat Zyazikov, who, as deputy presidential envoy to the South Russia Federal District, was widely believed to enjoy strong backing by the Kremlin.[68] Ingushetiya has suffered and continues to suffer tremendously from the influx of displaced persons, mostly Chechens, from neighboring Chechnya, where hostilities continue between the federal armed forces and the Chechen militarized groups. The following chapters do not return to the Ingush case, as the period of its investigation was limited to the two-year phase of local government power. The present chapter, however, informs the investigation of the other cases and the broader comparative conclusions about local government's mobilization-constraining or -inducing role.

Notes

1. See "The Ingush-Ossetiyan Conflict in the Prigorodnyi Region," (New York: Human Rights Watch/Helsinki, 1996); and O. P. Orlov, "Cherez dva goda posle voyny: Problema vynujhdennykh pereselentsev v zone osetino-ingushskogo konflikta," (Moscow: Human Rights Center "Memorial, " 1994).

2. Data from the 1989 census. The figure was reduced following the Ossetiyan-Ingush conflict.

3. Michael McFaul and Nikolay Petrov, eds., *Politicheskiy al'manakh Rossii 1997*, vol. 2 (Moscow: Moscow Carnegie Center, 1998).

4. Robert Conquest, *The Nation Killers* (London: Sphere, 1972), 37.

5. Yu. Yu. Karpov, "K probleme ingushskoy avtonomii," *Sovetskaya etnografiya* (September-October 1990): 29.

6. Valery Tishkov, ed., *Narody Rossii: Entsiklopediya* (Moscow: Nauchnoe izdatel'stvo Bol'shaya rossiyskaya entsiklopediya, 1994), 161-2.

7. Karpov, "K probleme ingushskoy avtonomii," 29.

8. Karpov, "K probleme ingushskoy avtonomii," 29-30.

9. For a detailed account of the various administrative and status changes of Vladikavkaz, see I. B. Didigova, "Dvadtsatye-tridtsatye gody: Problemy administrativno-territorial'nogo ustroystva chechenskogo i ingushskogo narodov," in *Severnyy Kavkaz: Vybor puti natsional'nogo razvitiya*, ed. N. F. Bugay (Maykop, Russia: Meoty, 1994), 140-58.

10. Records of Soviet administrators in Vladikavkaz in the 1920s, cited in N. F. Bugay, "Dvadtsatye gody: Stanovlenie demokraticheskikh form pravleniya na severnom Kavkaze," in *Severnyy Kavkaz*, 62.

11. Bugay, "Dvadtsatye gody," 62.

12. Didigova, "Dvadtsatye-tridtsatye gody," 148.

13. Karpov, "K probleme ingushskoy avtonomii," 30.

14. Aleksey Zverev, "Etnicheskie konflikty na Kavkaze, 1988-1994," in *Spornye granitsy na Kavkaze*, ed. Bruno Koppieters (Moscow: Ves' mir, 1996), 10-76.

15. Karpov, "K probleme ingushskoy avtonomii," 30.

16. For an account of the deportations, see Conquest, *Nation Killers*.

17. Conquest argues that the Germans did raise units from amongst the Chechens, as from other minority groups and Russians who resisted Soviet rule (*Nation Killers*, 100).

18. Timur M. Muzaev and Zurab Todua, *Novaya Checheno-Ingushetiya* (Moscow: Panorama, 1992), 33.

19. Conquest, *Nation Killers*, 67.

20. For a concise history of Inguhshetia and the various administrative changes, see Timur M. Muzaev, *Etnicheskiy separatizm v Rossii* (Moscow: Panorama, 1999).

21. Muzaev, *Etnicheskiy separatizm*.

22. Muzaev, *Etnicheskiy separatizm*.

23. Zverev, "Etnicheskie konflikty na Kavkaze, 1988-1994," 70-1.

24. Valery Tishkov, *Ethnicity, Nationalism and Conflict in and after the Soviet Union: The Mind Aflame* (London: Sage, 1997), 156.

25. Tishkov, *Ethnicity*, 159.

26. Tishkov, *Ethnicity*, 160.

27. "Zakon RSFSR 'O reabilitatsii repressirovannykh narodov,'" in L. K. Gostieva and A. B. Dzadziev, eds., *Severnaya Osetiya: Etnopoliticheskie protsessy, 1990-1994: Ocherki, dokumenty, khronika*, vol. 3 (Moscow: Rossiyskaya akademiya nauk, Institut etnologii i antropologii, 1995), 80-3.

28. "Rezolyutsiya O pervoocherednykh merakh po natsional'nomu spaseniyu i vozrojhdeniyu osetinskogo naroda," in Gostieva and Dzadziev, eds., *Severnaya Osetiya*, vol. 2, 44.

29. L. K. Gostieva, A. B. Dzadziev, and A. A. Dzarasov, "Severnaya Osetiya: Ot vyborov do vyborov (1993-1995)," in *Razvivayushchiysya elektorat Rossii*, ed. G. A. Ko-

marova, vol. 3 (Moscow: Rossiyskaya akademiya nauk, Institut etnologii i antropologii, 1996), 131-2.

30. Gostieva, Dzadziev, and Dzarasov, "Severnaya Osetiya," 131.

31. Gostieva, Dzadziev, and Dzarasov, "Severnaya Osetiya," 132.

32. "Obrashchenie Prezidiuma Verkhovnogo soveta i Soveta ministrov Severo-Osetinskoy SSR k s'ezdu osetinskogo naroda," in Gostieva and Dzadziev, eds., *Severnaya Osetiya*, vol. 2, 41-2.

33. "Obrashchenie Prezidiuma"; and "Rezolyutsiya O pervoocherednykh merakh," in Gostieva and Dzadziev, eds., *Severnaya Osetiya*, 42-3.

34. "Rezolyutsiya O pervoocherednykh merakh po natsional'nomu spaseniyu i vozrojhdeniyu osetinskogo naroda," in Gostieva and Dzadziev, eds., *Severnaya Osetiya*, 43.

35. Muzaev, *Etnicheskiy separatizm*.

36. "Postanovlenie nazranovskoy rayonnoy izibratel'noy komissii O registratsii kandidatov v deputaty nazranovskogo rayonnogo soveta narodnykh deputatov," *Put' Lenina* (*PL*), 6 February 1990, 1-4.

37. "Postanovlenie nazranovskoy rayonnoy izibratel'noy komissii."

38. Tishkov, *Ethnicity*.

39. A. Muradov, "Esli poschastlivitsya," *PL*, 1 March 1990, 2.

40. A. Sagov, "Udovletvoryaya spros pokupatelya," *PL*, 1 March 1990, 5.

41. M. Mikhaylov, "Doverie opavdaet," *PL*, 1 March 1990, 5.

42. To give another example, the platform of a candidate for the Nazran' regional soviet read: "As the main goal of my deputy activity I consider active participation in the restoration of Ingush autonomy in its former borders and as part of the USSR." He then went from the general to specific, pledging to "renovate the secondary school Number One, and to improve the condition of the V. I. Lenin, Trudovaya, Bytyrina, and Kommunisticheskaya streets."

43. S. Sagov, "Slovo o kandidate v narodnye deputaty," *PL*, 23 January 1990.

44. Allegation made by Beslan Kostoev in "Zyorna i plevely: Zametki o problemakh v ingushskom dvijhenii," *Golos Checheno-Ingushetii*, 20 February 1991, 3.

45. The following discussion is based on an examination of the two newspapers.

46. "Postanovlenie Ispolkoma narodnykh deputatov Ingushetii O naznachenii vyborov narodnykh deputatov v parlament Ingushskoy respubliki," *Leninskoe znamya* (*LZ*), 2 November 1991, 1.

47. "Obrashchenie k ingushskomu narodu," *LZ*, 7 September 1991, 1.

48. Interview by author with Ingush activist, tape recording, Moscow, 10 September 1999.

49. "Obrashchenie," 1.

50. Interview by author with Ingush activist, tape recording, Moscow, 18 September 1999.

51. I. Kodzoev, "V poiskakh pravdy," *PL*, 31 July 1990, 2.

52. Kodzoev, "V poiskakh," 2.

53. B. Bekov, "O voprosakh formirovaniya narodnoy respublikanskoy gvardii Ingushetii," *LZ*, 19 October 1991, 2.

54. "Na kogo rabotaet Niyskho," *Ingushskoe slovo* (*IS*), no. 12, December 1991, 1, 3.

55. Doug McAdam, *Political Process and the Development of Black Insurgency, 1930-1970* (Chicago: University of Chicago Press, 1982); Anthony Oberschall, *Social Conflict and Social Movements* (Englewood Cliffs, N.J.: Prentice Hall, 1973); and Bert Klandermans, "The Social Construction of Protest and Multiorganizational Fields," in *Frontiers in Social Movement Theory*, ed. Aldon D. Morris and Carol McClurg Mueller (New Haven, Conn.: Yale University Press, 1992), 77-103.

56. A. A. Tsutsiev, *Osetino-Ingushskiy konflikt (1992- . . .): Ego predystoriya i faktory razvitiya* (Moscow: Rosspen, 1998), 101.

57. Klandermans, "Social Construction of Protest."

58. McAdam, *Political Process.*

59. "Tretiy s'ezd ingushskogo naroda," *IS*, no. 11, November 1991, 2.

60. M. Gelatho, "Est' predel terpeniyu," *IS*, no. 10, September 1991, 1.

61. "Tretiy s'ezd ingushskogo naroda," 3.

62. "Rezolyutsiya cherezvychaynogo s'ezda ingushskogo naroda," *Narodnoe slovo* (*NS*), 13 August 1992, 3.

63. Fiona Hill, "'Russia's Tinderbox': Conflict in the North Caucasus and Its Implications for the Future of the Russian Federation," (Cambridge, Mass.: Harvard University, John F. Kennedy School of Government, Strengthening Democratic Institutions Project, 1995), 44.

64. In the aftermath of the conflict, the Vladikavkaz city soviet took a special decision to impose a moratorium on the return of Ingush refugees ("Gorsovet prinyal reshenie," *Severnaya Osetiya* [*SO*], 2 December 1992, 1).

65. S. Djhizakov, "O demokratii i demokratakh," *Mozdokskiy vestnik* (*MV*), 26 September 1992, 6; and V. Aparin, "Kto govoril iskrenne?" *MV*, 20 August 1992, 3.

66. Concerned by Mozdok's possible secession, the Ossetiyan authorities held meetings with the Mozdok soviet chairman, who lamented the region's economic conditions. The chairman was also criticized by the Ossetiyan authorities for not holding enough "explanatory work" with the local populations ("Vstrecha v Verkhovnom sovete," *SO*, 10 January 1992, 1).

67. I. Chernoglazov, "Dva iz semi," *MV*, 21 July 1992, 1,4.

68. Norwegian Institute of International Affairs Database on Russian Regions, www .nupi.no/cgi-win/Russland/krono.exe?5105 (accessed 18 July 2003).

Chapter 6

Local Self-Government or Government Gone Local? Municipal Control of the Citizenry, 1992-2000

The August 1991 coup led to a series of institutional changes at the local level, culminating with the dissolution of the soviets in 1993. The most important change was the appointment of local executives and the emasculation of representative bodies, the soviets. The present chapter investigates the impact of the changing institutional structures on the incentives of the local actors and their resource bases. The chapter argues that the new institutions altered the structures of accountability and the local bodies' jurisdiction over public life and their resource bases, and that the changing structures of accountability in turn affected the way the resources and jurisdiction over public life were likely to be used by the respective actors in the local governing bodies. The result was that the local bodies assumed a different role vis-à-vis the social agencies, negatively affecting levels of ethnic mobilization and civic and social activism.

The key motive behind Yel'tsin's drive to reform the soviets was the perceived *political* role of these bodies during and before the August 1991 coup. The soviets were regarded as bastions of conservatism, an association that stemmed from the conflict between the RSFSR's chief executive and the largely conservative Supreme Soviet and its speaker, Ruslan Khasbulatov. Many of the republic-level Supreme Soviets and their presidia had indeed tacitly or explicitly supported the coup plotters. Yel'tsin, however, failed to appreciate the role of the lower-level councils in the large urban centers, which tended then and still tend to be more democratic than the other localities within the respective regions. In such cities as Ufa and Maykop, and in the other republic capitals, the local soviets with varying degrees of success were able to subvert efforts to introduce emergency rule locally, and had challenged the Supreme Soviets through their city presses. Yel'tsin, however, equated strong representative power with conservatism and antireformist political opposition across the board.

While Yel'tsin saw local government reform as a weapon against conservative forces on a regional level, the titular regimes utilized it against the municipal agencies that had challenged the republic bodies on democratic and national-ist grounds. In the ethnically diverse settings, plagued by controversies over nationalizing institution building, Yel'tsin's local self-government reforms therefore served to deprive the political opposition of the means to contest the republic policies.

In the aftermath of the August coup an RSFSR Supreme Soviet decree au-thorized the President to dismiss *oblast'*, autonomous *oblast'*, and *kray* execu-tives and introduce the post of head of administration (HA), or key local execu-tive, as the "successor" to the respective *ispolkomy*.[1] While the decree did not concern the republics, a subsequent provision introduced the presidency on re-public levels, which was to form part of the "common system of executive power in the RSFSR."[2] Another decree, ostensibly aimed at furthering "radical economic reform" banned elections to representative organs of all levels.[3] The decree made no explicit orders regarding the appointment of the local govern-ment chief administrators in the republics; however, from early 1992 onwards appointment became the norm, rather than the exception. Executive power was further strengthened by a provision of subordination of the lower organs to the higher ones, and the higher executives' right to dismiss decisions of the lower executive organs.[4]

The demise of the soviets was finalized in the aftermath of the October 1993 coup after the passage of a series of special decrees by Yel'tsin. Although the decrees did not concern the republics, many ethnic entities were quick to "desovietize."[5] Local self-government, as some have argued, had already been weakened after the Federal Treaty assigned authority over the institution to both the federal- and constituent-unit levels, with the subnational entities free to ex-periment with local institutional choices as long as they did not violate the broad federal requirements.[6] Against the background of federal stress on strong repub-lic presidencies, this meant executive control over local self-government makeup and its subordination to the republic chief executives.

The practical outcome of the above reforms was that local self-government virtually ceased to exist in the republics. In many cases, new local representative organs would not be elected for months. Many localities would be administra-tively merged and the powers of the respective councils would be transferred to the higher organs. By the end of the decade, there would be only 8,000 elected organs of local self-government,[7] compared to over 28,000 in 1993, that is, be-fore the October crisis.[8] Instead of the assemblies and their elected administra-tors, it was now the appointed figures, subordinate to republic executives, who wielded authority and power at a local level.

On paper, the above phase of the executivization of local government only lasted until 1995. In the context of regional "legal separatism," Yel'tsin and his advisors had come to think of local self-government as a potential check on re-gional regimes.[9] The 1995 law On Common Principles of Local Self-Government in the Russian Federation separated it from both the regional and federal levels of power, while also strengthening the representative branch and stipulating the election of local executives.[10]

In practice, the implementation of the law was slow. Even where the republics formally complied with some of the key provisions of the law, they have tended to sabotage them, maintaining de facto control over local government, and continuing to appoint or otherwise control local executives. A survey of local government practices in Russia's other constituent entities may be found in chapter 7. The following sections discuss the impact of Yel'tsin's reform of local government on ethnic activism in the two republics of Adygeya and Bashkortostan.

Institutional Changes at the Local Level

Adygeya

In Adygeya, the republic regime made an explicit link between the soviets and ethnic and political challenge to Adygeya's nationalizing agenda through the movements that they fostered. Accordingly, it opted for institutional arrangements that would subordinate the municipalities to the republic bodies. The newly elected president Aslan Djharimov's most important decree, adopted a mere five days after he took the oath in January 1992, concerned the appointment of heads of administrations. While the first decree was a populist statement with regard to an increase in social spending, the second decree concerned a common postelection formality of the dissolution of the old republic executive committee, the third and most substantive edict was On the Order of Appointment and Certain Issues Pertaining to the Work of Heads of Administrations.[11] While most of the old soviet executives were reappointed, the removal of some of the old "prefects" and *ispolkom* heads was specifically linked to their involvement with the nontitular movement activities prior to the elections. An *oblast'* presidium meeting assembled after the elections recorded the following:

> There is evidence of a purposive work in the Maykop *rayon* aimed at boycotting the elections. Because of the neglect [*popustitel'stvo*] of the officials, numerous flyers were posted in public places and in production units, openly calling for boycott of the elections and interethnic conflicts. There and in Maykop facts of verbal agitation for boycott of the elections were recorded, which negatively reflect on the public and political situation in the republic. The presidium has considered it inappropriate that V. V. Krokhmal' maintain the position of chairman of the Maykop *rayon* soviet of people's deputies and has decided to forward to the procuracy materials which confirm the purposive work aimed at organizing the boycott of the elections in the Maykop *rayon*, and the responsibility of certain officials, including V. V. Krokhmal'.[12]

Other officials in the lower soviets, such as the deputy chairman of Maykop city soviet, were reprimanded for failing to actively advocate parity in the elections. The chairman of the Maykop city soviet, Simatov, failed to be appointed as head of Maykop city administration amidst widespread speculation of retribution against him.[13] In his place the republic appointed Mikhail Chernichenko, an engineer by profession and for seven years an *oblast'* soviet executive committee functionary of the "tough administrator" type, who had not been involved in political opposition. Chernichenko stressed that his work principle was "strict one man rule" (*edinonachalie*).[14]

The January decree initiated a series of successive executive initiatives aimed at bringing the soviets under the control of the chief executive and his appointed figureheads. An edict on Adygeya's government structure stipulated: "Heads of administration of cities, *rayony*, village and town soviets form a unified system of executive power." The decree empowered the Adyge government to "suspend decisions of executive power organs . . . if they contradict the constitution and laws of the Republic of Adygeya and the Russian Federation, as well as dismiss the officials of these power organs should they violate the relevant legislation."[15]

The stress on the executive power was subsequently cemented in the law concerning the president.[16] This was followed by the establishment of a policing agency within the presidential administration whose task was to "monitor compliance with presidential decrees by ministries, as well as administrations of cities and *rayony*."[17] A special provision on "disciplinary responsibility" of heads of administrations threatened dismissal of those failing to comply with presidential directives.[18] In October 1993, Djharimov shifted powers away from the city and *rayon* soviets and assigned them to the appointed heads of administrations.[19] Adygeya's new legislation also distinguished between "local self-government" and "local government," *mestnoe samoupravlenie* versus *mestnoe gosudarstvennoe upravlenie*. A law for the "transitional period" provided for the appointment of heads of administrations in the largest cities, Maykop and Adygeysk, as well as in the *rayony*. Local self-government proper was only retained at the smaller administrative units of towns and villages.[20]

Although under federal pressure the principle of election of local executives was incorporated into Adygeya's constitution adopted in 1995, the elections did not take place until 1997. When they did, it was only after a hedge decree had been passed, stipulating that "heads of city and *rayon* administrations . . . bear personal responsibility for the state of discipline in . . . the cities and *rayony* in the Republic of Adygeya."[21]

Bashkortostan

In Bashkortostan, local heads of administrations began to be appointed in early 1992. As in Adygeya, the debates on local institutional reform and the strengthening of the republic executive hierarchy were linked to the question of the adoption of the republic constitution and the prevention of potential political challenge to this and other sovereignty legislation from below. A Supreme Soviet presidium decision having immediate effect cited the "need for executive discipline" and for doing away with the situation whereby "local soviets . . .

serve as arenas of clashing political opinions and platforms." The Supreme Soviet then amended the local self-government law to allow "the presidium the
right of appointment of heads of *rayon* and city administrations and dismiss
them at its initiative."[22]

In turn, the heads of administrations of cities and *rayony* were given the
right to appoint heads of administrations of the lower administrative-territorial
units.[23] While the soviets would still be elected,[24] henceforth the real decision-
making and executive authority would lie with the appointed administrative
heads. In a further move to undermine the representative organs, the new provisions also allowed the combining of the posts of the soviet chairmen and the
heads of administrations.[25] The fusion of executive and legislative powers at the
local level eliminated the remaining controls the soviets might have had over
their executives.

The Administration: Changing Roles and
the Mechanisms of Control

The above broad structural reforms substantially affected the lines of accountability of the local executive and legislative bodies. These factors in turn influenced the nature of the business of local self-government and the perceptions of
its role. Unlike the council members, the heads of administrations, by virtue of
their appointment from above, were now linked into the "formal" structures of
accountability and control. These HAs tended to have been or become "tough
administrators," whose credentials as such were stressed. They would have risen
through the party and local soviet *ispolkom* hierarchies, and would have shown
their loyalty to the republic regimes in the process. The other executives in the
local administrations appointed by the HAs tended to have had similar careers as
administrators. As late as 1999, local administrations in both Adygeya and
Bashkortostan were staffed by such members of the former apparat, who were
largely selected for their apolitical credentials and "professionalism."

An archetype of the apolitical administrator who had risen through the party
ranks and soviet administration is Vladimir Ivanov,[26] an Ufa administration
functionary. Ivanov had worked in the *obkom* for a number of years before being
elected to the Ufa soviet. He had been subsequently reelected to the Ufa soviet
in 1990, 1995, and 1999. As chairman of the soviet, he is also a deputy head of
administration, which is a full-time administrative post. Ivanov had apparently
never been involved in big politics, opposition or otherwise, even at the heyday
of the democratic and nontitular upsurge of the early 1990s. Ivanov's approach
to the mission of city government focuses on service, rather than politics. The
1990 soviet, he maintains, "had for two years suffered from the malaise of politics, that is, we deputies at the time tried to politically assess what was happening in the country, and paid less attention to things happening in the city pertinent to maintenance of normal conditions for life." Finally, he concludes, "the

soviet started to deal with what the representative organ is supposed to be doing, namely, city administration." Even in its nonpartisan form, however, he maintains that the council is an inconvenience from the point of view of efficiency: it lacks "technocrats." Otherwise, "for thirty council deputies we need over seventy real administration professionals."[27]

The greater powers of the administration vis-à-vis the council were also augmented by the administrators' increased specialization and social service responsibilities. Rather than diminishing compared to Soviet times, these responsibilities have reportedly increased, due to the shortage of local funds for the provision of basic services and mounting social problems. Despite attempts at privatization, most assets continue to be in state hands. This means that salaries to local enterprise employees are paid out of municipal budgets. The budgets in turn depend on levels of allocation from republican funds. These prerogatives are substantially wider than those exercised by municipalities in the West. The views of Ivanov, who frequently travels to Ufa's twin city in Germany, Halle, are typical of local administrators:

> When we are, say, in the West and ask a burgomaster or a mayor a question, what do you do if some food products are absent in the shop, he stares and says, "What do I have to do with this? Not my problem." Here, in contrast, we are responsible for all now . . . because in our country the redistribution of property has not occurred, and the main share of property remains in state hands. . . . In the West, he [the mayor] is not concerned with how enterprises, firms, and companies are working. It is not his problem. It is the problem of those who work there, who own these places, who founded them. Here we have a headache today about even this, because today we don't have a real owner; it appears that everybody is the owner.[28]

Ivanov's counterpart in the Maykop city administration, Georgiy Petrov,[29] maintains in a similar vein: "All the questions in the city have to be regulated by the authorities, which means that the city should have real power over many issues, beginning with the birth of a child and ending with the lack of bread in the shops."[30]

The republic bodies manipulate local budgets, exercising political influence over the administrations: "If the mayor shows defiance, the republic says: Deal with the salaries yourself," claims Ivanov.[31] The administrations, in turn, manipulate the disbursal of funds to enterprises to achieve the same goal, observed in other regions as well and described as "pseudo-socialist activities."[32] Enterprise managers in turn manipulate payment of salaries to individual employees. As such, their role has not changed since the soviet period, when "the management of factories and farms . . . exercised police functions over their respective workforces, visiting threats and penalties on those choosing to participate in 'unsanctioned' political activities."[33]

The social expectations of the municipalities' role are likewise much greater than of those in the West. "In contrast to the West," maintains Ivanov, "when salaries are not paid here, even at privatized enterprises . . . workers come here, criticizing the administration: Why don't you pay us salaries? We have to interfere."[34] This view echoes the observations of scholars of local politics in other regions. In Sverdlovsk *oblast'*, for example, during a student protest demonstration, "the demands of the students concerning the reform of higher education were directed at the mayor and the governor, even though these officials were not included in the formulation of that series of reforms."[35] The control of the budgetary tool, as well as the social perceptions of the local governments as all-powerful entities, facilitates the manipulation of the issue of sanctions for deviating behavior, since punishments could be tangible.

The Local Councils

The scaled-down local councils continued to be popularly elected. Although power was now vested in the administrative bodies, the councils preserved formal authority over a number of important areas, such as the approval of local budgets. No formal mechanisms for the removal of local councilors had been put in place. Increasingly, however, local council members tended to be part of what may be referred to as both the formal and the informal frameworks of control and accountability.[36]

The formal lines of accountability stem from the fusion of executive and legislative power. Local councilors, as, indeed, members of the republic-level legislature, could combine executive posts in local administrations with councilor positions in other areas.[37] As full-time appointees in local administrations, their primary accountability lies with the bodies appointing them, rather than in the part-time council positions. Aside from those formally under direct control of the executives, it is possible to distinguish several categories of those within the "informal" control networks.

The Ufa council elected in 1999 is representative of the distinctions between those forming part of the various control networks one could observe in the scaled-down councils elected between 1995 and 1999. Out of fifty-eight elected deputies, the largest categories are seventeen, or 29.3 percent, managers in the ranks of heads of enterprises; fourteen, or 24.1 percent, heads of medical establishments; eight, or 13.8 percent, heads of educational institutions, mostly schools; and five deputies, or 8.6 percent, directly connected to council administrations; the council also has one head of administration of a lower-level *rayon*. Thus, while only six deputies are directly connected to the administration, and linked to the formal executive chain of command, on close scrutiny, the majority of the remaining deputies also form part of executive lines of accountability or are subject to less formal executive control.

The deputy corps could be divided into five categories.[38] The first is that forming part of the common system of executive power, such as the head of administration and other local executives. The second category is the directors of state enterprises. These tend to be appointed by the republic Cabinet of Ministers, or enter into paid contracts with it. This category is subject to both formal and less formal accountability. The informal aspect stems from their vulnerability to the tax inspectorate, the police, and other law enforcement agencies, which may or may not be de jure subordinate to the republic or local administrations, but are de facto under the control of local HAs. The next category is the so-called business entrepreneurs. An examination of their activities and affiliations reveals that they tend to perform services vital to the city, and enjoy a certain status within the municipal services private contracts hierarchy. For example one deputy runs an enterprise for sanitary and technical works, and has an exclusive contract with the city to do so. His dependence on the administration is an informal one, as he is subject to material rewards, rather than direct accountability.

The two categories after entrepreneurs are heads of medical and educational establishments. In chapter 4, I made the distinction between doctors and teachers on the one hand and heads of their respective establishments on the other. The distinction is an important one, and prevents us grouping the latter into the broader "professional" or "intelligentsia" categories.

The "colonization" by these two groups, which has increased in the Ufa council from 1995 to 1999, is an interesting phenomenon, also observed to a

Table 6.1. Composition of Ufa and Maykop City Councils, 1990-1999

Deputy category	Ufa city council (%)			Maykop city council (%)		
	1990	1995	1999	1990	1995	1999
Soviet administration	4.1	15.0	8.6	5.6	0	5.5
HA		3.3	0			0
Engineer	8.1	6.7		4.0	15.0	0
School head	4.6	16.7	13.8	6.4	20.0	11.1
Hospital head	3.6	16.7	24.1	0	5.0	5.5
Lower-level manager	20.8	5.0	5.2	7.2	0	0
Manager	10.2	31.7	29.3	16.0	10.0	33.3
Worker	21.3	0	3.4	20.8	15.0	5.5
Public association member	3.6	0	3.4	7.2	5.0	0
Teacher	8.6	0	3.4	7.2	10.0	33.3
Lower-rank party official	4.1	N/A	N/A	5.6	N/A	N/A
Military	0	0	0	4.8	0	0
Other	11.2	5.0	8.6	15.2	20.0	11.1

Sources: Compiled from *Adygeyskaya pravda*, *Sovetskaya Bashkiriya*, *Vechern - yaya Ufa*, and *Maykopskie novosti*.

lesser extent with regard to school heads in the Maykop 1995 city council. Some local interviewees believe that their electoral success stems from the generally high priority accorded to health care and education.[39]

School directors and hospital heads are successful at convincing the electorates that council positions would benefit the respective institutions in the form of greater financial and other rewards. According to some views, they may thus represent certain large "lobby" groups in the council, aggregating the preferences of their constituencies. However, hospital heads, as a local councilor maintained, are not mere doctors; they are entrepreneurs, "tsars and gods" within their institutions.[40]

Although school directors could not be described as entrepreneurs, they are the most powerful individuals within their institutions and enjoy status and prestige in the republics' educational hierarchies. Considering the amount of gatekeeping and "selectorates" involved in council elections, their high representation is unlikely to be accidental. Rather than being a reflection of constituency preferences, their election is a result of the republic elites' efforts to ensure that a high proportion of these "notables" get in.[41] Hospital staffs are in regular contact with district constituencies. Unlike in countries with privatized health care, in Russia hospitals continue to be attached to districts and one is affiliated with it according to where one holds the *propiska*, or residence permit. Those who opt for free health care have to go through the local hospital, rather than the equivalent of the general practitioner (GP) of their choosing. I was told that before the 1999 Ufa council election, GPs campaigned during patient visits for the election of certain candidates.

The same holds true for school heads. One is attached to a school according to where one holds the *propiska,* although since 1991 some flexibility has been introduced into the system and there are many privatized schools now. However, most people continue to send their children to the official state schools. School heads, however, can exercise leverage as to who gets in, who is attached to what classes, and the grades obtained. In Bashkortostan, Adygeya, and elsewhere, school heads become important in the political process. Schools are used as polling stations during the elections. They are also a convenient venue for information and agitation. These two categories are both subject to formal and informal lines of accountability. The appointment of school heads is done through the local administrations' *nomenklatury.* Heads of hospitals are appointed either by local administrations or by the Ministry of Health.

What unites all of the above categories is (1) their more or less formal dependence on the executive chain of command; and (2) their key positions within organizations representing business, social, professional, and other networks. The lines of accountability continue downwards as we move on to the next level. The most straightforward formal control framework is the influence over appointments within the organization, vested in the respective heads or managers. The second, an informal one, is the control over payment of salaries. Heads of municipal organizations do not control this, but local administrations do. Heads of institutions are vehicles through which the sanctions system is spread: "We will not get wages if we do not do this or that." These heads, considering their regular network contacts, status, and influence, are thus notoriously crucial players in the local political process. Finally, one could also infer that social sanctions might be applied to those within these professional networks who deviate from a general political line, since as a result, the whole organization might be penalized. People involved in opposition activities generally keep quiet about them for fear of sanctions and undermining their associates and family members; those who donate money for such activities do not disclose their identities or professional affiliations, for the same reason.

The Maykop city council elected in 1995 is similar to that of Ufa in that the council has a large proportion of either local "notables" or regular employees of state bodies, controlled by the executive. The Maykop council, however, is more diverse in its composition, reflecting the more competitive electoral process in the republic. Out of the council's twenty deputies, the largest single category is comprised of heads of educational establishments, with 20 percent; heads of hospitals comprise 5 percent, and 10 percent are managers. Teachers, who are *kontraktniki* (dependent on municipal contracts), comprise 10 percent, and workers 15 percent, of the deputy corps. There is one voluntary association member and three engineers. Four deputies, whom I included in the category of "other," include pensioners and a deputy listed as unemployed.

The council's 45 percent municipal employees and managers are subject to the same structures of control as in Bashkortostan. The body has not made many politically sensitive statements throughout its tenure. The Communists have a large presence in the council, but their opposition to the republic bodies has been limited to economic concerns. Still, considering its diversity, the council is freer of administrative constraints compared to Ufa. One of its deputies was active with the Union of Slavs in 1990-1992, and continued to cooperate with the Union throughout the 1990s. As the head of a small private enterprise, he is less vulnerable to sanctions than the other deputies.

Changing Jurisdictions over Public Life: The Fostering of "Ethnic Peace"

In addition to the reform of the institutional structure of local self-government, important changes were also introduced into the formal jurisdictions of the respective local agencies. In time, this included the informal levers, now firmly vested in the hands of the local executives. This could be summarized as a shift of prerogatives over public life and the influence over public opinion from the representative or legislative agencies to the executive ones. The previous chapters have described how much of the gatekeeping over public activities was vested in the presidia. These were in turn elected by the soviet deputies from within their ranks. In 1990, they often included the most active council deputies, as well as the most visible public figures, which helped shape the image of the councils as the "conscience of the city." By 1993, these gate-keeping prerogatives had shifted to the executive organs, the HAs, and the impersonal departments within the local administrations subordinate to the HAs.

The most notable formal jurisdictions concerned the sanctioning of mass protest acts and other forms of social activism; the registration of local chapters of public associations and political parties; the formalization of the rules for logistical support to the public associations, with the administration put in charge of giving out premises; and the ownership and control of the local news-paper, the key molder of local public opinion, such as *Maykopskie novosti* in Adygeya and *Vechernyaya Ufa* in Bashkortostan.

Mass Acts

Between 1992 and 1993, when HAs began to be appointed and the soviets were disbanded, the executive arm acquired the prerogative for the sanctioning of mass political acts, originally vested in the representative organs' presidia. They had thus acquired a substantial gatekeeping tool against any potential opposition activities.

In Adygeya, the head of Maykop city administration personally approves public associations' applications after a preliminary review by the deputy HA. The applications are of an informative (*zayavitel'nyy*) nature, and the HAs, according to the administration officials I spoke to, are bound to approve them unless they grossly violate certain "public order" or "ethnic hatred" criteria. The administration reviews the proposed slogans, and then uses its discretion to influence them, and to allocate space and time for the act. According to the Union of Slavs activists, the administration consciously strives to move the locations for public acts to the most remote locations, unsuitable from the point of view of attracting attention.

In 1990-1992, much of the opposition activity took place in the Lenin Square, between the buildings of the former *obkom* on the one hand, and the Maykop city council on the other. This giant space, as in all provincial cities in the Soviet times used for May demonstrations and other formal occasions, was perfectly suited for mass gatherings. According to the Union of Slavs' leader, it is also most appropriate, because policy makers, both at the Maykop city and republic levels, are prime targets for opposition acts and pressure tactics. However, the location subsequently became exclusively reserved for official regime activities. Alternative mass gatherings were driven out into the shady wooded area of the Maykop city park, away from the center of town.

In Bashkortostan, where local government also exists on city-district level, the decision making over protest acts is formally more decentralized, and is the prerogative of the various lower-level administrations, depending on where the act is to be held. It thus ostensibly gives more leeway to public associations. In practice, since local HAs form part of the common system of executive power, they are likely to give a uniform response to a given application or else face executive sanctions. Even when in isolated instances a given district HA exercises a more lenient attitude, the sanctioned protest act is easily subject to sabotage by the administrative bodies.

A case in point is an incident relating to TOTs's opposition to the language law. A Tatar activist recalls his organization's efforts to get authorization for a protest demonstration, held in January 1999 in Ufa: "At first we did not get a sanction . . . for example, the Sovetskiy *rayon* administration explained the refusal on the grounds that they do not have such problems. One of the pickets we planned was by the Ufa Department Store [a central location] and this is the answer they [the administration] gave us: 'The Ufa Department Store and the language law are not in any way connected.' So they prohibited the holding of the picket." After a series of similar refusals, an authorization was obtained from one of the Ufa district administrations.[42] Yet, according to the organizers of the event, even then the location that they were offered was the least convenient one from the point of view of access. It was by the Friendship Monument, an isolated location on the city outskirts facing the river with very little public transportation services. Moreover, the operation of the main transport link, a trolleybus, was suspended an hour before the event. The TOTs activist claims that this was done in order to limit the possibility for the public of getting to the location. The city's public transportation is controlled by the city administration. Thus, the formal decentralization of decision making in local government structure is overwritten by the de facto overall executive control, which can be used to subvert opposition activities.

Registration of Public Associations and Logistical Support

After 1992, administrative jurisdiction over public associations and their activities was also extended to the areas of registration and the allocation of premises. In Adygeya, the prerogative over the registration of public associations became vested in the republic Ministry of Justice. The municipalities, however, were put in charge of allocating premises to PAs due to their continued control over the vast majority of unprivatized municipal real estate. According to a local administration official, PAs are entitled to twenty meters of free space, with any excess paid by the PAs themselves.[43] The Union of Slavs activists claim, however, that a large measure of selectivity is exercised in the allocation of premises.

Between 1992 and early 1999, despite numerous requests to the administration, the Union of Slavs was denied office space under the pretext of lack of suitable vacant premises. The dependence on the administration for the allocation of premises stems not only from their control over most municipal assets: private property holders refuse to rent out space to opposition groups for fear of administrative punishment. This is likely to be monitored by the Soviet-era-style Committees on Local Self-Government of Microdistricts, *Komitety samoupravleniya mikrorayonov* (KSMy), which have acquired notoriety for being watchdog agencies at the very lowest, neighborhood levels. The acquisition of premises in any case requires official administrative sanctioning and approval.

In Bashkortostan, only the official "public associations" of a cultural nature are given premises. The degree of repression is much higher than in Adygeya, and opposition PAs rely on clandestine locations, which are often subject to surveillance and searches. Local administrations, however, unlike in Adygeya, are formally in charge of registering the local chapters of PAs, which, in addition to the informal repressive mechanisms, provides them with legitimate gatekeeping instruments. Every local administration has a department within it in charge of relationships with PAs, including their registration. A member of the political party Yabloko in charge of registering the party's local chapter maintains: "Whether we get registered or not will depend on the republic's position."[44] Local administrations are thus instruments for the furthering of the republic political line at the local level through, among other things, the prevention of the possibility of the legal operation of PAs and parties.

The Local Newspaper

Finally, the local government's administrative control over public life was established through the acquisition of partial or complete jurisdiction over the most important instruments for shaping public opinion. Scholars of local self-government in the Western settings have noted the role of the "local" newspaper.[45] This role becomes particularly salient when few alternative presses are allowed to exist. Even when they do, their impact is restricted by the limited circulation and problems with distribution. Most importantly, many "independent" newspapers continue to depend on state sources with all the obvious consequences stemming from such dependence. Michael Urban and his collaborators write: "State subsidies [in Russia] are not doled out without strings attached. Consequently, independent publications—especially (but not exclusively) regional or city newspapers—are forced to exchange editorial autonomy for government financing."[46] In the post-Soviet settings, these problems stem from the continued inadequacy of private resources to help sustain alternative publications, and the reluctance of prospective donors to associate themselves with the opposition.

In 1990-1991, the city newspapers like *VU* and *MN*, given their virtual monopoly in the local press market, had enormous public resonance and influence. While they continue to be virtual monopolies, their coverage of public affairs had been altered substantially, given the loss of control over them by the representative organs. In Adygeya, *MN* was created at the initiative of the city soviet's liberal Deystvie group; the soviet also approved its key editor. In the aftermath of the October crisis in 1993, when the soviets were disbanded, the jurisdiction over the paper passed on to the appointed city administration. After the election of the Maykop soviet in 1995, the soviet reacquired partial jurisdiction over the paper as its original founder, with the administration also having partial legal ownership. De facto, however, the paper continues to be under the control of the administration. "What used to be the mouthpiece of the deputies," maintained a former Deystvie deputy, "is now 100 percent the mouthpiece of the

head of the administration."[47] The deputy, reelected to the 1995 Maykop council, said, "We insist that the paper be returned to us, as cofounders, or cease to
exist, because for some time it has not been covering our activities, only those of
the administration."[48]

The fate of Bashkortostan's *VU* was not much different from that of *MN*.
The city soviet, together with the editorial staff, was the cofounder of the paper.
However, control over it had completely passed on to the city administration.
The result was a turnaround from being a press organ of the opposition to one of
the republic regime. Politics as such was driven out of *VU*. The editor's dis-
claimers and disparaging comments increasingly accompanied the rare instances
of editorial letters written by deputies exercising their right to be published.
These too, however, ceased to appear by the end of 1992. The quest to purge the
newspaper of politics went as far as misrepresenting Ufa soviet deputy affiliations despite the soviet's partial ownership of the newspaper. Thus an activist of
Rus' and one of the editors of its newspaper *Otechestvo* was listed in the register
of deputies elected to the 1999 council as "journalist." He claimed that the
vagueness of the affiliation was not accidental. He had originally presented himself as a journalist for *Otechestvo*. The omission of this important detail, according to him, was to mask the embarrassment suffered by the regime because he
had somehow gotten into the council, and to spare *VU* trouble from disclosing
the party activist's opposition identity.[49]

Theoretical Reflections

It is now important to step back and reflect theoretically and comparatively
on the detail presented in the above sections. To the extent that the changes concerned "professionalism" and the reduction of "politics" and partisanship in local administration, the changes that were introduced into local government in
1992 have some parallels in Western settings. One example is the late nine-
teenth- early twentieth-century Reform Movement in America aimed at making
local government more efficient. The reformers in America had of course other
motivations for driving "politics" out of local government, namely the perception that local decision making suffered from divisive party or ethnic and racial
politics damaging to efficient administration.

The Russian regional contexts and the motivations of advocates of reformed
institutions are of course completely different from those in the United States. In
Russia, the key motive for "driving politics out of local government" was the
regional regimes' effort to establish control over the localities and to prevent
opposition to their rule from below. But for all their differences, there are some
similarities in the *formal* institutional changes that were introduced in an effort
to "depoliticize" local government, as well as the actual power gains that they
may have brought to the interests pushing for reforms in the guise of "nonpartisanship." Important aspects of the reforms carried out in Russia's republics
broadly conformed to the thrust of the Reform Movement, most notably con-

cerning the reduction of partisanship. Executives were now appointed, rather than elected, and their professional and administrative, rather than political, credentials were stressed. The councils too were made less partisan, although not necessarily through the same system as in the United States. Edward Banfield and James Wilson define nonpartisanship as a "system of elections . . . in which no candidate is identified on the ballot by party affiliation."[50] No explicit provisions to this effect exist either in the Russian federal law On the Common Principles of Local Self-Government or in the republic legislation. Bashkortostan's local self-government legislation leaves it up to the charters of the respective municipalities. In Adygeya, electoral blocks and associations are allowed to nominate candidates, and no explicit restrictions as to partisanship in elections are laid out.

In practice, however, the "selectorates" put in place and the system of formal and informal sanctions had the effect of depoliticizing these bodies. This is particularly true in Bashkortostan. Such restrictions apply both to the Bashkir and non-Bashkir nationalist groups, although the latter suffer much greater sanctions. Those from the opposition like the editor of *Otechestvo* who do manage to get in suffer from the misrepresentation of their opposition identity: his affiliation with Rus's newspaper was simply not mentioned. Instead, he is presented as an impersonal "journalist." Within the Ufa soviet, the HA has used his power to prevent the formation of deputy factions by simply failing to place the issue on the council's agenda. The same holds true for Adygeya. A limited degree of opposition and regime criticism is permitted in the council, but only as it relates to economic and administrative matters. The Communists have a large presence in the Maykop council, and a faction of their own. Their opposition to the administration and the republic bodies, however, has been limited to questions of social welfare and budgetary redistribution between the city and the republic.

In the West, driving partisanship out of local government and the centralization of executive control have been generally viewed as a means to achieve efficient local administration. A city cannot run effectively, according to Banfield, without a large degree of centralization since there would be too many "civic controversies."[51] Executive functionaries in the republics have actively propagated views along these lines. According to another view, however, the "depoliticization" of local bodies in fact represents the concentration of political decision making in the hands of a narrow group of powerful local actors. Potential civic or ethnic controversies are not avoided, but are being decided in advance in favor of a more powerful party in a potential conflict.

There are two ways in which this result is achieved. The first is the prevention of conflicts and issues from entering into the public domain. According to Peter Bachrach and Morton Baratz, "To the extent that a person or group—consciously or unconsciously—creates or reinforces barriers to the public airing of policy conflicts, that person or group has power."[52] The second related method is the employment of the institutional and informal mechanisms for centralization that "nonpartisanship" brings about, for the attainment or enforcement of political, policy, or public agenda-setting aims.

The institutional mechanisms include formal lines of accountability and subordination. The informal mechanisms would involve potential material rewards or other informal sanctions. Banfield refers to these as "structures of control." He writes: "When two or more actors come under the control of another on a continuing basis, i.e., from proposal to proposal, a *structure* of control exists." This would include the mayor's control over the city council, the newspaper's control over "civic leadership," and the governor's control over the legislature. According to Banfield, "centralization of control therefore necessitates a linkage of structures where structures exist."[53]

The preceding empirical sections have identified the formal and informal structures of control that exist in the republics. The most straightforward structure is the vertical chain of executive power. The president appoints heads of administrations of larger areas, which in turn appoint the executives of lower-level local administrations. Formal executive control also largely extends to the legislature. While in municipalities with strong mayors the mayor de facto exercises power over the weaker representative bodies, here a large percentage of councilors are subject to direct lines of executive accountability in their professional capacities as appointed functionaries.

These functionaries, in turn, extend the structure of executive control to those subordinate and accountable to them within the large enterprises or other organizations that they head. The executives do not exercise formal control over the social agencies, but they have jurisdictions over activities and functions crucial for their work. These jurisdictions effectively allow for the silencing of opinions alternative to those of the most powerful actors and for the prevention of their public airing. The linkage of the structures of control is further exercised through the system of "private-regarding" and "public-regarding" benefits disbursed by the power elite.[54] The first is achieved through the tangible private benefits or costs that accrue to those who conform or deviate. Banfield defines it as "power which makes its effect by offering gains or losses which the responding actor values for his own sake or for the sake of some small private circle belonging to him (e.g., family, friends)." The second, public-regarding power, is "power which makes its effect by offering gains or losses which the responding actor values for the sake of something (e.g., value, group, public) that transcends (although it may include) him and his small private circle."[55] Usually, according to Banfield, power is not spent; it is invested. In other words, it is the threat of sanctions and the constant promise of the flow of rewards which make the actual regular exercise of sanctions redundant.

Banfield's insights came from observations of community politics in democratic settings. In statist or undemocratic settings, the "structures of control" are much more formal and rigid because of the high degree of administrative ordering of the social activity by the state. Harry Eckstein's concept of "directiveness" is a convenient device for describing the jurisdictional power of the state vis-à-vis the society in Russian localities.[56] Directiveness might indirectly affect movement resources, as it significantly increases the costs of activism, particularly of the radical and oppositional kind. The concept is more appropriate than "repression,"[57] and captures better the contexts that may not be overtly repressive, but that nevertheless serve to stifle movement activism by other means.[58] Allen Kassof described the extreme version of such a system as "totalitarianism without terror" made possible due to the colossal dependence of the "administered society" on the state.[59]

In the Russian federal and regional settings, control is further exercised through a juxtaposition of such "public-regarding" values as professionalism against politics. Politics is presented as leading to "conflict" and upsetting "consensus"—rhetoric illustrated by the quote from the local Ufa functionary Ivanov. Ivanov is typical of Russia's local functionaries who project an image of themselves as *pragmatiki* (pragmatists) and *krepkie khozyaystvenniki* (tough administrators) in an effort to undermine political opponents.[60] Such forms of Weberian self-legitimization could not exactly be described as ideologies. Juan Linz, in his study of authoritarianism, describes them as "mentalities," designed to justify a given regime and to influence public perceptions thereof.[61] Harmon Zeigler contrasts such a mentality and its stress on social conflict as "pathological," with pluralism, whose premise is that "conflict is either healthy or unavoidable."[62]

Pluralist systems have of course also suppressed conflicts from entering into the public domain with the ostensible aim of fostering "consensus." "Gag rules," however, as Stephen Holmes indicates, can foster democracy to the extent that the polity as a whole is self-regulating.[63] It is a way of preventing conflicts potentially damaging to the polity as a whole, rather than, as in authoritarian settings, preventing those damaging only to the narrow unrepresentative regime in question, seeking to undermine "collective alternatives" to its rule.[64] In strong statist settings, such as Russia, the state is able to impose agendas with little or no social input. To paraphrase Holmes, to "gag" in the Russian context has precisely meant to "choke"—both the particular social movement or civic actors and democracy in general.[65] The state projected apolitical "mentality" dooms or undermines the social agencies' efforts because it affects the attitudes of the ordinary citizenry toward the organized social actors. Opposition activism is presented as threatening the community at large in terms of material rewards. It is also presented as posing a threat to the nontangible value systems like "ethnic peace" and "social harmony." The following sections return to the microlevel of investigation in order to illustrate how the system works at very small town and village community levels.

Public Agenda Setting in Small Towns

Orchards

The leafy rural town of Orchards is located several kilometers outside of the city of Maykop.[66] The mostly Russian, Armenian, and Ukrainian town has a population of 3,300 people. It is the administrative center of the Maykop *rayon*'s larger district, *sel'skiy okrug*, which includes a number of other small towns and villages. Orchards is the seat of the district head of administration and the village soviet consisting of seven deputies, most of whom come from Orchards itself. As in other small towns, the part-time council, largely composed of appointed *kontraktniki* (employees depending on municipal contracts and salaries) from among the village intelligentsia, such as teachers and doctors, is considered a defunct rubber-stamp body. It is the full-time local head of administration who is the major player and decision maker in the locality. The administration is housed in the former village soviet, and is the administrative heart and center of the village.

The HA, Dmitriy Semyonovich,[67] an ethnic Russian, is a retired military officer. He had returned to Russia after much travel in the former Soviet republics as part of the quest to reestablish his Russian roots and enjoy retirement on his native soil. He has been much disillusioned since. Personally, he holds strong views about the situation of ethnic Russians in Adygeya, and is keen to express them privately.[68] Dmitriy Semyonovich presides over an administration which includes an Armenian and two Russian aides. One of the administration's contractors is an Adyge, and Dmitriy Semyonovich is eager to point him out as the "representative of the indigenous nationality." A certain ethnic balance is thus observed in the local administration.

Unlike the heads of city and *rayon* levels, Dmitriy Semyonovich is a popularly elected figure as a head of a village district. Republic functionaries like to point him out as a rebel and as a walking case against the election of local HAs even at the township levels. He is known to have fought for a greater budget for the locality and has openly opposed the higher Maykop *rayon* HA. Dmitriy Semyonovich is a renegade, and only one other HA of his kind apparently exists in Adygeya. The fact that he is a renegade, however, is interesting in and of itself as an indication of the submissive status of the other local HAs. Close scrutiny reveals that Dmitriy Semyonovich, in fact, operates under a system of tough constraints, both formal and informal, and in many ways plays by the rules of the game. His conflict agenda is strictly within the bounds of "policy" and "administration," and he has kept politics, and, most importantly, ethnicity, out of local government as best as he has been able.

The formal constraints include those in line with amendments to local self-government law specifically aimed against local functionaries like him. One amendment, passed in June 1999, allows *rayon* HAs to nominate local HAs from amongst local council deputies, while another threatens the possibility of the removal of popularly elected HAs. Dmitriy Semyonovich's battles with the *rayon* head thus risk him his position when he stands for the next term. The local budget, virtually completely dependent on allocations from the Maykop *rayon*, is the most important informal constraint on his actions. Dmitriy Semyonovich claims he must constantly go cap in hand: "All the time we go to him [*rayon* HA] and ask: Give, give."

According to Dmitriy Semyonovich, the *rayon* administration is quick to use this lever of influence. It also fosters a strong sense among the local population that Dmitriy Semyonovich's political conflicts with the higher bodies reflect on their social and material well-being in the locality. "The mentality is such that if the head of the *rayon* is unhappy, then who would be the first to suffer? He will definitely deprive us of something, like he will prevent construction of a road, will not pay for the telephone line, gas, or water . . . such is the mentality of the people. Since one is not friendly with the *rayon* head that means [one] will have problems."

Local public opinion is shaped by the one major *rayon* newspaper, subsidized by the appointed *rayon* administration. According to the HA, the paper has tried to organize a campaign against him. Dmitriy Semyonovich claims he does not subscribe to it "out of principle" because of its biased nature; he claims the paper refuses to publish his views despite his status as the head of administration of a lower level. He would have loved to run a local newspaper, but lacks funds in the local budget to start one.

Dmitriy Semyonovich sees his goal as changing the local popular mentality and fostering greater decision-making responsibility at a local level. He takes pride in his efforts to invigorate local self-government and to rid the towns of the malaise of popular apathy and passivity. He frequently resorts to the *skhody* or popular gatherings to decide on local matters as a means of getting the people involved in local decision making. Dmitriy Semyonovich maintains that the *skhody* have served as a means of schooling in civic efficacy in conditions where lack of appropriate resources for administration and decision making are universally blamed for inaction across Russia's locales. Dmitriy Semyonovich is proud of what he has accomplished, however little it might seem to an outside observer. When the locality needed a water pipeline and there were no resources in the budget, Dmitriy Semyonovich called a *skhod*. He had to use some persuasion to convince all the locals to chip in an equal amount of money for a common pool. This was later successfully used to construct the pipeline. Dmitriy Semyonovich was thus able to overcome the potential coordination and "free-rider" problems.

More sensitive issues are also placed at *skhody* at the HA's discretion, as a means of avoiding rather than fostering controversies. A Gypsy family was about to move into a neighborhood after Dmitriy Semyonovich had granted them *propiska* (residence registration). Some local families protested. "So I called a *skhod* and put it to a vote, and they [the people] voted in favor, so I said: your objection is overruled," recalls Dmitriy Semyonovich. The Gypsies have never been a source of a major ethnic cleavage in the republic, however. The issue was a strictly local one, and had no potential for expanding its resonance outside of the locality.

Dmitriy Semyonovich's decision making in the above case contrasts with another local issue, this time involving the ethnic Adyge. Dmitriy Semyonovich refers to this case as a "massive controversy," which had at one point allegedly bred ethnic hostilities on an unprecedented level. An open field area was chosen on the territory of the district for building a settlement for Adyge repatriates from Kosovo. The republic government initiative was part of the broader effort to repatriate ethnic Adyge scattered throughout the former Ottoman Empire. The single largest group, over 150 ethnic Adyge, came from war-torn Kosovo. Of these, sixty families were to be resettled in the district. After a protracted search, in which the repatriates were given the opportunity to choose the preferred location, a large open tract of three hectares of land was selected in a very picturesque area. Although the Adyge were warned against the rather bad soil, they insisted on the location due to its proximity to the main highway leading into Maykop, which would facilitate trading activities. The Adyge village was to be built on an elevated hill spot, overlooking several other existing settlements— Russian and Armenian.

The village, however, was to have an unhappy beginning. As the local head of administration, Dmitriy Semyonovich claimed he and not the republic bodies had jurisdiction over the chosen area. Moreover, he claimed, the local vox populi should have had an influence over this decision. The local communities, and not the settlers, were supposed to get the land rights, which had earlier been promised to them by Dmitriy Semyonovich as part of a plan to expand existing villages. Still worse, a part of an existing *khutor* (village) had been included with the originally allocated area without input from local residents. From below, the aggrieved townspeople watched with envy as the spacious two-story redbrick mansions gradually rose up on the hill, and they grumbled about injustice and unfair treatment.

To Dmitriy Semyonovich the injustice stemmed from his feeling of the republic encroaching on his turf. The republic, he maintained, "created a commission and I wasn't included in it. So they decided all in advance, came here, measured it all, and then came to me and said: Sign." The fact that his signature was required, even if it was entirely pro forma, however, appeared to have given Dmitriy Semyonovich certain leverage over the republic functionaries.

Dmitriy Semyonovich's initial reaction was twofold: to get the people involved, rallying them behind him, and to play up the ethnic dimension of the issue. He initially refused to sign the document: "I say: I am sorry, this is against the law, I have to gather people and see if my people want to live nearby. Practically, there is only one Cherkes [Adyge] *aul* [village] in the district." Dmitriy Semyonovich was thus pointing to the potential problem of close coexistence of the various ethnic communities, implying that it might lead to conflicts. In practice, the above course of action was not pursued.

I asked him if he ended up having a *skhod* in the end. In response Dmitriy Semyonovich laughed out loud: "Who would [allow] that sort of a thing!" Although the HA is not supposed to ask formally for permission to hold a *skhod*, his response indicates his anticipated reaction and the constraints he felt against holding the meeting. When he did tell the republic functionaries that he wanted to do it, they explicitly warned him against "inciting ethnic tensions." The way the issue was finally decided is instructive. Dmitriy Semyonovich's initial concerns over ethnic coexistence appeared to have evaporated. He was able to spin the issue in a way that stressed the material benefits of mutual coexistence. Prior to signing the paper, Dmitriy Semyonovich was able to wrestle an agreement from the republic bodies to give part of the land to people from adjoining settlements: now they would be living even closer together than had been originally intended by the republic planners. He also secured a gas supply for the neighboring towns from the newly created, richer, village. What might have been presented as an ethnic controversy had suddenly acquired the matter-of-fact air of division of spoils. Once this had been settled, the issue had gone away altogether.

The above case is an illustration of how a potentially mobilizable issue had been turned into a "nonissue." There was an "aggrieved elite" factor and mass ethnic grievances among the constituencies the aggrieved HA controlled. He could have also used a mass forum in the form of a *skhod* to shape public opinion and foster mobilization. But the issue had already been decided by the powerful republic elite bodies, enforcing their will through the system of formal and informal structures of control.

The most important was the use of the threat to the public-regarding benefits, such as ethnic peace. The second was their control over private-regarding benefits, which the HA lacked, such as the possibility of providing the community with gas. If Dmitriy Semyonovich had mobilized the towns he controlled, he risked depriving the communities of both these public- and private-regarding benefits, and hence his own status and position. Even if the "threat to ethnic peace" was a public relations strategy used by the higher bodies, Dmitriy Semyonovich did not control local public opinion to the same extent that the higher bodies did in order to challenge it.

The Town of Peach Valley and the Bashkir "Genealogical Tree"

The town of Peach Valley lies some 120 kilometers northwest of Bashkortostan's capital, Ufa.[69] It is a rural town surrounded by hills and green farmland, and its fertility and efficient exploitation by the collective farms has made it one of Bashkortostan's most economically successful and self-sufficient localities. It is the administrative center of Peach Valley *rayon*, and is the seat of the *rayon* administration. The town's 10,000-strong population is overwhelmingly Tatar, and Tatar is the predominant language spoken here: some of the interviewees had trouble expressing themselves in Russian, and had to rely on their colleagues for interpretation. Although the official percentage is lower (82 percent), its residents claim as much as 95 percent of its population is ethnic Tatar. The rest are Bashkirs, Russians, and the other smaller Volga groups. Peach Valley, with its strong Tatar identity, thus represented a definite interest from the point of view of investigating local Tatar mobilization to counter Bashkortostan's ethnic policies and the way the local administration handles situations.

Yet, unlike its counterpart in Adygeya, Peach Valley is more of a typical case despite the potentially mobilizable Tatar constituency. Its local governing bodies had not established any notoriety for themselves as bastions of opposition to the more powerful republic actors. Even in the heyday of the soviets' activism, when Tatar soviets one after another were challenging Bashkirization and Bashkortostan's language polices and even threatened to secede and join Tatarstan, Peach Valley remained a quiet political backwater, engrossed in its rural agricultural concerns. The town has been rewarded from above in the form of the stability of its political elite and has avoided the kind of scandalous removals of HAs observed in some of Bashkortostan's other locales. The head of administration, an ethnic Tatar, is known to be on good terms with Bashkortostan's president Murtaza Rakhimov, and is bent on preserving the status quo.

The main source of insights on the role of the local administration was not the HA, but the deputy head, or number two, in the *rayon* administration; the HA was not available for meeting. The deputy HA is Raya Raisovna.[70] Her name first came to my attention a year before the trip to Peach Valley, during the Bashkir presidential elections. It is here, in Peach Valley, according to the opposition ethnic Russian and Tatar presidential hopefuls, that their aides were prevented from collecting signatures required to register their candidacies. A stern woman greeted the aides and instructed them to leave. This was because the local soviet had allegedly voted overwhelmingly in favor of the Bashkir president Murtaza Rakhimov; hence no signature collection for the other candidates was allowed.[71]

Raya Raisovna is the local equivalent of Vladimir Ivanov in Ufa. She is steely and self-consciously maintains an air of professionalism; she uses the jargon and has the air, at the very least, of a senior Komsomol functionary, if not that of a middle-ranking *obkom* official. She has indeed risen through the Komsomol and party *nomenklatura* ranks following her completion of the Higher Party School, and has served as secretary for ideology in the *raykom*. Like Ivanov, she had been elected to the soviet in 1990, and had been in the local administration system since then. She talks about the need to "work with cadres" and the *nomenklatura*, the need for professionalization of local government.

The deputy HA, however, is not just there to "professionalize" and depoliticize local government, or indeed to suppress any potential conflicts from entering or expanding in the public domain. Instead, she combines this function with a self-consciously political and ideological role, albeit one ostensibly concerned with preserving "interethnic peace and the development of culture of those living in the *rayon*." Raya Raisovna, an ethnic Tatar, is the head of the Executive Committee (Ispolkom) of the *rayon* Peach Valley branch of the republic-sponsored Kurultay (Congress) of Bashkirs. The Ispolkom's main function, according to her, is to promote Bashkir culture in the *rayon*. Its main preoccupation has been the introduction of Bashkir language in the local schools. The instruction until now has been voluntary, although parents are encouraged to send the children for bilingual instruction. Furthermore, she maintained:

> The Bashkir Kurultay also pays attention to the study of the genealogical tree.
> And truly, on close inspection of the genetic tree, one discovers that in the
> olden times, naturally, it was the Bashkirs who lived here. . . . We even had a
> scientific conference, . . . and the Bashkir Kurultay invited scientists from the

state university and people from the central archives, archaeologists . . . and we came to a conclusion that Bashkirs lived here in these villages, and so in the future, should parents wish, especially now that the law is passed . . . if there is such a wish among parents and children, let them learn the Bashkir language. . . . Therefore, we have to promote this genealogical tree, the classes of history and culture of Bashkortostan, so a student will know his genealogical tree and will think and reflect, and each parent will have to know . . . not forcibly, but with the help of explanatory work.[72]

Ideology is just one function of the administration. Social control here is formalized through the maintenance of *nomenklatura,* which serves the same function as it did in the Soviet times. The person in charge of *nomenklatura,* Faiz Murtazovich,[73] has the rank of deputy head of administration for cadres. His function: "The selection, placement, and upbringing of the cadres."[74] Faiz Murtazovich maintains personal files (*lichnye dela*) for top administrative posts in the locality, as well as reserve cadre. These are in turn divided into three categories: those appointed by the decree of the HA, those appointed "in consultation with the HA," and chairmen of collective farms. Although the latter are formally elected, they are usually recommended by the administration as well. "Incidentally," proudly remarks Faiz Murtazovich, "there was not a single case when our cadre had been turned down." Overall, the *nomenklatura* includes 113 appointive posts ranging from the heads of the lower-level soviets, to heads of municipal enterprises and such agricultural service enterprises as Agropromservice and Agropromtrans, to directors of cultural institutions and the *rayon* media and school heads. The latter are scrutinized before the administration's commissions every year and their reappointment is coordinated with the HA. Heads of the local enforcement agencies, such as the MVD (Ministry of the Interior), although nominally subordinate to the higher agencies, work under the direct control of the HA. "It has to be like this," maintains Faiz Murtazovich, since "one man rule [*edinonachalie*] brings discipline."

The effectiveness of these control mechanisms is evident when one goes down to the level of agencies controlled by the administration through the appointments system. A group discussion involving a local newspaper editor, a local TOTs branch head, and a private businessman, is instructive.[75] One of the participants is the administration's appointee Timur Timurovich Musin, the editor of Peach Valley's Tatar language newspaper. Musin is shortly up for retirement, and the administration is already looking in the reserve *nomenklatura* for someone to replace him. Musin, a former first secretary of the local Komsomol, is the local intellectual. He is an archetypal gatherer of knowledge about the locality, or a *kraeved*; his main hobby is the painstaking collection of data on famous people from Peach Valley for his book *Born in Peach Valley.*

Musin is the main "notable" in the discussion, and the other participants respectfully defer to him. Musin sees his official public role as the editor of the major public opinion organ as a peace broker in Peach Valley, responsible for maintaining ethnic stability. He illustrates the sensitivity of the ethnic situation:

a group of Tatar school children were praised for their success in a local school Olympiad. A Bashkir teacher wrote protesting, why had Bashkir children, who had also done well in the Olympiad, not been mentioned in the paper? An article in the paper criticizing alcoholism in a Chuvash village provoked protests about implicit stigmatization of the group at large. As an editor, Musin claims, he takes great pains to moderate such concerns. Yet, while he starts off with the usual references to ethnic peace in the locality, Musin increasingly expresses his bitterness about Bashkirization. As a *kraeved*, he brims with facts about the actual, as opposed to official, numbers of ethnic Tatars in Peach Valley, the origins of Tatar settlements in the locality, and so forth. Clearly, he does not subscribe to Raya Raisovna's views about the "genealogical tree."

Now that the main semiofficial figure has broken the ice, the other participants join in. Roza Il'gizovna is Musin's employee at the newspaper, a correspondent. She is also the head of the local chapter of TOTs. As such, she is supposed to be defending the interests of the Tatars in the locality. Yet, the impression she gives is passive apathy. Roza Il'gizovna complains: "There is the official Tatar Ispolkom here, which does nothing for the Tatars; they say we have no ethnic problems here." The Bashkir Kurultay, she complains, is the one body that is active here, in this overwhelmingly Tatar area. "Our Tatar Kurultay does not work; the Bashkir one does, although we have no Bashkirs here." "If they instruct from above to teach Bashkir in schools no matter what you do it will be so." Roza Il'gizovna is cautious about criticizing anyone in the administration, although the reference to the Bashkir Kurultay is clearly aimed against the deputy HA. The reality is that she cannot go against the official figures, and has to deal with them to get anything at all done, hence the passiveness of her organization. "We are thinking of creating a TOTs radio," she says. "I went to speak to Raya Raisovna; she supports [the idea], and promised to speak with the HA."

Thus, the setting up of an independent radio station requires the preliminary approval of the deputy HA, who in turn needs the sanction from the key figure in the *rayon*. Marat El'mirovich, the local *kommersant* (businessman) is a potential contributor to the radio station, but his private credentials do little to make TOTs activities more independent. There was actually a radio station before, which used the newspaper's printing house, but "our tax inspectorate works so well that they said we need a license," says Roza Il'gizovna with sad irony. The *kraeved* wraps up the discussion: "The problem is this: when people are poor and hungry, democratization is not possible. We are all worried about our positions, myself included, because if they throw me out, how will I feed [my family]? Same with the head of the administration: although he understands, he can't do anything, and all the other staff and us too."

The participants in the discussion illustrate how potentially mobilizable resources fail to be used for mobilizing the existing pool of grievances into opposition activities, and are in fact, as in the case of the editor, used to enforce executive agenda setting. The editor, considering his vast knowledge of local history, could have been the potential intellectual resource for mobilization or for countermobilization against Bashkir claims of being indigenous to what he considers to be his native Tatar land. He also controls the key instrument of public opinion in Peach Valley. Roza Il'gizovna, as the correspondent for the paper, could likewise influence public opinion. She is also in charge of an independent public association, not connected to the official Tatar Kurultay. As such, she has the support of a small but committed group of Tatar activists.

Marat El'mirovich is more independent from the establishment than any of the above actors. As a *kommersant,* he does not depend on a state salary, and is not constrained by affiliation with establishment institutions. He has financial resources, crucial for any social movement activity, which he has indeed used in the past to support the local TOTs. TOTs, however, is prepared to go only so far in its activities. Roza Il'gizovna, affiliated with the official newspaper, depends on the editor for her position, and is subject to constraints and his approval as to what she can publish and how far she can go in her TOTs activities. Even if Marat El'mirovich were to provide money for the Tatar radio, its existence would still depend on the HA. The *kommersant* could also suffer penalties in the form of meddling by the tax police. The result is that the main target for opposition activities, the local governing institutions, are also key decision makers as to how much Tatar activity is permitted in the locality. Such a situation makes the existence of any opposition redundant. The result is passive acceptance and resignation to the few handouts of the local administration.

The View from the Grassroots

The above sections have focused largely on the institutional mechanisms of control over public life and suggested the links between them and the final outcomes: the depoliticization of local government, the fostering of local "consensus," and popular acceptance of the status quo. This section focuses on the effects of these control mechanisms on public associations and their struggle to overcome them to influence public life. Public associations are here viewed as actors occupying an intermediate place between the institutional actors on the one hand, and the broader society on the other. One would expect that the degree of repression and control over public life would have naturally led to the slow death of the nationalist associations and other PAs, which emerged to contest the nationalizing policies in the early 1990s. Most have indeed perished or have acquired the form of classical phantom associations. Ten years later, however, the most visible and strong associations of 1990-1992 still exist, which is a remarkable fact in and of itself. This section focuses on the main nationalist associations, which have survived into the present: the Union of Slavs in Adygeya, and TOTs, and to a lesser extent, Rus', in Bashkortostan. The section is based on a series of interviews conducted with the respective leaders and activists, past and present. The interviews were conducted in 1998 and 1999.

The first problem after the collapse of the soviets' institutional structures of support was that of resources and logistics. It was particularly felt in Adygeya, where there was a near fusion between the soviets and the PAs. Virtually overnight, the Union of Slavs lost the premises that it had occupied previously, as well as access to the Maykop soviet office for its campaign activities. Between 1993 and 1998, the city administration kept refusing the Union premises despite numerous requests. The official excuse was the lack of vacant municipal property. According to a Union of Slavs activist, this was one of the most substantial blows to the Union: "Where there are premises, there is work with the people,"[76] she maintained. The second problem was the loss of access to the city presses, and hence the major source of publicity for the PAs. In Bashkortostan a TOTs leader could not even publish an announcement for a TOTs plenary meeting, let alone any program documents, statements, or appeals. In Adygeya, between 1993 and 1999 not a single of the Union of Slavs's opposition appeal was featured in *MN*. Lacking regular contact with the public or access to the media deprived the PAs of the means of working to enhance or promote their public image. The monopolization of the media by the republic bodies and the controlled local administrations facilitated the uncontested stigmatization of the social actors as "loonies" and "people from the street." The PAs could no longer rely on the establishment actors to promote their image either by associating themselves with the movement or serving as its advocates in the press. The "professionalization" of local government made such advocacy at a local level unfeasible.

At the same time, many of the more colorful establishment figures, who had supported the PAs in their opposition activities, had been forced to leave the republic, or had chosen to do so because of the repressive climate. Their promotions blocked at the republic level, they chose what might be referred to as the "bypass" option of advancing at the federal level or in the neighboring regions. Their departure deprived the movements of authoritative leadership with establishment credentials, elite networks, and resources, as well as an intellectual potential to influence movement course and actions. Albert Hirschman refers to such a phenomenon as the "exit" of the "quality consumer."[77]

In Adygeya, the mastermind of the Slavic movement, Valentin Lednev, left after his election to the State Duma. He remained in Moscow even after his deputy term ended. Lednev unsuccessfully tried to run for the Adyge presidency in 1997, excluded from the race due to his lack of fluency in the Adyge language. Lev Simatov, the former Maykop soviet chair, was likewise squeezed out of the republic following his outspoken criticism of Adygeya's nationalizing laws in the Adyge parliament in the capacity of republic-level deputy.

In Bashkortostan, Rus' leader Alexandr Arinin, like Lednev, was elected to the State Duma, and reelected for a second term. He was also prevented from running for republic presidency in 1999 for lack of Bashkir language fluency. Although Lednev and Arinin tried to influence local public opinion by making statements in the Duma and other federal agencies and the press, a conscious effort was made to prevent them from entering into the republic media. The latter, in turn, enjoyed monopoly power to challenge their credentials as those of old *nomenklatura* officials who had chosen to go to Moscow for material reasons, and are using the nationalist umbrellas to advance their narrow personal agendas. The TOTs leader, Kerim Yaushev, eventually resigned due to frustrations stemming from the movement's failure to achieve its goals for lack of establishment support.

The importance of the loss of these establishment figures is evident from the changing strategies of the weakened and demoralized nationalist groups. Changing levels of institutional support led to an increasing appreciation of the fact that the movements would not be viable without the support of the establishment elite actors with political grievances. A Tatar activist refers to them as the "aggrieved *nomenklatura*." "I am more and more convinced," he bitterly maintained, "that a leader could only be someone from the aggrieved *nomenklatura*, a Tatar."[78] "Day by day," he continued, "the numbers of such people are increasing. . . . The Tatars are being squeezed out of power. It is they, with their connections, resources, etc., who can become exactly the sort of opposition force that is needed, but not the national movements. I am absolutely convinced of that." The Tatar activist thus acknowledged his own weakness and that of the new TOTs leader, a former sports coach and a small trader, as not belonging to the high-powered elite or what he calls the "heavyweights," and hence lacking the relevant movement resources.

The above fact led to increased levels of cooperation with Rus', whose leader's *nomenklatura* credentials were much appreciated in the Tatar movement. Rus's leader, Arinin, enjoyed the kind of financial backing by powerful aggrieved business and political elite interests that TOTs lacked. Similar frustrations were expressed in Adygeya. A Union of Slavs activist maintained with respect to leadership: "The problem with the leader is that he has to be well known, he has to be 'spun out,' but the well-known Russians here are quite manageable. . . . So for us the leadership problem is probably the most important one. . . . It is the same problem for all ethnic republics, since the most active ones [personalities] are being squeezed out."[79]

The strategic response to the loss of establishment support was an effort to enter the establishment itself, and to work through state channels in order to influence decision making. In Adygeya, the Union of Slavs enjoyed some success in working through institutional venues, while in Bashkortostan none of the opposition figures could gain such access, due to the more repressed political environment. In Adygeya, one activist was able to obtain a seat in the Adyge parliament. The Union also boasted a number of its other activists in both the republic legislature and the local council levels. The deputy from the Union of Slavs takes credit for blocking a number of potentially discriminatory legislative provisions from being passed, or for using the assembly floor to challenge them.

The Linkage of Local Self-Government with Movement Work

Significantly, in both Adygeya and Bashkortostan, the lobbying or legislative efforts of movement activists had come to focus on changing the legislation on local self-government. Their program statements, goals, and the limited activities they are able to pursue link effective movement work with local self-government independent from the republic bodies. A Union of Slavs activist maintains: "Here you need a program to dispel ignorance [*programma likvidatsii bezgramotnosti* or *likbez*], because for them [the people] local self-government is limited to this: Djharimov [republic president] gathers people and gives them an order to do this and that . . . based on the understanding that if tomorrow they rebel . . . they will be deprived of their salary or something else." In terms of work with the people, the Union has thus focused on information campaigns about the need for local self-government. In limited instances where sympathizing heads of administrations allow the holding of *skhody*, LSG *likbez* has been accorded a priority.[80]

The legislative work of deputies that managed to get elected to the republic legislature likewise prioritized local self-government reform. A Union of Slavs deputy maintains that, together with several other Russian-speaking deputies in the Hase (Adygeya's parliament), she was able to delay the passage of amendments which would have further limited the independence of local governing bodies. These clauses were eventually passed after the activist's deputy status had been illegally suspended based on her critique of the republic regime. The clauses, passed in the summer of 1999, allow for the election of village settlement and town-level HAs from amongst local council deputies following "recommendation" from the *rayon* HAs. Another clause allows for combining the posts of council chair and HA in one person.

In Bashkortostan, the improvement of the situation of ethnic Tatars has been tied to the question of local self-government. The development of local self-government is regarded as a tactical move which would allow movement campaign work for the broader strategic goal of the achievement of Tatar political autonomy. The questions prepared for a TOTs-organized planned referendum are instructive. While dealing with the issue of Tatar rights, they identified as their goal the development of broadly defined local government, rather than the narrowly defined cultural autonomy for the Tatars. The first question read: "Do you consider that in order to realize the principle of the division of executive and legislative power, enshrined in the constitution of the Republic of Bashkortostan, the combining of deputy status with that of a head of administration should be made unlawful?" The second question read: "Do you consider that in order to fulfill the principle of peoples' power, accountability, and responsibility to the population, heads of administrations of *rayony* and cities in Bashkortostan need to be popularly elected?" Only in the third question did the issue of official status for the Tatar language came up, while the fourth item dealt with the symbolic issue of the change of the name of the republic.[81]

These strategies reflect the general frustrations of having to go through the local administrations for the pursuit of even the most mundane, let alone substantive, activities in the localities. They also reflect the recognition of the administrations' powerful impact on local public opinion, whereby local bodies' position is taken at face value, hence the Russian movement's stress on the need for *likbez*.

Conclusion

The centralization of executive power in the republics, fostered by Yel'tsin's reforms of local self-government, from 1992 onwards significantly affected the makeup of the local governing bodies and the incentives of its actors. In addition to strengthening the overall weight of the executive, the reforms also shifted the jurisdictions over public life from the representative to the appointive executive bodies. Aside from these formal jurisdictions, the local bodies have continued to dominate the public and private spheres of production and local services, which makes the local societies dependent on them. These factors, as the examples from Orchards, Peach Valley, Maykop, and Ufa demonstrate, have allowed for the monopolization of the local agenda setting and the suppression of any potential challenge from below. The result was the weakening of the nationalist groups who had previously challenged the nationalizing policies. They now stressed the need to work with the establishment and the development of genuine local self-government to enable effective movement work.

Notes

1. "Postanovlenie Verkhovnogo soveta RSFSR O dopolnitel'nykh polnomochiyakh Prezidenta RSFSR po obespecheniyu zakonnosti deyatel'nosti sovetov narodnykh deputatov v usloviyakh likvidatsii posledstviy popytki gosudarstvennogo perevorota v SSSR," *Vedomosti Soveta narodnykh deputatov RSFSR* 34, no. 22 (1991): 1403-4.

2. "Postanovlenie Verkhovnogo soveta RSFSR O glavakh ispolnitel'noy vlasti respublik v sostave RSFSR," *Vedomosti Soveta narodnykh deputatov RSFSR* 42, no. 17 (1991).

3. "O dopolnitel'nykh polnomochiyakh."

4. For a discussion of the reforms, see Vladimir Gel'man and Grigorii V. Golosov, "Regional Party System Formation in Russia: The Deviant Case of Sverdlovsk Oblast," *Journal of Communist Studies and Transition Politics* 14, no. 1 (1998): 31-53; Vladimir Y. Gel'man, "Regional'naya vlast' v sovremennoy Rossii: Instituty, rejhimy, i praktiki," *Polis* 1 (1998): 87-105; and John F. Young, "Zakonodatel'stvo Rossii po mestnomu samoupravleniyu," in *Tret'e zveno gosudarstvennogo stroitel'stva Rossii: Podgotovka i realizatsiya federal'nogo zakona Ob obshchikh printsipakh organizatsii mestnogo samoupravleniya v Rossiyskoy Federatsii*, ed. Kimitaka Matsuzato (Sapporo, Japan: Slavic Research Center, Hokkaido University, 1998), 109-29.

5. Vladimir Todres, "De-Sovietization: The Parliament from Sakha: The Dissolution of the Soviets as a Method of Self-Preservation," *Segodnya, The Current Digest of the Post-Soviet Press* 65, no. 41 (1993), 15-16.

6. "Aktual'nye problemy formirovaniya mestnogo samoupravleniya v Rossiyskoy federatsii ('Kruglyy stol' v Institute gosudarstva i prava Rossiyskoy akademii nauk)," *Gosudarstvo i pravo* 5, no. 1997 (1997): 32.

7. In 1999, the total number of municipal bodies was 13,669 (P. A. Goryunov et al., *Formirovanie organov mestnogo samoupravleniya v Rossiyskoy federatsii: Elektoral'naya statistika* [Moscow: Ves' mir, 1999], 9).

8. Goryunov et al., *Formirovanie organov*, 28.

9. For a discussion of the numerous violations of Russia's legislation and the constitution by the regions, see Alexandr Arinin, "Problemy razvitiya rossiyskoy gosudarstvennosti v kontse dvadtsatogo veka," in *Federalizm vlasti i vlast' federalisma*, ed. Michael N. Guboglo (Moscow: Inteltekh, 1997), 6-107.

10. "Federal'nyy zakon Ob obshchikh printsipakh organizatsii mestnogo samoupravleniya v Rossiyskoy federatsii" (Moscow: Yuridicheskaya literatura, 1995).

11. "Ukaz Prezidenta SSRA O povyshenii zarabotnoy platy rabotnikam sfery obrazovaniya, zdravookhraneniya, kul'tury, sotsial'nogo obslujhivaniya," *Sovetskaya Adygeya (SA)*, 21 January 1992, 1; and "Ukaz Prezidenta SSRA O prekrashchenii polnomochiy ispolkoma soveta narodnykh deputatov SSRA," *SA,* 23 January 1992, 1.

12. "V prezidiume Soveta narodnykh deputatov SSRA," *SA,* 11 January 1992, 1.

13. R. Ashinov, "Ruslan Hadjhibiekov: Oppozitsiya eto neplokho, no rabotat' soobscha luchshe," *SA,* 10 June 1992, 1.

14. "Manny nebesnoy ne budet," *SA,* 22 February 1992, 2.

15. "Ukaz Prezidenta SSRA O strukture pravitel'stva i nekotorykh voprosakh deyatel'nosti organov ispolnitel'noy vlasti v SSRA," *SA,* 5 March 1992; *SA,* 7 March 1992, 3.

16. "Zakon Respubliki Adygeya O presidente Respubliki Adygeya," *SA,* 25 March 1992; *SA,* 31 March 1992, 1.

17. I. Jhad'ko, "Dlya kogo zakon ne zakon," *SA,* 12 August 1992, 2.

18. "Polojhenie O distsiplinarnoy otvetstvennosti glav administratsiy," *SA,* 28 October 1992, 2.

19. "Ukaz prezidenta RA O merakh po osushchestvleniyu reformy mestnogo samoupravleniya v RA," *SA,* 30 October 1993.

20. "Zakon RA Ob osnovakh organizatsii i deyatel'nosti mestnogo gosudarstvenogo upravleniya i mestnogo samoupravleniya v RA na perekhodnyy period," *SA,* 7 April 1994, 1.

21. "Ukaz prezidenta RA O merakh po ukrepleniyu distsipliny v sisteme ispolnitel'noy vlasti RA," *SA,* 18 July 1996, 1.

22. "Postanovleniye VSRB O moratorii na vybory v vysshyye i mestnyye organy gosudarstvennoy vlasti v RB," *VU,* 30 October 1992, 1.

23. R. Ayupov, "I za zemlyu pridyotsya platit'," *Vechernyaya Ufa (VU)*, 3 March 1992, 1.

24. A subsequent decree, based on "consultations" with heads of other republics, set a moratorium on elections to the soviets and heads of administrations until the expiration of their terms ("Postanovleniye VSRB O moratorii na vybory v vysshyye i mestnyye organy gosudarstvennoy vlasti v RB," *VU,* 30 October 1992, 1).

25. R. Ayupov, "M. Rahimov: Ya otkazalsya uchastvovat' v rabote s'ezda," *VU,* 10 March 1992, 1.

26. Name has been changed to preserve the anonymity of respondent.

27. Interview by author, tape recording, Ufa, 4 June 1999.

28. Interview by author, tape recording, Ufa, 4 June 1999.

29. Name has been changed to preserve the anonymity of respondent.

30. Interview by author, tape recording, Maykop, 29 July 1999.

31. Interview by author, tape recording, Ufa, 4 June 1999.

32. Matsuzato found that in Kotovsk city in Tambov *oblast'* the city administration's Department of Control and Audit, "going beyond its ordinary competence to audit municipal accounts, tries to regulate economic activity within the city" by auditing the accounts of local companies to reveal their ability to pay municipal taxes (Kimitaka Ma-

tsuzato, "Local Elites under Transition: County and City Politics in Russia 1985-1996," *Europe-Asia Studies* 51, no. 8 [1999] 1367-400).

33. Michael E. Urban,Vyacheslav Igrunov, and Sergei Mitrokhin, *The Rebirth of Politics in Russia* (Cambridge: Cambridge University Press, 1997), 194. For similar evidence from *perestroyka*-era politics, see also M. Steven Fish, *Democracy from Scratch: Opposition and Regime in the New Russian Revolution* (Princeton, N.J.: Princeton University Press, 1995).

34. Interview by author, tape recording, Ufa, 4 June 1999.

35. Yaroslav Startsev, "Gubernatorial Politics in Sverdlovsk Oblast," *Post-Soviet Affairs* 15, no. 4 (1999): 349.

36. For a discussion of the mechanisms of control in American settings, see Edward C. Banfield, *Political Influence* (New York: Free Press, 1961).

37. For a discussion of the dependence of the regional legislatures on the executive branch, see Darrell Slider, "Elections to Russia's Regional Assemblies," *Post-Soviet Affairs* 12, no. 3 (1996): 243-64, 258.

38. Based on conversation with opposition activist, Ufa, 3 June 1999.

39. I am grateful to Oleg Tsvetkov for providing the deputy lists for the 1999 Maykop city council.

40. Interview by author, tape recording, Ufa, 3 June 1999.

41. For a discussion of "machine politics" in Bashkortostan's elections, see Henry E. Hale, "Machine Politics and Institutionalized Electorates: A Comparative Analysis of Six Duma Elections in Bashkortostan," *Journal of Communist Studies and Transition Politics* 15, no. 4 (1999): 70-110.

42. Interview by author, tape recording, Ufa, 8 June 1999.

43. Interview by author with deputy of Maykop City Representative Assembly, tape recording, Maykop, 6 August 1999.

44. Interview by author, tape recording, Ufa, 12 June 1999.

45. Banfield, *Political Influence*.

46. Urban, Igrunov, and Mitrokhin, *Rebirth of Politics*, 299.

47. Interview by author, tape recording, Maykop, 9 August 1999.

48. Interview by author, tape recording, Maykop, 12 August 1999.

49. Interview by author, tape recording, Ufa, 12 June 1999.

50. Edward C. Banfield and James Q. Wilson, *City Politics* (New York: Vintage, 1963), 151. For a discussion of the impact of electoral arrangements on partisanship in local government, see also Sidney Tarrow, *Between Center and Periphery: Grassroots Politicians in Italy and France* (New Haven, Conn.: Yale University Press, 1977).

51. Banfield, *Political Influence*, 258-9.

52. Peter Bachrach and Morton S. Baratz, "Two Faces of Power," *American Political Science Review* 56, no. 4 (1962): 949.

53. Banfield, *Political Influence*, 311.

54. Banfield, *Political Influence*, 315.

55. Banfield, *Political Influence*, 315.

56. Harry Eckstein, "Congruence Theory Explained," in *Can Democracy Take Root in Post-Soviet Russia? Explorations in State-Society Relations*, ed. Harry Eckstein, Jr., Frederic J. Fleron, Erik Hoffmann, and William M. Reisinger (Lanham, Md.: Rowman & Littlefield, 1998), 3-33.

57. For a discussion, see Charles Tilly, *From Mobilization to Revolution* (Reading, Mass.: Wesley, 1978).

58. Repression is of course also a feature of some Russian regional settings, a case in point being Bashkortostan. Scholars have noted that the more repressive a regime, the

greater the costs of opposition activism. Ashutosh Varshney notes: "In democratic systems, the costs of collective action are significantly lower because repression cannot normally be exercised with impunity" (Ashutosh Varshney, *Democracy, Development, and the Countryside: Urban-Rural Struggles in India* [Cambridge: Cambridge University Press, 1995], 199). India, Varshney's subject of study, is an example of how mass mobilization is possible even in poor, but politically open and democratic settings.

59. Allen Kassof, "The Administered Society: Totalitarianism without Terror," *World Politics* 16, no. 4 (1964): 558-75.

60. For a discussion of such rhetoric, see Marie Mendras, "How Regional Elites Preserve Their Power," *Post-Soviet Affairs* 15, no. 4 (1999): 295-311; Marie Mendras, "L'Etat, L'Argent, La Clientèle," *La Revue Tocqueville/The Tocqueville Review* 19, no. 1 (1998): 35-54; Jean-Charles Lallemand, "Gouvernance Introuvable à Briansk et à Smolensk," *La Revue Tocqueville/The Tocqueville Review* 19, no. 1 (1998): 75-102; Jean-Charles Lallemand, "Politics for the Few: Elites in Bryansk and Smolensk," *Post-Soviet Affairs* 15, no. 4 (1999): 312-35.

61. For a discussion, see Juan J. Linz, "An Authoritarian Regime: Spain," in *Mass Politics: Studies in Political Sociology* (New York: Free Press, 1970), 257-66.

62. Harmon Zeigler, *Pluralism, Corporatism, and Confucianism: Political Association and Conflict Regulation in the United States, Europe, and Taiwan* (Philadelphia: Temple University Press, 1988), 22. For a discussion of the correlation between acceptance of conflict and democracy, see also Stefan Szuks, *Democracy in the Head: A Comparative Analysis of Democratic Leadership Orientations among Local Elites in Three Phases of Democratisation* (Goteborg, Sweden: Center for Public Sector Research, Goteborg University, 1998). Juan Linz maintains that such mentalities are characteristic of authoritarian regimes: rather than enthusiastic support, they expect "passive acceptance" of the regime, while the regime itself stigmatizes "politics" (Linz, "Authoritarian Regime").

63. Stephen Holmes, "Gag Rules or the Politics of Omission," in *Constitutionalism and Democracy*, ed. Jon Elster and Rune Slagstand (New York: Cambridge University Press, 1988), 24.

64. Adam Przeworski, "Democracy as a Contingent Outcome of Conflicts," in *Constitutionalism*, 60; and Adam Przeworski, *Democracy and the Market* (Cambridge: Cambridge Univeristy Press, 1991), 54.

65. Holmes wrote: "Issue suppression sounds tyrannical: to gag is to choke. But self-denial may be indispensable in self-regulating polities" (Holmes, "Gag Rules," 24).

66. The name of the town has been changed to preserve the anonymity of respondents.

67. The name has been changed to preserve the anonymity of the respondent.

68. Interview by author, tape recording, 6 August 1999.

69. The name of the town has been changed to preserve the anonymity of respondents.

70. The name has been changed to preserve the anonymity of the respondent. Interview by author, tape recording, 17 June 1999.

71. For an account of the elections, see Tomila Lankina, "Showcase of Manipulated Democracy: Shadow-Puppet Elections in Bashkortostan," *Transitions* 5, no. 8 (1998): 62-4. For a discussion of the political developments in the republic, see also Tomila Lankina, "Local Government and Ethnic and Social Activism in Russia," in *Contemporary Russian Politics: A Reader*, ed. Archie Brown (Oxford: Oxford University Press, 2001), 398-411.

72. Interview by author, tape recording, 17 June 1999.

73. Name has been changed to preserve the anonymity of respondent.

74. Interview by author, tape recording, 17 June 1999.

75. The names of the people in the discussion have been altered to preserve the anonymity of respondents. Interview by author, tape recording, 17 June 1999.

76. Interview by author, tape recording, Maykop, 4 August 1999.

77. Albert O. Hirschman, *Exit, Voice, and Loyalty: Responses to Decline in Firms, Organizations, and States* (Cambridge, Mass.: Harvard University Press, 1970).

78. Interview by author, tape recording, Ufa, 7 June 1999.

79. Interview by author, tape recording, Maykop, 4 August 1999.

80. Interview by author, tape recording, Maykop, 9 August 1999.

81. Interview by author with Tatar activist, tape recording, Ufa, 8 June 1999.

Chapter 7

Is Local Government Becoming Local?

In recent years, the Russian media has featured numerous accounts of rebellious local governments, usually at the level of the regional capital, challenging regional authorities. The "mayor versus governor" has reportedly become the main regional cleavage replacing the earlier line of conflicts between the executive branch on the one hand, and the representative branch on the other.[1] The battles between Evgeniy Nazdratenko and Viktor Cherepkov and between Nikolay Kondratenko and Valeriy Samoylenko[2] became soap operas closely followed by observers nationwide, including Moscovites usually indifferent to provincial chronicles. Elsewhere, as in the Novgorod region, local governments have reportedly sought the inputs of the grassroots, actively aiding the development of civic activism.[3] Finally, the mayor of the capital city in one of Russia's most diverse ethnic republics, Karachay-Cherkessiya, emerged as a champion of the republic's politically and culturally marginalized groups, the Cherkes and Russians. Such events suggest that local government is becoming increasingly independent, and now has sufficient power to mobilize enough resources to challenge regional authorities, to support ethnic movements, and to foster the development of civil society. Most importantly, the early postelection pronouncements of Russia's new president Putin, as well as his actions against some notoriously anti-LSG governors, indicated his own preference for a stronger and more institutionally independent local self-government.

How representative of the entire regional scene, however, are these much-publicized instances? Is local self-government becoming "local," independent from the regional executive hierarchies? Is it really becoming responsive to the local civic, cultural, and minority ethnic pressures, rather than serving as an instrument of social control? Finally, is the idea of a stronger and more independent local government just rhetoric, or does it truly enjoy the support of the new Putin administration?

The purpose of this chapter is threefold. First, it extends the comparisons of cases to include Russia's other entities. Second, it further probes the conceptual arguments about state-society relations in Russia by discussing local governments' influence over other aspects of social activism. Third, it highlights the key aspects of Putin's reform of LSG in an effort to ascertain their implications for democracy in the Russian polity as a whole.

The discussion will roughly follow the lines of inquiry pursued with regard to Adygeya and Bashkortostan. The preceding chapters have established that despite the vast differences along a number of dimensions—cultural, ethnic, political, socioeconomic—Adygeya and Bashkortostan's local governments were strikingly similar in many respects. After a brief period of "local power" when the lower bodies cooperated with the social agencies, local government turned into the regional regimes' instrument of social control. Such control has been possible due to LSG's institutional structure, its makeup, and the socioeconomic features that Russia inherited from its Soviet past. If the above institutional features, council makeup, and systemic features affect levels of social activism in our "most different" cases, then we ought to regard these features as the main independent variables accounting for levels of social mobilization and ethnic, civic, and other forms of independent social activism, or lack thereof, throughout Russia. The questions, then, are as follows. Is "executivization" of local government and its fusion into regional hierarchies a typical feature of Russia's republics? To what extent do councils in the other entities conform to the pattern of high "netness," i.e., of the predominance of notables in charge of large professional networks, that we observed in Adygeya and Bashkortostan? Is there evidence to suggest that elsewhere, local governments also use their resources to stifle, rather than encourage, local social activism? Do the republics differ from the nonethnically defined regions along the above dimensions? Finally, will Putin's reform of local government help to reverse or, alternatively, reinforce the above tendencies?

Regional Variations

Regime Differences between Republics and Regions

One way of establishing whether municipalities, at least at the higher city or *rayon* levels, enjoy substantive independence from the regional authorities is to examine the regional political cleavage lines. Scholars have distinguished between "uniactor" versus "multiactor" Russian regional regimes. Adygeya and Bashkortostan could be easily classified as regimes with "one actor," that is, where the president controls the political situation in the republic and does not face any significant challenge from other actors.

As an indication of the number of uniactor entities, I made use of a study by Sergei Ryzhenkov, which attempted to devise a representative sample of different regional regimes. Out of the sample of twenty-one entities, which included both republics and regions, seven had one main actor, Tatarstan being a typical example. Nine had two main actors (mayor and regional head), of which Udmurtiya was a famous case, and the remaining five cases had an "uncertain" configuration of actors.[4] Thus, it may be inferred that close to half of Russia's regions maintain uniactor political regimes and hence maintain control over municipalities. If one distinguishes between the regions and republics, however, it emerges that the republics are more likely to conform to the uniactor pattern than the regions.[5] Of the twenty-one republics, only two, Udmurtiya and Karachay-Cherkessiya, have had significant conflicts between the regional and local levels of government. Russia's republics in general have also been identified among entities with the "highest resistance" to the implementation of federal legislation on LSG. A recent effort to classify local government institutional practices has singled out many of the republics for having statified and abolished the crucial *rayon* level as a unit of local self-government altogether, a practice which was only observed in six "Russian" regions.[6]

Kimitaka Matsuzato's comparative study of regional regimes confirms the above findings. In terms of the local government institutional differences, he specifically distinguishes between the "ethnically Russian" regions and the other political regimes.[7] Matsuzato cites Tatarstan as a regime type broadly representative of the ethnic republics. He writes that although in the "Russian" regions chief executives at all levels of government are elected, Tatarstan "statified not only counties but also cities."[8] The political consequences of the institutional setup are that local HAs serve as "boss politicians responsible for running electoral machines for the sake of the higher authorities."[9]

Another significant distinction between the republics on the one hand and the Russian regions on the other relates to patterns of revenue distribution within these entities. A recent study has shown that the republics strongly conform to the redistributive pattern of revenue allocation, with the republic bodies concentrating decision-making authority on local expenditures. The study contrasts this with the "Russian" regions, where local governments retain more local revenue, and possess much greater levels of authority over it.[10] Such fiscal control enhances the republics' institutional levers of influence over their localities, including the rich urban capitals.

The redistributive pattern of revenue allocation corresponds to the anecdotal evidence from the republics: the republic elites are often accused of channeling funds to their native areas of origin, or to the localities with predominantly titular populations. These practices may represent an extension of the republic elites' nation-building initiatives. One can also regard them as an effort at demonstrating the concern for the titular ethnie as a whole, rather than its narrow elite segment, in the context of frequent accusations of republic elites' corruption and nepotism.

Local Government Institutions in the Republics

Having established the broader institutional and regime differences between the republics and regions, this section discusses in greater detail the local government institutional organization in the republics in order to generalize further from Adygeya and Bashkortostan to other cases. In virtually all of the republics, heads of local administrations continue to be fused into local republican hierarchies and to be dependent on the republican chief executives. The Kremlin's efforts to ensure compliance with the 1995 law On Local Self-Government, which mandates the election of local executives, have resulted in some de jure modifications of local government organization.

In practice, however, the republics have continued to sabotage this requirement and have devised subtle ways of evading it. For example, according to the official CEC report on local government in the republics, all of Adygeya's local governing bodies are popularly elected, while those in Tatarstan are elected by the councils.[11] In fact, most of the republics in the report appear to have complied with the law by either electing HAs popularly or through the local councils. A more nuanced reading of the republics' local governing laws reveals a

Table 7.1. Legal Provisions on Heads of Administrations, 1993-1998

Legal provisions	Republics
Nomination of lower-level HAs by higher-level local government HAs.	Adygeya Altay Komy Sakha-Yakutiya Udmurtiya
Appointment of HAs by republic president or subject to his "presentation" of a candidate.	Bashkortostan Komy Mariy El Sakha-Yakutiya
Republic president does not appoint HAs, but is allowed to remove them.	Buryatiya Kalmykiya
No explicit provisions for appointment; vague wording leaves possibility of various interpretations.	Kabardino-Balkariya Mordoviya Tatarstan
Local government or its separate levels listed as part of a system of state power, suggesting possibility of HA appointment by republic bodies.	Adygeya Khakasiya Tatarstan

Source: Compiled from *Konsul'tant-plyus* electronic database of Russian legislation.

different picture. Adygeya is a typical example of how the republics violate federal legislation on local government. As I have discussed above, Adygeya has introduced an elaborate distinction between local *state* government and local *self*-government.[12] It can thus justify to the federal center that all of its local governing bodies are elected. But the most important local figure, the mayor of Maykop, is legally part of local state government rather than self-government, and is a minister in Adygeya's government. He thus forms part of the republic's executive chain of authority.

In other republics, the presidents can remove popularly elected mayors, or raise the issue in the local councils dependent on them. In a number of republics, while local HAs are elected at lower levels, they continue to be subordinate to the republican chief executives at the most important large city, *rayon*, or capital city levels. Table 7.1 summarizes the legal provisions in some of the republics that serve to illustrate how the respective regimes subvert federal LSG requirements. The summary covers the periods from 1993 until 1998, and is based on a search of the Russian regional law database, *Konsul'tant-plyus*.

The two cases that stand out are Udmurtiya and Karachay-Cherkessiya. In both cases local governing actors have been sufficiently independent to challenge republic authorities, and, as in the case of Karachay-Cherkessiya, to mobilize the public behind the local mayor. Udmurtiya's conflict, however, has been pacified with the help of the federal institutions, such as the Constitutional Court.[13] The Court ruling, although ambiguous and subject to conflicting interpretations, was seen as having a prorepublic bias, depriving the local government actors of key federal support. In Karachay-Cherkessiya, by contrast, Moscow played an important role in supporting mayoral elections, and did not explicitly endorse any side in the struggle between the rival regional and mayoral factions.

The Deviant Case of Karachay-Cherkessiya

In 1998-1999, the tiny North Caucasus republic of Karachay-Cherkessiya became a focus of national and international media attention. The republic was rocked by ethnic tensions which threatened to spill over to other North Caucasus republics. Between January 1998 and April 1999, the republic witnessed mass mobilization on a scale not seen since the early phase of Russia's democratization in 1990-1992. Thousands of people protested against Karachay-Cherkessiya's Communist-era leadership headed by Vladimir Khubiev and demanded his resignation and the holding of presidential elections. The mass movement, uniting mostly Cherkes and Abazin groups, but also Russians and Cossacks, acquired a distinctly ethnic dimension. Although the republic has two main titular groups—the Karachay and the Cherkes—the latter, along with the republic's sizeable Russian-speaking populations, expressed grievances about political and cultural discrimination by the Karachay leadership, headed by Khubiev. Protest demonstrations were held in the capital city Cherkessk, involving thousands of people. Disruptive tactics were used to obstruct the work of the republic's People's Assembly. Abazin and Cherkes autonomies were proclaimed, and appeals made to the neighboring Stavropol' *kray* to incorporate the republic's Russian areas. Worse still, leaflets appeared in the city warning of terrorist acts, and rumors were spread to the effect that the "Wahabbites"—a common Russian reference to extremist Islamic groups—were "recruiting and preparing for battle."[14]

In April 1999, submitting to pressure from Moscow and the local population, the republic finally held presidential elections, in which Vladimir Semenov, an ethnic Karachay, narrowly won against the other main contender, Stanislav Derev, an ethnic Cherkes. Derev also happened to be the mayor of the republic's capital, Cherkessk. He had been elected in November 1997 after the republic conceded to federal pressure to separate local government from republic organs. The non-Karachay groups challenged the outcome of the presidential election on the grounds that Khubiev had manipulated the elections to ensure the victory of his anointed heir. For days, tens of thousands of people gathered in Cherkessk to protest amid widespread allegations of electoral fraud, further exacerbating an already tense situation.

Ethnic discrimination was doubtless a crucial reason for these people to abandon their day-to-day preoccupations for days and weeks to engage in a sustained political protest which lasted from late 1997 to the end of 1999. However, their involvement raises a host of questions, which came up repeatedly in interviews with groups in Adygeya and Bashkortostan. Who authorized the demonstrations that lasted for days and weeks? Who paid for the buses and gas to bring the protesters to the main square in such an organized fashion? Who provided the participants with food and water? Who allowed their absence from work for days? Finally, why did they protest at that particular point in time?[15]

The resources that the mayor controlled were crucial for the outcome of the movement. Not only was the mayor a popularly elected figure, which made him institutionally independent from the republic regime, he was also a powerful enterprise notable in charge of the republic's largest enterprise, the Mercury firm, controlling vast production and trade networks in his city and beyond. According to some estimates, Mercury's mineral water and vodka production generated up to 25 percent of the republic's income.[16] Derev's election as mayor in November 1997 provided him with the political resources crucial for mass mobilization which his wealth alone could not have generated. The institutional resources that came with the mayor's office, combined with his private control over industrial networks, allowed him to rally thousands of people for a highly visible and effective protest movement.

The mayor's control over resources explains why this enterprise tycoon with no prior record of involvement in nationalist activities, rather than the Cherkes nationalist groups, was the prime moving force behind the nationalist mobilization. When I visited the republic in the summer of 1997, it was a quiet backwater, boasting "ethnic harmony" and "consensus." The Cherkes nationalist leaders I interviewed thought otherwise. Such expressions as "bloodshed" and the coming of "violence" to end the discrimination of the non-Karachays peppered their diatribes against the Khubiev regime.[17] Yet, these statements seldom found their way into the national press, and the nationalist groups failed to launch large-scale mass protest acts. It took the popular election of the mayor to enable locally and nationally visible mass mobilization.

In essence, Derev's conflict with Khubiev and his loyalists was not different from the mayor-versus-governor struggles observed in the nonethnically defined regions. The struggle was over political office, the republic presidency, and, indirectly, over economic spoils derived from control over key republic institutions. In the regions, however, the politicians do not have easy recourse to such mobilizable issues as ethnicity, although some, like the notorious anti-Semite Kondratenko, the former governor of Krasnodar *kray*, have frequently employed anti-Jewish rhetoric, while others, like Moscow's mayor Yuriy Lujhkov, have railed against "persons of Caucasian nationality." Karachay-Cherkessiya demonstrates how in the ethnic republics, the mayor-versus-governor political cleavage observed in the regions and made possible by the mayors' greater independence becomes transformed into a divisive ethnic issue with a potential for ethnic conflict. Karachay-Cherkessiya could thus be regarded as the exception that confirms the rule that mass mobilization in the localities, or any social activism that has the potential for unseating regional regimes, is only possible where local government is at some levels institutionally separate from the regional level.

"Netness"

In addition to the imposition of executive hierarchies with top-bottom subordination, the "netness" of the local councils is another way of ensuring the fusion of society and the state and the latter's control over the former.[18] Adygeya and Bashkortostan demonstrate continuity with the Soviet period in terms of the predominance of the established actors from large professional networks, often dependent on the executive branch, in their local councils. How representative are these findings of the other republics?

Table 7.2 contains official CEC information on the composition of local governing bodies in all of Russia's republics except for Bashkortostan and Ingushetiya, as of 1998. Bashkortostan was not listed in the report, while Ingushetiya has abolished its local governing bodies. The table reveals that organized social and political interests continue to be represented weakly in the local bodies; in many cases not at all. Instead, the table reveals the continued "executivization" of local councils, as well as the predominance of the managerial elite.[19] State and municipal employees form large proportions of the local deputy corps in all the republics. In Altay, for example, they constitute over half of all councilors, and almost a third in Buryatiya. Heads of enterprises constitute as much as or even more than half of the deputy corps in Altay, Buryatiya, Kalmykiya, Mariy El, and Chuvashiya. The CEC report does not disaggregate the "municipal employees" category, and it is difficult to judge what percentage represents the "notability" in charge of educational, medical, and other net-works. However, case studies of other regions indicate that further generaliza-tions might be possible not just to the republics, but to regions as well.[20]

A study of municipal elections in several cities indicates that candidates coming from "education" and "medical" professions constitute 64 percent in Pskov, 53 percent in Kirov, 52 percent in Ryazan', and 61 percent in Samara.[21] As in Adygeya and Bashkortostan, the enterprise and other network notables tend to be dependent on municipal administrations in one way or another, which also makes them vulnerable to random sanctions and penalties. Despite years of

Table 7.2. Composition of Local Representative Bodies in Russia's Republics, 1998

Republic	Population	Total LSG deputies	Nomi-nated by elec-toral blocks	State and municipal employ-ees	Enter-prise heads
Adygeya	432,046	397	9	59	81
Altay	190,831	207		107	122
Buryatiya	1,038,252	341		108	155
Dagestan	1,802,188	5,156		1053	749
Ingushetiya	No LSG				
Kabardino-Balkariya	753,531	1,410	9	239	340
Kalmykiya	322,579	830		109	378
Karachay-Cherkessiya	414,970	614	10	76	189
Kareliya	790,150	413	46	5	72
Komy	1,250,847	413	8	25	165
Mariy El	749,332	438		32	170
Mordoviya	963,504	5,478		838	784
Sakha-Yakutiya	1,094,065	523		91	191
North Ossetiya	632,428	1,055		58	152
Tatarstan	3,641,742	6,937			125
Tyva	308,557	329	4	73	72
Udmurtiya	1,605,663	864	77	47	311
Khakasiya	566,861	698		13	97
Chuvashiya	1,338,023	571	19	76	283

Source: Compiled from P. A. Goryunov et al., *Formirovanie organov mestnogo samou-pravleniya v Rossiyskoy federatsii: Elektoral'naya statistika* (Moscow: Ves' mir, 1999).

privatization and efforts to create an independent entrepreneurial sector, local economic processes continue to be "administrative" in nature.[22]

The state-imposed licensing further facilitates the subordination of private agencies to the local bodies. Licensing exists in other more pluralist settings, but it is the extent to which the state continues to "direct" the society through the imposition of license requirements that makes Russia and some other postcommunist states stand out.[23] Consider the following example. It refers to a political issue discussed at the national level. However, its policy impact would be felt most at the micro levels involving the interaction of the individual and the state's outreach agencies in the localities.

At the time of the work on this book a battle was being waged between Russia's liberal economics minister German Gref and the state bureaucracies over their power to issue permits for private activity. Over 1,500 types of private activities are subject to licensing, from publishing, to primary, secondary, higher, and vocational training, to the setting up of investment funds.[24] Gref's battles notwithstanding, the threat to licensing other hitherto unlicensed agencies looms large as various state bureaucracies fight for the right to cover more areas of activity. The Ministry of Press demands the right to license publishing; the State Technical Inspection Agency—to "inspect" sixty more types of activity in addition to those already covered; the State Committee on Sport—the production, distribution, and sale of mineral water; and the Ministry of Culture—the featuring of films.[25] Licenses may be withdrawn at random and their costs increased, but licensed agencies may also enjoy privileges in the form of financial subsidies, access to the state resources, or other lucrative arrangements.

There is substantial evidence to suggest that the local bodies abuse their control over the private sphere for political or other ends. A 1997 letter by the prosecutor general to the Duma listed over 70,000 violations of the law by local administrations, identifying the following as the most widespread: illegal licensing and taxation; illegal imposition of financial penalties; and interference with the economic activities of enterprises, among others.[26] Such facts have led some scholars to conclude, "the underdeveloped market economy in Russia adds the most fundamental economic opportunities . . . to this category of 'resources' exploited by local administrations for political (electoral) purposes."[27] The fact that the enterprise notables in becoming local deputies might be motivated by the desire to avoid penalties and to lobby for favors does not diminish the argument of their vulnerability to the local organs and their resultant hesitance to espouse political opposition to the regional regimes.

Local Government and Civil Society

If organized civic and political groups are weakly represented in the local councils, perhaps they influence local affairs indirectly, through cooperation with the local institutions. There is a dearth of systematic academic work on the relationships between public associations and local government in Russia's regions—a puzzling omission considering that this aspect is considered one of local government's key functions in democracies. A notable exception is Nicolai Petro's study of the Novgorod region, which specifically examines relationships between civil society groups and municipal institutions. Petro argues that civic associations are engaged in meaningful public decision making through the local governing bodies.[28] As an example of their participation in decision making, Petro cites the existence of official "social chambers" at both regional and municipal levels, uniting Novgorod region's civic groups into discussion bodies, whose opinions are sought out by the local administrations.[29]

However, evidence from this and other regions indicates that even where such consultative forums exist, local government preferences and institutional support or lack thereof crucially affect the survival rate and activities of nonstate actors. Thus, even in the more "civic" Novgorod region, only the registered associations can participate in the official "social chamber," chaired by the governor, while agencies not officially recognized become marginalized.[30] "After the administration formed its own social chamber," writes Petro with regard to a social agency not integrated into formal structures, "the importance of the unofficial chamber waned."[31] A study of feminist groups in Russia found that in such different cities as Moscow, Ivanovo, and Cheboksary, well into the post-Soviet period, some groups continue to suffer from a failure to obtain registration and from lack of access to office space, telecommunications, and other crucial facilities still concentrated in the municipal state organs.[32] By contrast, "integrat[ion] into the local power structures" was found to be crucial for groups' success.[33] Another scholar wrote, based on a comparative study of several regions: "Organizations without patronage had relatively little political influence," while "any impact they had was generally linked to their dependence on local political figures."[34] Similarly, a recent study published in an influential policy-oriented volume on Western civil society building efforts in postcommunist states found that in Russia "the success of regional women's groups depends mostly on the personalities in charge of local government, the personalities in charge of local women's organizations, and the connections between the two."[35]

If we use Larry Diamond's criteria of civil society, we may conclude that the civil society observed in Russia's regions is far from being "voluntary," "self-generating," largely "self-supporting," and "autonomous from the state."[36] Instead, it is actively incorporated into the state's local structures, a feature making it less like democracy and more like dictatorial regimes in so far as "they cannot and do not tolerate independent organization," or patrimonial regimes, which, as Richard Rose and Doh Chull Shin aptly put it, view society as an "extension of the ruler's household."[37] It represents co-optation of semiautonomous groups rather than substantial policy input by a plurality of independent social agencies.

Other postcommunist states confirm these findings, supporting the contention that even where more independent local government structures are in place, the systemic socialist socioeconomic features and the bureaucratic infrastructures linger on, increasing the society's dependence on the state. In Hungary, which is often praised for having progressed the furthest in local government reforms compared to the other postcommunist countries, the state continues to envelop public associations in a web of regulations, while patronage of local governing organs is central to the survival of some agencies at the expense of others. The welfare ministry, for example, requires NGOs to have contracts with local governments, but the latter may refrain from entering into a contract for personal, political, or other reasons, risking closure of NGOs.[38]

Local Government in Putin's Russia

During his presidential campaign and the first months in office, Putin showed remarkable ambivalence toward local government. His statements and actions were inconsistent, and, in sharp contrast to the overall thrust of his policies on federalism, demonstrated much less of a commitment to a coherent set of reforms. Some of Putin's early decisions suggested a preference for stronger municipal government as a check on regional regimes, a policy pursued by his predecessor, Boris Yel'tsin. For example, in what appeared to be a highly symbolic act on a preelection trip to Tatarstan, Putin advocated the independence and increased power of municipalities. In this bastion of "regionalism," where the republican president continued to appoint heads of local administrations in defiance of federal law, which required that they be popularly elected, he stated: "It is necessary to share power with people and to develop the municipal level of administration."[39] In another apparent expression of support for local government in April 2000, Putin attended a Union of Russian Cities' congress in Nijhniy Novgorod amid extensive official media coverage. He also publicly instructed his aides to bolster the Congress of Municipal Authorities, and to promote policies that would strengthen local government's financial and political independence.[40]

Shortly after his election, however, Putin disbanded the numerous government agencies created in the context of Yel'tsin's local government reforms, such as the office devoted to this issue in the presidential administration.[41] He also marginalized the governmental and nongovernmental agencies previously favored by Yel'tsin.[42] In addition, Putin floated a series of proposals in the Duma that sought to deprive municipalities of most of their institutional powers. There was also a perceptible change in Putin's rhetoric, as he began to stigmatize mayors as "corrupt," "overpoliticized," and "inefficient."

By 2001 a much more consistent line on local government emerged; moreover, local government was identified as "the main task of the Russian government." In the summer of 2001 the president set up a commission headed by Dmitriy Kozak, a senior official from the presidential administration, to delimit powers between federal, regional, and local government. He ordered the commission, consisting of eight working groups, to prepare proposals by the summer of the following year.[43] Kozak's appointment emphasized the importance of the commission since he had earlier been considered for the post of Russian procurator general and had just finished preparing a plan to overhaul the country's judicial system.

In the fall of 2002, the commission submitted draft legislation to the public "for discussion," and in January 2003, the president submitted it to the Duma. Despite much criticism from the civic, academic, and intellectual communities, and, most importantly, the municipal practitioners, the pro-Kremlin Duma majority on 21 February 2003 approved the draft in the first reading, on 11 June in the second, and on 16 September in the third and final reading, retaining most of the original substantive provisions.[44]

Although ostensibly concerned with efficiency, transparency, and local democracy, the law serves to institutionalize local government dependence on both regional and federal bodies of authority. As such, it is bound to reinforce the tendencies of institutional control over local citizenries discussed in the preceding chapters. To begin with, according to the new law, the municipalities are to undergo a process of redistricting corresponding with the setting up of new types of municipal structures—the settlements—(*poseleniya*), the municipal districts—(*munitsipal'nye rayony*), and the city districts—(*gorodskie okruga*). It is the republics and regions that will possess the right to determine the boundaries of the new municipal formations.[45] These provisions have already been much criticized for their potential to strengthen the regions' influence over the localities because they leave much room for manipulation of electoral and administrative boundaries for political purposes.

The republics and regions will also now have significant influence over the appointment of key local executives and control over their decision making. Aside from the possibility of having a popularly elected mayor, the law provides for an additional figure, a head of local administration, appointed by contract following a competitive selection process for a period of time set by the charter of the municipality. According to Kozak, the difference between the popularly elected mayor and the city manager-type head of local administration is that the mayor would be the "political face" of the locality, and the manager, a "professional" with managerial qualifications that the elected figure may lack.[46] Institutionally, the key local executives will now strongly depend on the regional structures of power. While the "manager" on the settlement level is to be appointed by a *konkursnaya komissiya* (selection commission) approved by the settlement council, the *konkursnye komissii* on the municipal and city district levels are to be approved both by the respective district councils and the regional legislature. In these cases, the regional legislature makes its appointment at the recommendation of the governor. The region's influence is also strengthened by provisions that allow it to delegate up to one third of the members of the commission.

The governor and regional legislature will now also have extended powers to remove not just the appointed managers, but also popularly elected mayors, to disband local councils, or set up temporary regional administrations in the localities, albeit largely subject to approval by the "appropriate courts." The extensive list of causes for which the LGs may be penalized ranges from such commonly occurring situations as deficits exceeding 30 percent of their locally generated budget revenues in a given year, to actions leading to "mass violation of human rights and civil freedoms," to the even more curious possibility of a town adopting a decision containing a "threat to [Russia's] territorial integrity, national security, [or] defense potential."[47] It is not difficult to imagine how the regional authorities may use any of these (even the most extreme) provisions to penalize politically disobedient municipalities.

Not only does the law serve to institutionalize the localities' de facto dependence on the regions, it also ensures a degree of fusion of local government into central state power structures. Critics of the reform have already pointed out that the law drafters have essentially regarded local government as an extension of state power in the localities.[48] This is because the localities will now be reduced to performing many state-delegated tasks, while having significantly smaller budgets to perform local functions. The performance of the state-delegated functions will be funded through subventions and other federal or regional transfers. Much of this funding is likely to be targeted, and local governments will have little discretion as to how it is to be spent. Should the central government find that the money has been misappropriated the localities can suffer from state-imposed penalties such as the dissolution of local bodies and imposition of "external rule," provisions which could be abused by the state and regional bodies for political purposes.[49]

The state mobilizational function is also evident in provisions that essentially oblige the local citizenry to engage in "public" activities. These provisions are reminiscent of the Soviet "voluntary-coerced" (*dobrovol'no-prinuditel'noe*) practice of requiring public participation, which I have discussed in chapter 2. In the first draft the provision referred to so-called public duty (*obshchestvennaya povinnost'*). In the draft approved in the second and final readings "public duty" was replaced with the term "socially important works" or *sotsial'no-znachimye raboty*. The relevant provision is worth reproducing in full. Article 17.2 reads: "Settlement and city *okrug* local governments may decide in accordance with the charter of the municipal formation on engaging citizens on a voluntary basis in works (including duties) socially important for the settlement and city *okrug*. . . . The goal of conducting socially important duties justifies summoning work-age adults outside of regular work or study hours on a noncompensatory basis no more often than once in three months." An earlier, October 2002, draft, even contained a reference to "administrative responsibility" for failure to perform the duties. Although the provision has not elicited much public reaction, at least one concerned agency, the Congress of Municipal Authorities, has already pointed to its anticonstitutional nature. The Congress in particular noted that the provision allows for the use of "forced labor," which is prohibited by Article 37.2 of the Constitution and by the labor code, which stipulates that public works are to be carried out only pursuant to a paid work contract.[50]

The weak and subordinate status of local government, which can only worsen in Putin's Russia following the implementation of his municipal reforms, has powerful implications for the country's democracy. The preceding chapters have demonstrated that local government's institutional dependence on the republics' power structures has undermined the potential for the emergence and viability of alternative political or civil society actors and of political pluralism central for the existence of a healthy democracy. An increase in the municipalities' financial and institutional dependence on the regional bodies fostered by the new legislation will lead to an even greater reluctance of civic and political actors to aggregate and articulate local social and political preferences should they be in opposition to the ruling regional regimes. At the same time, the Kozak reform's etatization of local government, whereby it will now perform mostly state functions, implies that the central state, and not just the regions, will now have powerful mechanisms of political control over the localities. Already the government has submitted a draft law to the Duma that would endow municipalities with the state function of monitoring political demonstrations, a practice which, as discussed in previous chapters, has long existed in the republics, but may now acquire the status of federal legislation.[51]

The preceding chapters have suggested numerous analogies of post-Soviet local government with that of its Soviet predecessor. The one analogy that until recently would not have been entirely appropriate is the municipalities' function of projecting the central state's political programs into the grassroots. This is because until now the municipalities, while often fused into the regional structures, have not actually formed part of the central state's institutional "power vertical." Authoritarian-style "mobilized participation" was possible at the regional, and particularly republic level, but could not be imposed by the central state uniformly in a Soviet fashion because the 1993 Constitution and the 1995 local self-government legislation made local government independent from central state power.

Although local government continues to be legally separate from the state, aspects of the Kozak reform suggest the fusion of local government into a centralized power vertical. Already weak and dependent on regional bodies, the etatized local government risks reinforcing the undemocratic tendencies evident at the federal level. Not only does the president now control the Duma, the Federation Council, and Russia's key television channels, he can also with greater facility rely on the network of municipal institutions to project central state political preferences into the grassroots and to repress or undermine political opponents at all territorial levels throughout Russia. A lack of "institutional pluralism" will lead to a greater deficit of civic and political pluralism, further undermining Russia's future as a democratic state.

Conclusion

Local government control is a feature of the Russian regional scene as a whole. Local organs continue to be fused into regional executive hierarchies, and the local councils have high percentages of enterprise and other notables from state-controlled professional networks. At the same time, the local bodies continue to have jurisdiction and administrative means of control over the local organized groups. As a result, throughout Russia, the local bodies continue to have a powerful impact on organized social activism. A striking finding, however, is that the ethnically defined republics appear to outdo the nonethnic regions along the above parameters, being entities with the "highest resistance" to local government's separation from regional control.

These features confirm the broad thrust of the book. The republic regimes seek to maintain a tight grip on local government as a means to prevent ethnically based or ethnically defined challenges to their rule. Throughout the federation's constituent entities, local government control has been crucial to outcomes of battles over privatization, electoral struggles, and political institution building.

The ethnic republics, however, have had to confront an additional group of ethnically based contenders. Irrespective of whether their agendas have been purely cultural or nationalist in nature, or whether they masked political and economic interests, these contenders could mobilize the broader nontitular publics around issues with a powerful emotional appeal. In such circumstances, control over local governments becomes an instrument for undermining the nontitular nationalists by fashioning rival ideologies projected through the local bodies. It also facilitates the building of support bases among representatives of the titular group itself by channeling resources from rich, ethnically diverse urban areas to the rural localities in an uncontested fashion.

The above features of local government, facilitating social control, are likely to persist in Putin's centralist state. His reforms have further undermined the financial independence of LSG from the higher regional bodies. Moreover, they have served to make LSG institutionally more dependent on the central state, as well as on the regional bodies by endowing the higher levels of authority with substantial powers to remove even popularly elected local officials.

This finding, along with those of previous chapters, does not bode well for a Russian democratic society. If national elections are routinely rigged with the help of the local bosses and if the local social and political actors cannot freely conduct pressure-group and awareness-increasing activities, then one must conclude that the local publics have been deprived of the possibility of voice as regards both national and local issues. These broad features apply throughout Russia's localities, with the difference that the ethnically defined entities experience a greater democracy deficit than the nonethnically defined regions. These tendencies are bound to increase throughout Russia's constituent entities, regions and republics alike, following the implementation of Putin's reform of local government.

Notes

1. For a discussion of these conflicts in various regions, see Anne Le Huerou, "Elites in Omsk," *Post-Soviet Affairs* 15, no. 4 (1999): 362-86; Leonid Smirnyagin, "Mayors against Governors?" *Russian Regional Report* (electronic version) 4, no. 9 (1999); Peter

Kirkow, "Regional Warlodrism in Russia: The Case of Primorskii Krai," *Europe-Asia Studies* 47, no. 6 (1995): 923-47; Pavel Romanov and Irina Tartakovskaya, "Samara Oblast': A Governor and His Guberniya," *Communist Economies and Economic Transformation* 10, no. 3 (1998): 341-61.

2. The governors and mayors of Primorskiy and Krasnodarskiy *kray*, respectively. Nazdratenko finally gave up the post after federal intervention, and was appointed as head of the federal fisheries commission.

3. Nicolai Petro, "The Novgorod Region: A Russian Success Story," *Post-Soviet Affairs* 15, no. 3 (1999): 235-61.

4. Sergei Ryzhenkov and N. Vinnik, eds., *Reforma mestnogo samoupravleniya v regional'nom izmerenii* (Moscow: Moskovskiy obshchestvennyy nauchnyy fond, 1999); Sergei Ryzhenkov, "Regional'naya elita i mestnoe samoupravlenie: Aktory, pravila igry i logika reformy," in *Reforma mestnogo samoupravleniya*, 96. For another discussion of the regimes with one and two actors, see Vladimir Gel'man, "Federal'naya politika: Reforma mestnoy vlasti v gorodakh Rossii" (paper presented at the Seminar on Russia's Regions, Centre d'Études et de Recherches Internationales, Sciences Po, Paris, 2000).

5. For discussions of "asymmetry" in Russian federalism and its impact on intraregional developments, see Andreas Heinemann-Grüder, "Der asymmetrische Föderalismus Russlands und die Rolle der Regionen," in *Russland unter neuer Führung: Politik, Wirtschaft und Gesellschaft am Beginn des 21. Jahrhunderts*, ed. Hans-Hermann Höhmann and Hans-Henning Schröder (Berlin: Bundeszentrale für politische Bildung, 2001), 78-86; Jeffrey Kahn, *Federalism, Democratization, and the Rule of Law in Russia* (Oxford: Oxford University Press, 2002); Jeff Kahn, "The Parade of Sovereignties: Establishing the Vocabulary of the New Russian Federalism," *Post-Soviet Affairs* 16, no. 1 (2000): 58-89; Daniel S. Treisman, "Russia's 'Ethnic Revival': The Separatist Activism of Regional Leaders in a Post-Communist Order," *World Politics* (1997): 212-49; and Daniel S. Treisman, *After the Deluge: Regional Crises and Political Consolidation in Russia* (Ann Arbor: University of Michigan Press, 1999).

6. The classification was done by Russia's Center for Fiscal Policy.

7. Kimitaka Matsuzato, "From Communist Boss Politics to Post-Communist Caciquismo," *Communist and Post-Communist Studies* 34, no. 2 (2001): 182-3.

8. Matsuzato, "From Communist Boss Politics," 183.

9. Matsuzato, "From Communist Boss Politics," 189.

10. Lev Freinkman and Plamen Yossifov, "Decentralization in Regional Fiscal Systems in Russia: Trends and Links to Economic Performance," (Washington, D.C.: World Bank, 1999).

11. P. A. Goryunov et al., *Formirovanie organov mestnogo samoupravleniya v Rossiyskoy federatsii: Elektoral'naya statistika* (Moscow: Ves' mir, 1999), 171.

12. For a more detailed discussion of Adygeya's local government legislation and practices, see Tomila Lankina, "Local Self-Government or Government Gone Local? The Case of Adygeya," *Russian Regional Report* (electronic version) 4, no. 33 (1999).

13. For a discussion, see Kimitaka Matsuzato, ed., *Tret'e zveno gosudarstvennogo stroitel'stva Rossii: Podgotovka i realizatsiya federal'nogo zakona Ob obshchikh printsipakh organizatsii mestnogo samoupravleniya v Rossiyskoy federatsii* (Sapporo, Japan: Slavic Research Center, Hokkaido University, 1998).

14. *British Broadcasting Corporation (BBC)*, 6 March 1999.

15. For a discussion of the importance of these seemingly mundane matters for explaining the dynamics of ethnic activism in other settings, see Paul R. Brass, *Theft of an Idol: Text and Context in the Representation of Collective Violence* (Princeton, N.J.: Princeton University Press, 1997).

16. "Karachay-Cherkessiya, in the Middle of Russia's Powder Keg," Barcelona Center for International Relations and Cooperation Crisis Watch database, www.crisiswatch.barcelona2004.org/observatorio/dossierCompleto_i.htm?num_dossier=67 (accessed 8 Se-ptember 2003).

17. Interview by author with Cherkes activist, Cherkessk, 13 August 1997.

18. Term "netness" borrowed from Charles Tilly, *From Mobilization to Revolution* (Reading, Mass.: Wesley, 1978).

19. Data compiled from Goryunov et al., *Formirovanie*. For case studies of smaller localities, see I. Kukolev, "Vybory v gorodke N," *Vlast'* 8 (1997): 27-33.

20. On the notablity and the old *nomenklatura* makeup of the local councils and the power of the local executives in the regions, see Jean-Charles Lallemand, "Politics for the Few: Elites in Bryansk and Smolensk," *Post-Soviet Affairs* 15, no. 4 (1999): 312-35; Anne Gazier, "Les Pouvoirs Locaux dans les Régions Russes du Centre-Terres Noires," *Les Cahiers du CERI* 5 (1993); and Boris Ovchinnikov, "Munitsipal'nye vybory: tendentsii i zakonomernosti," in *Reforma mestnogo samoupravleniya*, 107-33.

21. See, for example, Sergei Mitrokhin, "Relizatsiya munitsipal'nogo proekta v Rossii: Nekotorye aspekty federal'noy politiki," in *Reforma mestnogo samoupravleniya*, 26-43.

22. For a discussion, see Marie Mendras, "How Regional Elites Preserve Their Power," *Post-Soviet Affairs* 15, no. 4 (1999): 295-311; and Marie Mendras, "L'État, L'Argent, La Clientèle," *La Revue Tocqueville/The Tocqueville Review* 19, no. 1 (1998): 35-54.

23. Paul Kubicek, *Unbroken Ties: The State, Interest Associations, and Corporatism in Post-Soviet Ukraine* (Ann Arbor: University of Michigan Press, 1999); Paul Kubicek, "Variations on a Corporatist Theme: Interest Associations in Post-Soviet Ukraine and Russia," *Europe-Asia Studies* 48, no. 1 (1996): 27-46. For a discussion of business licensing in China, see Jean C. Oi, *Rural China Takes Off: Institutional Foundations of Economic Reform* (Berkeley: University of California Press, 1999), 128-9.

24. Georgiy Osipov, "Gref obmanul byurokratov: Pravitel'stvo v desyat' raz sokrashchaet litsenziruemye vidy deyatel'nosti," *Segodnya*, 15 March 2001.

25. Osipov, "Gref obmanul byurokratov."

26. Sergei Mitrokhin, "Realizatsiya," 32-3.

27. Matsuzato, "From Communist Boss Politics," 242. Other postcommunist states also demonstrate the persistence of socialist structural features. Rudolf L. Tokes, "Hungary: Elites and the Use and Abuse of Democratic Institutions," in *Elites after State Socialism: Theories and Analysis*, ed. John Higley and Georgy Lengyel (Lanham, Md.: Rowman & Littlefield, 2000), 71-85.

28. Petro, "Novgorod Region." For another article about democratic decision-making in the region, see Vladimir Jhovannik, "Nenujhnyy progress: Unikal'nyy opyt Novgoroda federal'nuyu vlast' ne interesuet," *Ekspert* 29, no. 22 (2000). For a critique of Novgorod politics, see Vladimir Y. Gel'man, "Federal'naya politika: Reforma mestnoy vlasti v gorodakh Rossii" (Paper presented at the Seminar on Russia's Regions, Centre d'Études et de Recherches Internationales [Sciences Po, Paris, 2000]). Gel'man in fact implied in his article that the region is a "uniactor" regime considering the staggeringly high vote (95 percent) the governor received in the 1999 gubernatorial elections.

29. Petro, "Novgorod Region."

30. Petro, "Novgorod Region." 245.

31. Petro, "Novgorod Region." 246.

32. Valerie Sperling, *Organizing Women in Contemporary Russia: Engendering Transition* (Cambridge: Cambridge University Press, 1999), 132.

33. Sperling, *Organizing Women*, 134.

34. James Alexander, *Political Culture in Post-Communist Russia: Formlessness and Recreation in a Traumatic Transition* (New York: St. Martin's, 2000), 162.

35. James Richter, "Evaluating Western Assistance to Russian Women's Organizations," in *The Power and Limits of NGOs: A Critical Look at Building Democracy in Eastern Europe and Eurasia*, ed. Sarah E. Mendelson and John K. Glenn (New York: Columbia University Press, 2002), 78.

36. Larry Diamond, "Rethinking Civil Society: Toward Democratic Consolidation," *Journal of Democracy* 5, no. 3 (1994): 4-17.

37. Richard Rose and Doh Chull Shin, "Democratization Backwards: The Problem of Third Wave Democracies," *British Journal of Political Science* 31, no. 2 (2001): 331-54.

38. Stephen P. Osborne and Aniko Kaposvari, "Nongovernmental Organizations, Local Government and the Development of Social Services: Managing Social Needs in Postcommunist Hungary" (Budapest: Open Society Institute, 1998), 10. For additional evidence from Russia and other postcommunist states, see also Bruce Parrott, "Perspectives on Postcommunist Democratization," in *The Consolidation of Democracy in East-Central Europe*, ed. Karen Dawisha and Bruce Parrott (Cambridge: Cambridge University Press, 1997), 48; David M. Olson, "Democratic and Political Participation: The Experience of the Czech Republic," in *Consolidation of Democracy*, 40-65; and Thomas F. Remington, "Democratization and the New Political Order in Russia," in *Democratization and Authoritarianism in Postcommunist Societies*, ed. Karen Dawisha and Bruce Parrott (Cambridge: Cambridge University Press, 1997), 109.

39. Natal'ya Panshina, "Putin Gives Instructions Promoting Local Government," *ITAR-TASS*, FBIS-SOV-2000-0412, 12 April 2000; Vyacheslav Bantin, "Republican, Federal Constitutions Should Not Differ," *ITAR-TASS*, FBIS-SOV-2000-0322, 22 March 2000, 16.

40. Sergei Mitrokhin, "V Otsutstvie pozitsii Prezidenta," *Munitsipal'naya politika* 10-11, no. 26 (2000): 3-7; "Putin on Local Self-Government Problems," *Rossiyskaya gazeta* (*RG*), FBIS-SOV-2000-0324, 21 March 2000.

41. *Kommersant* (*K*), 20 April 2001. For other aspects of Putin's federal reforms, see Nikolai Petrov, "Seven Faces of Putin's Russia: Federal Districts as the New Level of State-Territorial Composition," *Security Dialogue* 33, no. 1 (2002): 73-91; Nikolai Petrov and Darrell Slider, "Putin and the Regions," in *Putin's Russia: Past Imperfect, Future Uncertain*, ed. Dale R. Herspring (Lanham, Md.: Rowman & Littlefield, 2003), 203-24; Cameron Ross, *Federalism and Democratisation in Russia* (Manchester, England: Manchester University Press, 2002); and Cameron Ross, "Putin's Federal Reforms and the Consolidation of Federalism in Russia: One Step Forward, Two Steps Back!" *Communist and Post-Communist Studies* 36 (2003): 29-47.

42. Dmitriy Mikhaylin, "Shaymiyev Warns against Dividing Power 'Pie,'" *RG*, FBIS-SOV-2000-0522, 20 May 2000, 2.

43. For a discussion of the work of the commission see "Sovet predstaviteley organov mestnogo samoupravleniya obsujhdaet razgranichenie polnomochiy," excerpts of stenographic records of session of the Council of Representatives of Local Self-Government, State Duma, Moscow, 18 March 2002, www.rels.obninsk.com/Rels/Lg/0203/03-01.htm (accessed 7 April 2003).

44. For criticism of the draft, see Galina Koval'skaya, "Munitsipiya vtorogo sorta," *Ejhenedel'nyy jhurnal*, 20 August 2002, www.ej.ru/030/life/o3/01/index.html_printed. html (accessed 20 August 2002); Natal'ya Melikova, "Mery dosidyat do kontsa sroka," *Nezavisimaya gazeta* (*NG*), 23 April 2003, www.ng.ru/printed/politics/2003-04-23/2_kozak. html (accessed 23 April 2003); Irina Nagornykh, "Mery podderjhali reformu

mestnogo samoupravleniya," *K*, 19 June 2002; and Maksim Glikin, "Komissiyu Kozaka pokidayut eksperty," *NG*, 20 August 2002, www.ng.ru/printed/politics /2002-08-20/2_kozak.html (accessed 28 August 2002).

45. For a discussion, see Il'ya Bulavinov, "Dekabr' shagaet po strane," *K*, 20 January 2003, www.kommersant.ru/k-vlast/ (accessed 20 January 2003).

46. Natal'ya Gorodetskaya, "Tridtsat' tysyach odnikh munitsipalitetov," *Vremya novostey*, no. 86, 17 May 2002, www.vremya.ru/cgi-bin/print/2002/86/4/34831.html (accessed 28 August 2002).

47. Art. 75.3; art. 74.2. Text of the draft law available at http://www.yabloko.ru/ Themes/SG/index.html (accessed 31 January 2004).

48. "Protiv Kozaka eshchyo odno ogosudarstvlenie," interview with Nadejhda Kosareva, president, Institute of Urban Economics, www.urbaneconomics.ru/news/2002 1104.html (accessed 28 March 2003).

49. This contradicts the policy pronouncements surrounding the reform and the earlier policy documents, such as the Program for the Development of Budgetary Federalism. See "Programma razvitiya byudjhetnogo federalizma v Rossiyskoy federatsii na period do 2005 goda," *RG*, 21 Aug. 2001, 4-5. See also "Polnyy tekst poslaniya Prezidenta RF Vladimira Putina federal'nomu sobraniyu," *Strana.ru*, 25 April 2002, www.strana.ru/print/131967.html (accessed 1 August 2003).

50. www.urbaneconomics.ru/news/20021204_04.html (accessed 28 March 2003).

51. Ivan Rodin, "V Rossii poyavyatsya upolnomochennye po mitingam," *NG*, 30 April 2003, www.ng.ru/printed/politics/2003-04-30/2_meeting.html (accessed 5 May 2003).

Chapter 8

Conclusions and Implications

In the aftermath of the USSR's collapse, a noted scholar of ethnic politics wrote: "It is an old proposition in the sociology of ethnic relations that times of transition frequently provide occasions for serious ethnic conflict."[1] Fortunately, the violent Ossetiyan-Ingush conflict was not a harbinger of Balkanization of the ethnically diverse imperial core of Russia. The conflict was emblematic, however, of what was and is going on elsewhere in the republics in that it involved a nationalizing titular group and an oppressed nontitular minority. While the violence was exceptional, the peculiarities of the titular-nontitular interaction leading up to it are part of a larger, recurring pattern. The frequently contentious nature of interactions between a dominant subnational group, recognized through some form of autonomy, and other groups denied such status is also common in other ethnically plural federations.[2] The fact that the scholarly usage of the conceptual titular-nontitular distinction has been largely confined to the post-Soviet space need not obscure the salience of the question elsewhere.

In Western and non-Western federations, democratic and not so democratic, nontitulars express grievances at discrimination or even "tyranny" by the titulars, endowed by the respective federal centers with political powers locally.[3] Such practices frequently lead to mass movements against discrimination, though not always to violence. The intensity of these movements in turn forces those at the center to create boundary readjustment commissions, to set up new federal subunits, or to make special arrangements for representation of the nontitulars within the subunit or at the national level.

Postcolonial India, whose States Reorganization Commission engaged in elaborate studies of the appropriateness of boundaries between the various subunits following ethnic tensions there, is one example of a state's effort to address minority concerns.[4] The laborious work of the Commission resulted in a number of new linguistic states. While they could not perfectly "contain" a given ethnic group within the new states due to the country's immense ethnic complexity, the new boundaries certainly made more sense than those that existed under the British.

The establishment of the Jura province in Switzerland following ethnic conflict in the Bern canton, of which the Jura had formed a part, is another example.
The conflict, involving ethnic violence, was sparked when a French-speaking
member of the cabinet in the predominantly German canton was denied an important appointment as a public works official because of his language.[5] The
conflict led to the separation of the three northern districts of Jura from the canton in what has become a well-known principle of Swiss conflict management,
referred to as "rolling cantonization."[6]

Belgium, whose efforts to ensure a nearly perfect match between the administrative and linguistic/ethnic status of its various units have perhaps gone the
furthest, offers additional examples. The homogenization of the respective linguistic provinces here came in response to movements opposed to discrimination against minorities by groups enjoying special status within these units. This
was the case with the famous Voeren incident. The French-speaking mayor of
Voeren, a town with a 60 percent Walloon population, refused to use Dutch in
official proceedings and demanded the cession of the town to the Walloon province of Liege. In so doing, he was tapping into the grievances of local Francophones that had existed for several decades.[7] The outcome was the "Voeren
compromise," with voters in Voeren being given special privileges to cast their
vote in Walloonia for federal and European elections.[8] Even the above arrangements do not eliminate the nontitular problem, but they do illustrate the salience
of the nontitular issue in other federations.

Yet the movements against titular group discrimination emerged for only a
brief period of time in Russia, and did not sustain their momentum long enough
to force substantive federal reform. Their quick demise could not be explained
by lack of discrimination, as it had only intensified in the 1990s. An equally
poor attempt at explanation would be to seek peculiar accommodative arrangements that Moscow might have put in place to satisfy the nontitulars' demands.
There was no single instance of a boundary readjustment despite the frequently
noted randomness of Soviet "ethnic homeland" boundaries. No new regions
were created in response to nontitular grievances.[9] And no special voting
mechanisms were put in place. Overall, Moscow made no systematic effort to
address the nontitular issue, the post-Soviet Russian nationalities policy being
inconsistent, or, according to some observers, nonexistent. In short, the institutional mechanisms used to explain the consensual channeling of conflicts were
not put into place in Russia.

This project, concerned as it is with the political expression of ethnicity, began in earnest with an exploration of the vast body of literature on all things
ethnic and nationalist. Yet, the scholarship specifically concerned with ethnicity
has failed to provide adequate explanations for the Russian situation. Instead, it
began to appear that Russia's ethnopolitical developments could be largely explained by local self-government, a variable which has almost never entered
studies of Russia's ethnopolitical developments. As the research progressed, the
interest in the dynamics of nontitular mobilization, that is, the dependent variable, was gradually supplanted by a fascination with local government, the inde-

pendent variable. This was because, while the original scope of investigation remained confined to the nontitular question, research into local government suggested its overwhelming impact on social processes in Russia in general. As such, the findings of this book about the permeation of the society by the local state organs offer exciting possibilities for further research into and explanation of other aspects of social activism or passivity in the post-Soviet space.

Mobilization, as distinct from quiet lobbying or pressure tactics, usually connotes a grassroots phenomenon. While the movements or campaigns that it generates might involve large groups of people, these people are members of smaller units—neighborhood, town, village, or professional networks. While the question of "micromobilization" has been a subject of sociological studies, it has largely remained outside of the purview of the scholarship on Russia's republics.[10] I have tried to demonstrate that the factors identified by the sociological literature as providing incentives or disincentives for people to mobilize can be largely explained by the relationship between local government and Russian society and moreover that this is applicable in other states, including Western democracies.

Traditional orthodoxy has painted an idealized and normative picture of local government as a bulwark against state tyranny, as a means of engagement and schooling in civil society, and as the most efficient provider of services, since only the grassroots know what is best for them. Local government in fact has been seen as not a government at all, in the sense of an institution within the larger state; it was, instead, regarded as a bona fide representative body, or even the sum total of the local people. While much Western scholarship has been colored by these views, one body of literature on long-standing democracies in Europe and North America has served to debunk these premises. To begin with, local government is rightly approached as *the government* in the sense that it is an agency of the state or dependent on it in some way. It is not immune from common criticisms against state agencies or other organizations, which tend toward oligarchization.[11] An agency possessing important resources, it is also usually regarded as composed of people better endowed than the average public it purports to represent. Local concerns are frequently far off local functionaries' agenda, as studies, from Newton's Birmingham to the Russian regions, have shown that many of these "notables" regard their posts as stepping-stones into the higher political elite.[12]

Studies of Western community politics, like much contemporary scholarship on Russian local government, largely confined themselves to addressing two questions: Is local government really democratic and representative? and Is it really in a position to deliver services in the most efficient way? The insights they provided point to other implications of local government for local social development, and in this book I have sought to broaden the focus. Rather than investigating whether local government reflects social preferences or serves the society, I have sought to demonstrate how local governments control or manipulate social agencies given their resources, elite makeup, and the public relations advantage of association with the "people."

Russia's Local Self-Government: A Path-Dependent View

In terms of its social and political role, local government in Russia and even the Soviet Union need not be regarded as unique. Indeed, the noted scholar of the subject, Theodore Friedgut, drawing on Philip Selznick's investigation of the American "grassroots," perceived how even in democracies the mobilizational needs of the modern state encourage the manipulation and control of social agencies, through local institutions.[13] Yet while conceptual parallels between Western democratic and Russian settings are appropriate, local governments in the Soviet Union and even present-day Russia provide grotesque versions of the social role of local governments observed elsewhere.

The mobilizational character of the Soviet regime and the statist nature of the polity accorded a special role to local governing institutions as control agencies vis-à-vis the grassroots. Local government was looked upon as both a highly *political* and highly *administrative* agency. From the very origins of the soviets, the Bolsheviks regarded them as political, in the sense of their role in the projection of the regime ideology onto the grassroots and in the mobilization of the public for political campaigns. Consider Leon Trotsky's fascination with the original Petersburg strike committee soviet during the revolution of 1905: "The Soviet was the axis of all events, every thread ran towards it, every call to action emanated from it."[14] It "organized the working masses, directed the political strikes and demonstrations, armed the workers, and protected the population against pogroms."[15] The party, he wrote triumphantly, "succeeded . . . in transforming the Soviet—formally a non-party organization—into the organizational instrument of its own influence."[16]

At the same time, the soviets became hyperadministrative agencies, considering the socialist nature of the economy and their resulting vast amount of micromanaging and service functions. This administrative role in turn had very powerful social implications. Tocqueville observes: "Centralization of government acquires immense strength when it is combined with administrative centralization. Centralization in that way accustoms men to set aside their own wills constantly and completely."[17]

Yet, the soviets did not simply reproduce a system of social passivity; they created a system of forced dependence. The local publics, which the soviets permeated and controlled, had to "subject their own wills" not simply because they were made accustomed to being taken care of, but because of the material or other sanctions they might suffer from these agencies if they deviated from the regime line. The soviets' executive departments were in charge of the so-called administrative regime,[18] and they had jurisdiction over the territorial branches of the Ministry of Interior for its enforcement. Aside from these straightforwardly coercive mechanisms, they, together with other state agencies, controlled the system of local material sanctions and rewards, like the distribution of housing, payments of salaries to state employees, and so forth. These, as Stephen Whitefield notes with regard to the ministerial agencies, made coercion unnecessary.[19]

This situation did not significantly change in the post-Soviet period. Russia's current federal system, unlike that of the USSR, of course, ensures that local government organization and practices are not completely replicated from republic to republic. Although the authoritarian republic of Bashkortostan clearly differs from the Novgorod region, hailed as the democratic "success story" at Russia's regional level, the patterns of local government control are still broadly similar across Russia's subnational units.[20] While as in the case of Bashkortostan, local government goes as far as coercing political opposition or projecting Bashkir nationalist ideologies onto the grassroots, in other republics or regions it influences the social actors through its control over social benefits and services. In the post-Soviet period, in fact, many of the services hitherto controlled by other state agencies have passed on to local governments. This "municipalization" of state assets ensures the continued subordination of the social agencies at the very lowest levels to the state agencies.[21]

The "smallness" of the jurisdictions of the local councils likewise suggests an unorthodox view of the role of size. In Russia, as in a number of Eastern European states, local government bodies could be legitimately established at very tiny village levels with a population of just a few hundred. In this, it has been noted, they approximate southern European countries and France where local governing units range from approximately 1,600 in France to 7,000 in Italy. In northern Europe, the sizes are much larger, while "authorities with under one thousand inhabitants have been virtually organized out of existence." The average in the British Isles, for example, ranges from 42,000 in Ireland to 127,000 in the United Kingdom. In the other northern European states, it ranges between approximately 9,400 in Norway and 30,250 in Sweden.[22]

The orthodox approach to the choice of the variable size of these bodies across different countries is that they stem from "different principles and values." Thus, Alan Norton writes:

> The Latin countries value the self-regulating historical community as the basis of their structure of self-government. They are prepared to entrench it as fundamental to their way of life. This is seen as justified by the principle of keeping responsibility as close as possible to the individual and family and educating citizens in the art of self-administration.[23]

This book offers a rather different view of local government's relation to the local communities. One might infer from the evidence presented here that the smaller the unit of jurisdiction, the greater the degree of social control by municipal bodies. The town of Orchards is a case in point, where the HA is personally familiar with all the residents in his locality. Such forums as *skhody*, which might be hailed as normatively desirable paragons of community self-rule, in fact reinforce such familiarity and provide further means for the head of administration to influence decision making within his locality.

The role of the key local notables, of course, varies with institutional arrangements and depends on the constraints that political institutions place on local executives and councils; indeed, Orchards' head, an ethnic Russian, is not happy about his role as the enforcer of the Adyge regime. He would perhaps act otherwise were he not subject to sanctions by higher bodies. We have seen that in the early 1990s the elected nature of executives and local councils free from executive influence provided the elite actors with greater mobilizational resources. Their frustrated mobility encouraged the use of these resources for politicizing and mobilizing the local communities. The centralization of executive hierarchy in 1992 and the emasculation of the local councils encouraged the use of administrative resources for constraining opposition ethnic and political activism. Both the executives and local council actors now either formed part of executive lines of accountability, or became dependent on republic bodies in other ways. Such a system ensured a degree of reintegration of the former political and administrative elite into the new republic polities, while also constraining their room for political maneuvering.

Debates on Local Government in Russia

It is possible to identify broadly four predominant approaches to local government in Russia.[24] First, there is what we might call the "traditional-institutional-legal" approach. Studies of this kind have focused on examining the various legal provisions of the relevant Russian legislation, describing the legal debates surrounding local government reform, and comparing the laws to their Western counterparts.[25] A second body of literature is concerned with the economic power of local government, ascertaining the economic resource base of local governing bodies, the material facilities they control in their localities, issues of local taxation, and so forth.[26] A third approach, coming from the "community power" perspective, examines the composition of the local community elite or the relationships between the elite actors within the bodies that makeup local councils.[27] Finally, the "traditionalists," or pluralists, have examined the degree to which local government is used as a vehicle for the representation, articulation, and aggregation of community preferences.[28]

The first two bodies of scholarship, while providing interesting insights into the institutional structure of local government or political decision making surrounding local government reforms, could be criticized on the grounds of their policy and prescriptive focus, and an insufficient exploration of the theoretical implications of the studies' findings. For example, it is said that local government in Russia is weak because it has few independent economic resources, taxation powers, etc., so these resources have to be increased; the legislation is inadequate or confusing, so it has to be clarified. The strength of community power and pluralist studies in contrast lies in their theoretical and comparative orientation.

The theory-driven approaches may be also vulnerable to criticism, however. As I have suggested, studies of the local "power elite" do not always link the elite to the society or ascertain the elite's influence on social agencies—a weakness that Newton identified in works on Western local government as well.[29] The pluralists have a bottom-up approach to social processes which may be not always appropriate in post-Soviet settings, considering the continued weakness of the social agencies vis-à-vis the state.

Rather than looking at how local government agencies use their resources to influence the social actors, the pluralists focus on how the social agencies influence local governments. Studies that have examined the impact of local governing institutions on the social agencies have usually approached local government from the point of view of its role in providing the "schooling in civil society" and in increasing the local "social capital"; that is, they have also taken the bottom-up view of the institution.[30]

This book, while drawing on the rich theoretical and comparative insights of the above studies, has approached local government from a different angle. Not only has it identified the elitist makeup of local government in both the late Soviet and post-Soviet periods—a finding which agrees with some of the elite-centered works—it has also investigated the interactions between the local institutions and the organized social agencies, an aspect of local politics that has hitherto remained underresearched.[31] Moreover, it has found that rather than serving as an instrument of community participation in local decision making— a premise of pluralist studies—local government actively shapes, constrains, or represses social activism.

Restating the broad findings of the book: in the postcommunist era, much as they were in the Soviet system, local governing actors have been the stage managers of local activism. When the interests of the elites and the broader nontitular publics coincided and local governing bodies possessed independent mobilizational resources, local governing bodies provided the local publics with resources crucial for movement activism. When local government was integrated into the republics' executive hierarchies, the same elite actors used their administrative resources to suppress any opposition to the titular regimes from below. Yet, even in the early period of mobilization in 1990-1992, the local bodies, composed of former *nomenklatura*, even while fostering ethnic activism, had a generally moderating impact on the movements. Local government's control over social agencies enabled forms of ethnic and civic corporatism, which channeled all activism in ways preferable to the local organs.

These findings, therefore, have important implications for our understanding of ethnosocial activism or lack thereof in the post-Soviet space. If the state through its local organs has continued to have an overwhelming impact on society, and, as we have seen, the elite actors in these organs have generally had a constraining and moderating impact on movement activism even where they fostered or tolerated limited expressions thereof, then that might explain the generally peaceful nature of post-Soviet transformations. In the few deviant cases like North Ossetiya/Ingushetiya, the radical position of the local bodies was likewise crucial in affecting movement outcomes. This was because in Ingushetia the local bodies ceased to be part of centralized or semicentralized institutional hierarchies in the way that they continued to be elsewhere in the late

Soviet and post-Soviet periods. The local state organs are thus the key to explaining local ethnosocial outcomes throughout the post-Soviet space.

Debates on Nontitular Mobilization

How does this investigation into local government relate to scholarship specifically concerned with nontitular group mobilization in the post-Soviet countries? Despite the overwhelming evidence of the presence of the local bodies as
actors in instances of ethnic mobilization in present-day Russia as well as in the
perestroyka-era USSR, there have been no systematic studies of their role in
fostering or constraining ethnic mobilization, with scholars mostly focusing on
other explanatory variables.

It has been some time now since primordialism began to provoke something
of an allergic reaction from scholars of ethnicity; indeed, it is de rigueur to distance oneself from this approach, rightly perceived as naive and simplistic. Yet,
some studies critical of primordialism have continued to be colored by a cul-
tural-anthropological perspective. While stressing that ethnic mobilization does
not occur because of "ancient hatreds," mobilization in such studies is still often
seen through the prism of the need to preserve one's culture and the group as a
whole. Jeff Chinn and Robert Kaiser in their study of Russians in the post-Soviet
states maintain, for example, that the "the nation has a destiny to fulfill."[32] It is
argued that if this ambition is thwarted by the nationalizing states, then the nontitular nations will mobilize to defend their rights. Ian Bremmer's study of Russians in the Ukraine contains references to "ethnic attachment" to the land as
one of the central variables affecting potential for mobilization.[33] Of course, few
scholars, and certainly not the authors of these studies, consider only primordial
or cultural factors at the expense of other variables, such as economic, political,
and other forms of discrimination, which are seen as central to understanding
and predicting ethnopolitical dynamics. But they have essentially maintained a
grievance-based approach to these processes, explaining the propensity for collective action by a *lack* of resources, such as political access, facilities for the
development of culture, and so forth.

David Laitin's studies of the "Russian-speaking nationality" are quite different in approach altogether, explaining the choice of the "exit," "voice," or
"loyalty" options by individual rational actor preferences.[34] Laitin constructs a
complex argument about the Russian-speaking nationality in the newly independent states, but also in Russia's ethnic republics. His model includes historical variables, patterns of imperial incorporation of the titular ethnies, and other
factors. For the purposes of the present discussion, it suffices to distinguish his
work very broadly from the above and from the present study.

Laitin contends that even where discrimination or resource deprivation is
present, the nontitulars will not mobilize if they find it advantageous to assimi-
late or integrate. It differs from the present analysis in that Laitin argues that
even if the nontitulars *do* have mobilizational resources, they may not take ad-

vantage of them, because they have chosen the above two options. With reference to local government, Laitin argues that in the Baltics the Russian speakers enjoyed full access to local governing institutions and the resources that come with such access, and yet they did not use them for mobilizational purposes.[35]

There is evidence to the contrary in other studies of the Baltics and other newly independent states, marginally touching upon the local councils in the areas of predominant residence of Russian speakers. Paul Kolstoe wrote, for example, that an Estonian electoral law allowed only citizens to run for office, preventing the former Russian nationalist councilors, responsible for tensions between Narva and Tallinn, from returning to office in the October 1993 local elections.[36] Laitin himself notes that only citizens of Estonia fluent in the titular language could run for mayor in the 1993 elections.[37] Graham Smith and Andrew Wilson estimated that the law served to exclude five-sixths of the population from running for municipal elections.[38] These facts challenge the premise that the nontitulars enjoy access to local government, since such legislation excludes those who are not proficient in the language.

More importantly, those who do manage to win office under these conditions represent a segment of the population already well integrated, if not assimilated. These particular individuals will not have incentives to mobilize the local publics. By contrast, in 1991, when Russians still had unrestricted access to the local councils, they were extremely vocal, demanding special status for their areas, and sponsoring local referenda on the question of local autonomy for the Russian areas.[39] These facts confirm the broad thrust of this study about the correlation of local government access and organization with levels of ethnic mobilization.

Despite Laitin's and other studies' references to local political institutions, they do not regard institutional resources as the most crucial variable in mobilization. Such a lack of an emphasis on the role of political institutional variables when it comes to nontitular mobilization is puzzling considering the overwhelming evidence of the role of political institutional factors in fostering *titular* mobilization in the USSR and Russia. Indeed, the institutional and elite basis of the "nationalist revivals" that led to the collapse of the USSR and to the "parade of sovereignties" in Russia is now almost taken for granted. Yet only a handful of studies have appreciated the fact that nontitular mobilization might be subject to similar dynamics. Smith and Wilson wrote of Estonia: "In the late Soviet period, the preexisting local Communist party and municipal government (urban soviet) in the region's largest town, Narva, provided the diaspora with a local organizational base which its pro-Soviet political elite used as a platform to challenge the legitimacy of the inclusion of the north-eastern region in the new Estonia."[40]

Another case in point is Mark Beissinger's investigation of ethnic violence in the late Soviet and post-Soviet periods, involving titular and nontitular groups. In places like Azerbaijan's Sumgait and Nagornyy Karabakh and in Georgia's Abkhazia, he argued, violence was "institutionalized" in state structures and fostered by those in local party and soviet organs, who brought people to mass rallies and incited them to violence.[41] In the run-up to the conflict in

Moldova's Transdniestriya, the local state organs in the predominantly Russian localities supported the anti-Moldovan strikers and obstructed the directives of the Moldovan officials, doubtless contributing to the conflict that followed.[42] The Russian soviets also sabotaged Moldova's efforts to introduce a new flag and staged other incidents with high symbolic and mobilizational appeal.[43] We have seen how the Ossetiyan-Ingush conflict was influenced by local soviet structures. The degree of institutional access has also been used to explain the passivity, and not just the mobilization, of the nontitulars. The findings of Smith and Wilson about the nontitulars' passivity in Estonia and Ukraine are consistent with my own findings in that the nontitulars have lacked appropriate "political opportunity structures."[44] The examples they cite include lack of full access to or genuine control over local governing bodies.

Implications for Federalism and "Institutional Engineering"

There are some broader implications for the normative debates on federalism and a body of literature which may be generically referred to as "institutional engineering to accommodate diversity." The Russian Federation is a sobering indictment against the exhilaration of ethnically based federations as "accommodating diversities" and as fostering "toleration, respect, compromise."[45] While Russia may be an extreme case of the nationalization of the republics by titular groups, the titular-nontitular problem is salient for all ethnically based federations, and indeed, for nonethnically based ones where a particular subnational group is in a dominant position. The situation stems from the peculiarity of the institutions of a federal system.

Because federalism's "celebration of diversity" usually extends only to recognized groups, the other groups within the subunits, depending on the federation, could be placed along the continuum from marginalization to full-scale discrimination. To use Rogers Brubaker's term, ethnically based federations foster expectations of "ownership" of the subnational polities by titular groups.[46] Devolution usually entails the acquisition of control of the local political bodies by the titular regimes. The fact that the federal center devolves power to a particular group with the ostensible aim of the "preservation of culture" legitimizes its privileged position within the entity, and encourages the definition of local politics in ethnic terms. Local politics become perceived as an ethnic zero-sum game: if other groups are allowed to advance and enjoy similar status, then the titular group loses its capacity to "develop" and "preserve its culture."

Why, then, has the nontitular question remained marginal to studies of federalism and institutional engineering? This is because of the challenge that it presents to much of the normative scholarship and policy advocacy of decentralization, federalism, and "conflict management" projects currently being undertaken. "Like peace, freedom and the family," as Michael Goldsmith and Kenneth Newton rightly discern, "no modern politician dare express a dislike of decentralisation."[47] Writes another scholar: "Decentralisation has been declared a 'very fashionable idea' . . . and 'the fashion of our time.'" Its advocacy, however, he notes, has "rest[ed] more on faith than on . . . careful analysis of historical and comparative experiences."[48]

The above observation is very pertinent to studies of ethnically plural federations. For example, much has been made of the devolution of power to Tatarstan, hailed as a paragon of the "peaceful resolution of conflict." Yet, in terms of the degree of political discrimination of the nontitulars, it is not much different from the cases examined in this book. Another example: Arend Lijphart identified India of the 1960s as a "consociational democracy," where diversity was recognized, *inter alia,* through the linguistic state system. The findings of Paul Brass, the scholar of Indian politics, about caste, communal, and linguistic discrimination by the states' dominant elites against other groups, however, make such assertions vulnerable to criticism.[49] Will Kymlicka, the advocate of "multicultural citizenship," urges federalism as a preferable option "where national minorities are regionally concentrated." In such settings, he suggests the "drawing up" of boundaries "so that the national minority forms a majority in one of the subunits," which indicates an underestimation of the enormous complexity that such boundary readjustments entail in the real world.[50] Accordingly, while Kymlicka provides excellent insights into other aspects of politics in multicultural settings, he does not treat the nontitular problem in an extensive way. Instead, he sees the issue of accommodating diversity in liberal democracies largely in terms of interactions between "ethnic groups" native to, or long resident in, a polity on the one hand, and the recent migrants or immigrants, the "minorities," on the other. Daniel Elazar, one of the foremost advocates of federalism as a form of "self rule" and "shared rule," urged its adoption in the former Soviet Union in order to accommodate "internal diversity."[51] His factual handbook on the world's federations, however, does not discuss in detail the internal ethnic composition of the RSFSR's subnational entities, which likewise suggests an underestimation of the relevance of the nontitular question.[52] A statement by Anthony Smith illustrates the optimism associated with the federal project: "The main agency of containment has been, and remains, the fact and the hope of federalism."[53]

While not always specifically concerned with the titular-nontitular issue, the findings of a number of influential studies on the frequently discrimination-inducing nature of federal and other decentralist arrangements further support the arguments advanced here. In a recent survey of the literature on decentralization (broadly defined), Paul Hutchcroft cautioned against the continued association of decentralization with democracy.[54] More specifically, Alfred Stepan underlined the frequent "demos-constraining" nature of federations.[55] Erik Nordlinger wrote that federalism "allows or encourages the dominant segment in any one state to ignore or negate the demands of the minority segment."[56] Brass's studies of local politics in India, a federal democracy, allowed him to conclude: "Many of the states actually promote integration and assimilation of minorities rather than pluralism."[57] Echoing him, another noted scholar of Indian politics wrote: "We had had enough experience by now . . . to know that putting greater power at the disposal of [subnational] state leaders is by itself no recipe at all for democracy."[58] Ted Gurr commented on the results of federalization in Belgium: "The solution to one region's [Walloonia's] communal grievances created a minority [French speakers] . . . that was subject to discrimination."[59] Perhaps the harshest indictment of federations comes from William Riker, and it is particularly interesting because it concerns a long-standing democracy. Refer-ring to America's Southern states before the Civil Rights movement, he wrote that federalism in the United States served to perpetuate "segregation and racial oppression."[60] His verdict: "Federalism that grants *more* local autonomy than is necessary for freedom and civil liberty encourages local tyranny."[61]

None of this is to suggest that federalism is not a preferred option in multi-ethnic settings. In fact, I concur with those who argue that it may be the only option against secession by the powerful territorially based groups or to avoid internal ethnic conflict. It is only preferable, however, to the extent that it is a *stability*-inducing institutional arrangement. Yet stability is not always compati-ble with democracy. From this point of view, federations are closer to Ian Lus-tick's control model than to Lijphart's consociational model.[62]

Considering its normative implications, the model advanced by Lustick as a competing explanatory and descriptive device has not been as popular as Lijp-hart's consociational model. Indeed, the model grew out of Lustick's observa-tions of ethnic politics in, among other cases, South Africa under apartheid and the American South before World War II. While dubious as a prescriptive de-vice, it approximates reality very closely in many federal polities, including democratic ones. "A control approach," he wrote, "would focus on the emer-gence and maintenance of a relationship in which the superior power of one segment is mobilized to enforce stability by constraining the political actions and opportunities of another segment or segments."[63] In contrast to the "perfect" consociational system, whose "visual metaphor" is a "delicately but securely balanced scale, . . . that appropriate for a control system is a puppeteer manipu-lating his stringed puppet."[64] He cites such characteristics of the system as the deprivation of "facilities for united political action"; denial of "access to inde-pendent sources of economic support"; "penetration of the subordinate group"; and the endowment of the system with legitimacy "by an elaborate and well-articulated group-specific ideology; specific, that is, to the history and perceived interests of the superordinate sub-unit."[65]

Lustick's powerful descriptive model conveniently brings us back to the grassroots. A general device for explaining the puzzle of stability in divided polities, Lustick's model was not concerned with specific institutional arrange-ments serving to reproduce control relationships. Yet, in terms of the role they perform, the local governing arrangements that we saw in Maykop, Ufa, Or-chards, and Peach Valley are strikingly resonant with the somewhat metaphori-cal descriptions of the control model. After 1992, they served to deprive the nontitulars of the means for "united political action," ensuring that "access to sources of economic support" would be denied in case of protest activities. Through the accountable nontitular administrations they also served as mechanisms of the "penetration" of the nontitular groups, and as transmission belts for the titular "group-specific ideology."

Lustick's approach is also relevant for the purposes of the present discussion of federations and local government in his stress on the stability-inducing nature of control systems. The implications are that states, foreign democratic nations, and the wider policy-making community turn a blind eye to control systems because the alternative may be internal ethnic conflicts or, should the federal center intervene too much to protect the rights of the controlled groups, secession of the controlling group. Consider the role of the U.S. Supreme Court in perpetuating segregation in the United States, or Brass's assertion that the federal center in India "turned a blind eye to states' discriminatory policies."[66]

Local Government and the Federal State in Russia:
Yel'tsin, Putin, and Beyond

Under Yel'tsin, there was a broad consensus that Moscow would not intervene in the republics' internal politics too much as long as they toned down the secession rhetoric and delivered the pro-Yel'tsin vote. Moscow also relied on the republics to maintain stability within their own entities, as conflicts such as that of Ossetiya-Ingushetiya required politically costly federal intervention. Such stability, and the delivery of the pro-Yel'tsin vote, however, required the perpetuation of internal control systems. These control systems in turn served to strengthen the power and independence of regional regimes, which made Moscow increasingly wary. The result was a search for ways that would undermine regional power from below. In both these conflicting policy agendas, local government took center stage. It was viewed as central to either the perpetuation of internal control systems or the mobilization of opposition to regional regimes from below. The above dilemma is reflected in the seemingly ad hoc and uneven nature of local government reform policies in the Yel'tsin era, which differed across the republics and regions, the electoral cycles, and the political situation in Russia in general.[67]

Yel'tsin was prepared to postpone reforms of local government that would make it more independent from the regional regimes so long as through their control over local government the regions could deliver the pro-Yel'tsin vote. In other circumstances, he urged local government independence as a counter to particularly anti-Kremlin regional regimes. Yel'tsin, however, showed particular reluctance to enforce local government reform at the republic, as opposed to nonethnic regional, level, although the various federal agencies charged with enforcing federal legislation made efforts to do so. Indeed, while mayoral elections had been held in most regions, HAs at almost all levels continued to be appointed rather than elected in such powerful entities as Tatarstan and Bashkortostan. While these republics would concede to changing some of the other legislation that violated federal law, they fiercely clung to their prerogative to appoint local HAs. These facts point to the recognition of the importance of local government as a control tool at both the republic and federal levels.

This analysis elevates local government to the center stage of federal, regional, and center-periphery politics. Local government played, and continues to play, a crucial role in the perpetuation of republic ethnocratic regimes, in the republics' relations with the Kremlin, and in federal-level politics. Initially leaning towards Yel'tsin's strategy of strengthening local government's independence to counter regionalism and separatism, Putin subsequently embarked on reforms aimed at establishing greater institutional control over municipalities by both federal and regional levels of authority.[68] As such, local government in Russia under the Putin administration continues to play a role greatly different from the one ascribed to it by normative theorists of the rule of the grassroots.

Notes

1. Donald L. Horowitz, "How to Begin Thinking Comparatively about Soviet Ethnic Problems," in *Thinking Theoretically about Soviet Nationalities: History and Comparison in the Study of the USSR*, ed. Alexander J. Motyl (New York: Columbia University Press, 1992), 14.

2. The existence of tensions between the dominant Francophones on the one hand, and the Anglophones on the other, in Canada's Quebec, is a case in point. See Kenneth McRae, "Canada: Reflections on Two Conflicts," in *Conflict and Peacemaking in Multiethnic Societies*, ed. Joseph Montville (Lexington, Mass.: Lexington Books, 1990), 197-217.

3. Ivo Duchacek, a noted scholar of federalism, for example, argued against the coincidence of administrative borders with a subunit's ethnic composition in order to alleviate fears of tyranny by the ethnic majority of a given subunit. He recommended the dispersion of a given group among several units (Ivo D. Duchacek, "Comparative Federalism: An Agenda for Additional Research," in *Constitutional Design and Power-Sharing in the Post-Modern Epoch*, ed. Daniel Elazar [Lanham, Md.: University Press of America, 1991], 31). For a discussion of ethnic politics in plural federations, see Graham Smith, ed., *Federalism: The Multiethnic Challenge* (New York: Longman, 1995).

4. See Paul R. Brass, *The Politics of India since Independence* (Cambridge: Cambridge University Press, 1994). The findings and recommendations of the relevant commission are contained in Government of India Home Department, *Report of the States Reorganisation Commission, 1955* (New Delhi: Government of India Press, 1955). For a discussion of Indian states' ethnic politics during the country's postcolonial state building, see also Myron Weiner, ed., *State Politics in India* (Princeton, N.J.: Princeton University Press, 1968). For ethnic politics in other ethnically plural federal polities, see Donald L. Horowitz, *Ethnic Groups in Conflict* (Berkeley: University of California Press, 1985).

5. The conflict erupted in 1947. The bilingual Bern canton, of which the Jura province formed part, was composed of 85 percent German and 15 percent French populations. Jurg Steiner, "Power-Sharing: Another Swiss 'Export Product'?" in *Conflict and Peacemaking*, 112-3.

6. Steiner, "Power-Sharing."

7. Liesbet Hooghe, *A Leap in the Dark: Nationalist Conflict and Federal Reform in Belgium*, Western Societies Program Occasional Papers, vol. 27 (Ithaca, N.Y.: Cornell University Press, 1991), 1, 13-14, 18.

8. Hooghe, *Leap in the Dark*, 88.

9. Ingushetiya became separate from Chechnya after Chechnya's declaration of independence, and was only later recognized as a separate republic by Moscow. Some other entities, such as Adygeya, were elevated in status, but their boundaries were not altered. For a discussion of these and other administrative changes, see Fiona Hill, "'Russia's Tinderbox': Conflict in the North Caucasus and Its Implications for the Future of the Russian Federation," (Cambridge, Mass.: Harvard University, John F. Kennedy School of Government, Strengthening Democratic Institutions Project, 1995).

10. William A. Gamson, "The Social Psychology of Collective Action," in *Frontiers in Social Movement Theory*, ed. Aldon D. Morris and Carol M. Mueller (New Haven, Conn.: Yale University Press, 1992), 53-76.

11. This discussion is largely based on Gerry Stoker, "Introduction: Normative Theories of Local Government and Democracy," in *Rethinking Local Democracy*, ed. Desmond King and Gerry Stoker (London: Macmillan, 1996), 1-27.

12. Kenneth Newton, *Second City Politics: Democratic Processes and Decision-Making in Birmingham* (Oxford: Clarendon, 1976). For examples of mayoral positions serving as stepping-stones into the regional-level political elite, see Steven Solnick, "Gubernatorial Elections in Russia, 1996-1997," *Post-Soviet Affairs* 14, no. 1 (1998): 48-80.

13. Theodore H. Friedgut, *Political Participation in the USSR* (Princeton, N.J.: Princeton University Press, 1979), 16-19.

14. Leon Trotsky, *1905* (Bungay, England: Chaucer, 1971), 122.

15. Trotsky, *1905*, 264.

16. Trotsky, *1905*, 267.

17. Alexis de Tocqueville, "Townships, Municipal Administration, State Government," in *Democracy in America*, ed. J. P. Mayer (London: Fontana, 1994), 87.

18. Stephen Whitefield, *Industrial Power and the Soviet State* (Oxford: Clarendon, 1993), 174.

19. Whitefield, *Industrial Power*.

20. Nicolai Petro, "The Novgorod Region: A Russian Success Story," *Post-Soviet Affairs* 15, no. 3 (1999): 235-61.

21. For a discussion, see Nigel M. Healey, Vladimir Leksin, and Alexandr Svetsov, "The Municipalization of Enterprise-Owned 'Social Assets' in Russia," *Post-Soviet Affairs* 15, no. 3 (1999): 262-80.

22. Alan Norton, "What East European Democracies Might Learn from the West," in *Local Government in Eastern Europe: Establishing Democracy at the Grassroots*, ed. Andrew Coulson (Aldershot, England: Elgar, 1995), 270.

23. Norton, "East European Democracies," 270.

24. This discussion concerns the literature specifically dealing with local, as opposed to regional, politics in Russia.

25. See, for example, T. M. Bjalkina, "Die örtliche Selbstverwaltung in der Russischen Föderation: Lage, Probleme, Perspektiven," *Osteuropa Recht* 47, no. 1-2 (2001): 15-34.

26. For example, see Institut ekonomiki goroda, *Munitsipal'noe ekonomicheskoe razvitie* (Moscow: Institut ekonomiki goroda, 1999); Peter Kirkow, "Local Self-Government in Russia: Awakening from Slumber?" *Europe-Asia Studies* 49, no. 1 (1997): 43-58; and P. G. Tsitsin, *Problemy ustoychivogo sotsial'no-ekonomicheskogo razvitiya munitsipal'nykh obrazovaniy i puti ikh resheniya* (Moscow: Novyy vek, 2002).

27. For an example, see Kimitaka Matsuzato, "Local Elites under Transition: County and City Politics in Russia 1985-1996," *Europe-Asia Studies* 51, no. 8 (1999): 1367-400; and Sergei Ryzhenkov, "Regional'naya elita i mestnoe samoupravlenie: Aktory, pravila igry i logika reformy," in *Reforma mestnogo samoupravleniya v regional'nom izmerenii*, ed. Sergei Ryzhenkov and N. Vinnik (Moscow: Moskovskiy obshchestvennyy nauchnyy fond, 1999), 85-106. For elite-centered approaches to Russian local politics, see also Vladimir Gel'man et al., *Making and Breaking Democratic Transitions: The Comparative Politics of Russia's Regions* (Lanham, Md.: Rowman & Littlefield, 2003).

28. For examples, see Jeffrey W. Hahn, "The Development of Local Legislatures in Russia: The Case of Yaroslavl," in *Democratisation in Russia: The Development of Legislative Institutions*, ed. Jeffrey W. Hahn (London: Sharpe, 1996), 159-96; Jeffrey W. Hahn, "Local Politics and Political Power in Russia: The Case of Yaroslavl," *Soviet Economy* 7, no. 4 (1991): 322-41; Nicolai Petro, *Jumpstarting Democracy: The Novgorod Model of Rapid Social Change* (Ithaca, N.Y.: Cornell University Press, in press); and Petro, "Novgorod Region."

29. Newton, *Second City Politics.*

30. A classic study of local government's relation to social capital is Robert Putnam, *Making Democracy Work: Civic Traditions in Modern Italy* (Princeton, N.J.: Princeton University Press, 1993).

31. But see Petro, *Jumpstarting Democracy*; and Petro, "Novgorod Region."

32. Jeff Chinn and Robert Kaiser, *Russians as the New Minority: Ethnicity and Nationalism in the Soviet Successor States* (Boulder, Colo.: Westview Press, 1996), 23.

33. Ian Bremmer, "The Politics of Ethnicity: Russians in the New Ukraine," *Europe-Asia Studies* 46, no. 2 (1994): 264.

34. David D. Laitin, *Identity in Formation: The Russian-Speaking Nationality in Estonia and Bashkortostan*, Studies in Public Policy, vol. 249 (Glasgow: University of Strathclyde, 1995); David D. Laitin, *Identity in Formation: The Russian-Speaking Populations in the Near Abroad* (Ithaca, N.Y.: Cornell University Press, 1998); and David D. Laitin, "Language and Nationalism in the Post-Soviet Republics," *Post-Soviet Affairs* 12, no. 1 (1996): 4-24. For a critique of Laitin's approach, see Jerry F. Hough, "Sociology, the State, and Language Politics," *Post-Soviet Affairs* 12, no. 2 (1996): 95-117.

35. Personal e-mail communication with David Laitin, 24 May 1999. Laitin particularly referred to Estonia, and, as an example, mentioned that Russians did very well in the 1994 local elections in Tallinn.

36. Paul Kolstoe, *Russians in the Former Soviet Republics* (London: Hurst, 1995), 134. Kolstoe also notes that, ironically, the local Russian leaders were Communists.

37. Laitin, *Identity in Formation: The Russian-Speaking Nationality*, 182-3.

38. Graham Smith and Andrew Wilson, "Rethinking Russia's Post-Soviet Diaspora: The Potential for Political Mobilisation in Eastern Ukraine and North-East Estonia," *Europe-Asia Studies* 49, no. 5 (1997): 851.

39. Kolstoe, *Russians*, 133-5.

40. Smith and Wilson, "Rethinking Russia's Post-Soviet Diaspora," 851.

41. Mark R. Beissinger, "Nationalist Violence and the State: Political Authority and Contentious Repertoires in the Former USSR," *Comparative Politics* 30, no. 4 (1998): 410, 416, 418. The findings parallel those of studies of ethnic politics in other states, such as India, where Paul Brass uses the term "institutionalized riot systems" to refer to their elite-controlled nature (*Theft of an Idol: Text and Context in the Representation of Collective Violence* [Princeton, N.J.: Princeton University Press, 1997]).

42. William Crowther, "The Politics of Ethno-National Mobilization: Nationalism and Reform in Soviet Moldavia," *Russian Review* 50, no. 2 (1991): 196.

43. Another example that Crowther mentions is the local soviets' threat to recall the local deputies to the Moldovan Supreme Soviet ("Politics," 200).

44. Smith and Wilson, "Rethinking Russia's Post-Soviet Diaspora."

45. Michael Burgess, "Federalism and Federation: A Reappraisal," in *Comparative Federalism and Federation: Competing Traditions and Future Directions*, ed. Michael Burgess and Alaign G. Gagnon (New York: Harvester Wheatsheaf, 1993), 7.

46. Rogers Brubaker, *Nationalism Reframed: Nationhood and the National Question in the New Europe* (Cambridge: Cambridge University Press, 1996).

47. Michael G. Goldsmith and Kenneth Newton, "Introduction," *European Journal of Political Research*, Special Issue, "Centralisation and Decentralisation: Changing Patterns of Intergovernmental Relations in Advanced Western Societies," 16, no. 4 (1988): 359.

48. Paul D. Hutchcroft, "Centralisation and Decentralisation in Administration and Politics: Assessing the Territorial Dimension of Authority and Power," *Governance* 14, no. 1 (2001): 23-4.

49. Arend Lijphart, "The Puzzle of Indian Democracy: A Consociational Interpretation," *American Political Science Review* 90, no. 2 (1996): 258-68; Paul R. Brass, *Language, Religion and Politics in North India* (New York: Cambridge University Press, 1974), 202.

50. Will Kymlicka, *Multicultural Citizenship: A Liberal Theory of Minority Rights* (Oxford: Clarendon, 1995), 27-8.

51. Daniel Elazar, *Federal Systems of the World: A Handbook of Federal, Confederal and Autonomy Arrangements*, 2d ed. (Essex, England: Longman Current Affairs, 1994), ix.

52. Elazar, *Federal Systems of the World*, 276.

53. Anthony D. Smith, "Ethnic Identity and Territorial Nationalism in Comparative Perspective," in *Thinking Theoretically about Soviet Nationalitie*, 60.

54. Hutchcroft, "Centralisation and Decentralisation," 33.

55. For a comparative critique of federations, and of the Russian federation in particular, see Alfred Stepan, "Russian Federalism in Comparative Perspective," *Post-Soviet Affairs* 16 (April 2000): 133-76.

56. Erik Nordlinger, *Conflict Regulation in Divided Societies*, Occasional Papers in International Affairs, vol. 29 (Cambridge, Mass.: Harvard University Center for International Affairs, 1972), 31.

57. Paul R. Brass, *Language, Religion and Politics in North India* (New York: Cambridge University Press, 1974), 202.

58. Rajni Kothari, *The State against Democracy: In Search of Humane Governance* (Delhi: Ajanta, 1989), 194.

59. Ted R. Gurr, *Minorities at Risk: A Global View of Ethno-Political Conflicts* (Washington, D.C.: United States Institute of Peace, 1995), 9.

60. William H. Riker, *Federalism: Origin, Operation, Significance* (Boston: Little, Brown, 1964), 153.

61. Riker, *Federalism*, 143.

62. Ian Lustick, "Stability in Deeply Divided Societies: Consociationalism versus Control," *World Politics* 31, no. 3 (1979): 325-44.

63. Lustick, "Stability," 328.

64. Lustick, "Stability," 332.

65. Lustick, "Stability," 332, 344.

66. Paul R. Brass, "Ethnic Groups and Ethnic Identity Formation," in *Ethnicity*, ed. John J. Hutchinson and Anthony D. Smith (Oxford: Oxford University Press, 1996), 85-90.

67. For a discussion of the Kremlin's use of local government for political purposes, see R. F. Turovskiy, "Otnosheniya 'tsentr-regiony' v 1997-1998 gg.: Mejhdu konfliktom i konsensusom," *Politiya* 1, no. 7 (1998): 5-32. See also Eugene Huskey, "Political Leadership and the Center-Periphery Struggle: Putin's Administrative Reforms," in *Gorbachev, Yeltsin, and Putin: Political Leadership in Russia's Transition*, ed. Archie Brown and Lilia Shevtsova (Washington, D.C.: Carnegie Endowment for International Peace, 2001), 113-41.

68. For a discussion of Putin's federal reforms, see Peter Reddaway, "Will Putin Be Able to Consolidate Power?" *Post-Soviet Affairs* 17, no. 1 (2001): 23-44; and Archie Brown, "Vladimir Putin and the Reaffirmation of Central State Power," *Post-Soviet Affairs* 17, no. 1 (2001): 45-55.

Bibliography

Akkieva, Svetlana I. "Etnopoliticheskaya i sotsial'no-ekonomicheskaya situatsiya v Kabardino-Balkarii nakanune vyborov 17 dekabrya 1995 goda." Pp. 61-89 in *Razvivayushchiysya elektorat Rossii*, edited by G. A. Komarova. Moscow: Rossiyskaya akademiya nauk, Institut etnologii i antropologii, 1996.

"Aktual'nye problemy formirovaniya mestnogo samoupravleniya v Rossiyskoy federatsii ('Kruglyy stol' v Institute gosudarstva i prava Rossiyskoy akademii nauk)." *Gosudarstvo i pravo* 5 (1997): 24-45.

Alexander, James. *Political Culture in Post-Communist Russia: Formlessness and Recreation in a Traumatic Transition.* New York: St. Martin's, 2000.

Almond, Gabriel A., and Sidney Verba. *The Civic Culture: Political Attitudes and Democracy in Five Nations.* Newbury Park, Calif.: Sage, 1989.

Anchabadze, Yu. D., and N. G. Volkova. *Narody Kavkaza.* Moscow: Rossiyskaya akademiya nauk, Institut etnologii i antropologii, 1993.

Anderson, Barbara A., and Brian D. Silver. "Equality, Efficiency, and Politics in Soviet Bilingual Education Policy, 1934-1980." *American Political Science Review* 78, no. 4 (1984): 1019-39.

Anderson, Benedict. *Imagined Communities: Reflections on the Origin and Spread of Nationalism.* London: Verso, 1983.

Arinin, Alexandr. "Problemy razvitiya Rossiyskoy gosudarstvennosti v kontse dvadtsatogo veka." Pp. 6-107 in *Federalizm vlasti i vlast' federalizma*, edited by Michael N. Guboglo. Moscow: Inteltekh, 1997.

Azovkin, I. A. *Mestnye sovety v sisteme organov vlasti.* Moscow: Yuridicheskaya literatura, 1971.

Bachrach, Peter, and Morton S. Baratz. "Two Faces of Power." *American Political Science Review* 56, no. 4 (1962): 947-52.

Balme, Richard. "Councilors, Issue Agendas and Political Action in Two French Towns." Pp. 135-56 in *Local Politics and Participation in Britain and France*, edited by Albert Mabileau, George Moyser, Geraint Parry, and Patrick Quantin. Cambridge: Cambridge University Press, 1989.

Balzer, Marjorie M., and Uliana A. Vinokurova. "Interethnic Relations and Federalism: The Case of the Sakha Republic." *Europe-Asia Studies* 48, no. 1 (1996): 101-20.

Banfield, Edward C. *Political Influence.* New York: Free Press, 1961.

Banfield, Edward C., and James Q. Wilson. *City Politics.* New York: Vintage, 1963.

Beissinger, Mark R. "How Nationalisms Spread: Eastern Europe Adrift the Tides and Cycles of Nationalist Contention." *Social Research* 63, no. 1 (1996): 97-146.

———. "Nationalist Violence and the State: Political Authority and Contentious Repertoires in the Former USSR." *Comparative Politics* 30, no. 4 (1998): 401-22.

Bennett, Robert J. "Local Government in Europe: Common Directions for Change." Pp. 1-27 in *Local Government in the New Europe*, edited by Robert J. Bennett. London: Belhaven, 1993.

Bentley, Arthur F. *The Process of Government.* Cambridge, Mass.: Harvard University Press, 1967.

Berlin, Isiah. *Karl Marx.* Oxford: Oxford University Press, 1963.

Bialer, Seweryn. "The Changing Soviet Political System: The Nineteenth Party Conference and After." Pp. 193-241 in *Politics, Society, and Nationality inside Gorbachev's Russia,* edited by Seweryn Bialer. Boulder, Colo.: Westview, 1989.

Birnbaum, Pierre. *States and Collective Action: The European Experience.* New York: Cambridge University Press, 1988.

Bjalkina, T. M. "Die örtliche Selbstverwaltung in der Russischen Föderation: Lage, Probleme, Perspektiven." *Osteuropa Recht* 47, no. 1-2 (2001): 15-34.

Brass, Paul R. "Ethnic Groups and Ethnic Identity Formation." Pp. 85-90 in *Ethnicity,* edited by John J. Hutchinson and Anthony D. Smith. Oxford: Oxford University Press, 1996.

———. *Ethnicity and Nationalism: Theory and Comparison.* New Delhi: Sage, 1991.

———. *Language, Religion and Politics in North India.* New York: Cambridge University Press, 1974.

———. *The Politics of India since Independence.* Cambridge: Cambridge University Press, 1994.

———. *Theft of an Idol: Text and Context in the Representation of Collective Violence.* Princeton, N.J.: Princeton University Press, 1997.

Bremmer, Ian. "The Politics of Ethnicity: Russians in the New Ukraine." *Europe-Asia Studies* 46, no. 2 (1994): 261-83.

Brown, Archie. *The Gorbachev Factor.* Oxford: Oxford University Press, 1996.

———. "Vladimir Putin and the Reaffirmation of Central State Power." *Post-Soviet Affairs* 17, no. 1 (2001): 45-55.

Brubaker, Rogers. *Nationalism Reframed: Nationhood and the National Question in the New Europe.* Cambridge: Cambridge University Press, 1996.

Brudny, Yitzhak M. *Reinventing Russia: Russian Nationalism and the Soviet State, 1953-1991.* 2d ed. Cambridge, Mass.: Harvard University Press, 2000.

Bruk, S. I., and Valery Tishkov. "Rossiya: Formirovanie territorii gosudarstva." Pp. 5-16 in *Narody Rossii: Entsiklopediya,* edited by Valery Tishkov. Moscow: Nauchnoe izdatel'stvo Bol'shaya rossiyskaya entsiklopediya, 1994.

Bugay, N. F. "Dvadtsatye gody: Stanovlenie demokraticheskikh form pravleniya na severnom Kavkaze." Pp. 33-99 in *Severnyy Kavkaz: Vybor puti natsional'nogo razvitiya,* edited by N. F. Bugay. Maykop, Russia: Meoty, 1994.

Bunce, Valerie. *Subversive Institutions: The Design and the Destruction of Socialism and the State.* Cambridge: Cambridge University Press, 1999.

Burgess, Michael. "Federalism and Federation: A Reappraisal." Pp. 3-14 in *Comparative Federalism and Federation: Competing Traditions and Future Directions,* edited by Michael Burgess and Alaign G. Gagnon. New York: Harvester Wheatsheaf, 1993.

Busygin, Evgeniy. "Russkie v mnogonatsional'nom povoljh'e." Pp. 35-57 in *Yazyk i natsionalizm v postsovetskikh respublikakh,* edited by M. N. Guboglo. Moscow: Rossiyskaya akademiya nauk, Institut etnologii i antropologii, 1994.

Buzarov, A. S., and K. K. Khutyz. "Totalitarizm i natsional'nye otnosheniya: Uroki i sovremennost' (Na primere stanovleniya gosudarstvennosti adygskikh narodov severnogo Kavkaza)." Pp. 15-32 in *Severnyy Kavkaz: Vybor puti natsional'nogo razvitiya,* edited by N. F. Bugay. Maykop, Russia: Meoty, 1994.

Chinn, Jeff, and Robert Kaiser. *Russians as the New Minority: Ethnicity and Nationalism in the Soviet Successor States.* Boulder, Colo.: Westview, 1996.

Churchward, L. G. *Contemporary Soviet Government*. London: Routledge & Kegan Paul, 1968.

Cielecka, Anna, and John Gibson. "Local Government in Poland." Pp. 23-40 in *Local Government in Eastern Europe: Establishing Democracy at the Grassroots*, edited by Andrew Coulson. Aldershot, England: Elgar, 1995.

Connor, Walker. *The National Question in Marxist-Leninist Theory and Strategy*. Princeton, N.J.: Princeton University Press, 1984.

Conquest, Robert. *The Nation Killers*. London: Sphere, 1972.

Coulson, Andrew. "From Democratic Centralism to Local Democracy." Pp. 1-19 in *Local Government in Eastern Europe: Establishing Democracy at the Grassroots*, edited by Andrew Coulson. Aldershot, England: Elgar, 1995.

Crisp, Simon. "Soviet Language Planning." Pp. 23-45 in *Language Planning in the Soviet Union*, edited by Michael Kirkwood. London: Macmillan, 1989.

Crowther, William. "The Politics of Ethno-National Mobilization: Nationalism and Reform in Soviet Moldavia." *Russian Review* 50, no. 2 (1991): 183-202.

Dahl, Robert A. *Polyarchy: Participation and Opposition*. New Haven, Conn.: Yale University Press, 1971.

———. *Who Governs? Democracy and Power in an American City*. New Haven, Conn.: Yale University Press, 1966.

Davies, E. M., John Gibson, and John Stewart. "Grant Characteristics and the Budgetary Process." Pp. 207-24 in *New Research in Central-Local Relations*, edited by Michael Goldsmith. Aldershot, England: Gower, 1986.

Della Porta, Donatella. "Social Movements and the State: Thoughts on the Policing of Protest." Pp. 62-92 in *Comparative Perspectives on Social Movements*, edited by Doug McAdam, John D. McCarthy, and Mayer N. Zald. Cambridge: Cambridge University Press, 1996.

Denber, Rachel, ed. *The Soviet Nationality Reader: The Disintegration in Context*. Boulder, Colo.: Westview, 1992.

Diamond, Larry. "Rethinking Civil Society: Toward Democratic Consolidation." *Journal of Democracy* 5, no. 3 (1994): 4-17.

Didigova, I. B. "Dvadtsatye-tridtsatye gody: Problemy administrativno-territorial'nogo ustroystva chechenskogo i ingushskogo narodov." Pp. 140-58 in *Severnyy Kavkaz: Vybor puty natsional'nogo razvitiya*, edited by N. F. Bugay. Maykop, Russia: Meoty, 1994.

di Palma, Guiseppe. *To Craft Democracies: An Essay on Democratic Transitions*. Berkeley: University of California Press, 1990.

Djharimov, Aslan. *Adygeya: Ot avtonomii k respublike*. Moscow: Autopan, 1995.

Domhoff, G. William. *Who Rules America? Power and Politics in the Year 2000*. Mountain View, Calif.: Mayfield, 1998.

Dowding, K., P. John, T. Mergoupis, and M. Van Vugt. "Exit, Voice and Loyalty: Analytic and Empirical Developments." *European Journal of Political Research* 37, no. 4 (2000): 469-95.

Drobizheva, Leokadia. "Processes of Disintegration in the Russian Federation and the Problem of Russians." Pp. 45-55 in *The New Russian Diaspora: Russian Minorities in the Former Soviet Republics*, edited by Vladimir Shlapentokh, Munir Sendich, and Emil Payin. Armonk, N.Y.: Sharpe, 1994.

———. "Russians in the Republics of the Russian Federation." Paper presented at the Seminar on Interethnic Relations in Russia and the Commonwealth of Independent States, Moscow Carnegie Center, Moscow, 1995.

Duchacek, Ivo D. "Comparative Federalism: An Agenda for Additional Research." Pp. 23-40 in *Constitutional Design and Power-Sharing in the Post-Modern Epoch*, edited by Daniel Elazar. Lanham, Md.: University Press of America, 1991.

Durkheim, Emile. "Anomie and the Moral Structure of Industry." Pp. 173-88 in *Emile Durkheim: Selected Writings*, edited by Anthony Giddens. Cambridge: Cambridge University Press, 1972.

———. *Suicide: A Study in Sociology*. Translated by George Simpson. London: Routledge, 1952.

Easter, Gerald. *Reconstructing the State: Personal Networks and Elite Identity in Soviet Russia*. Cambridge: Cambridge University Press, 2000.

Eckstein, Harry. "Congruence Theory Explained." Pp. 3-33 in *Can Democracy Take Root in Post-Soviet Russia? Explorations in State-Society Relations*, edited by Harry Eckstein, Jr., Frederic J. Fleron, Erik Hoffmann, and William M. Reisinger. Lanham, Md.: Rowman & Littlefield, 1998.

Eisinger, Peter K. "The Conditions of Protest Behavior in American Cities." *American Political Science Review* 67, no. 1 (1973): 11-28.

Ekiert, Grzegorz, and Jan Kubik. "Contentious Politics in New Democracies: East Germany, Hungary, Poland, and Slovakia, 1989-93." *World Politics* 50, no. 4 (1998): 547-81.

Elazar, Daniel. *Federal Systems of the World: A Handbook of Federal, Confederal and Autonomy Arrangements*. 2d ed. Essex, England: Longman Current Affairs, 1994.

Esadze, Semyon. *Istoricheskaya zapiska ob upravlenii Kavkazom*. Vol. 1. Tiflis, Georgia: Guttenberg, 1907.

Fainsod, Merle. *Smolensk under Soviet Rule*. Cambridge, Mass.: Harvard University Press, 1958.

Fearon, James D., and David D. Laitin. "Explaining Inter-Ethnic Cooperation." *American Political Science Review* 90, no. 4 (1996): 715-35.

Fish, M. Steven. *Democracy from Scratch: Opposition and Regime in the New Russian Revolution*. Princeton, N.J.: Princeton University Press, 1995.

Fox, Jonathan. "Latin America's Emerging Local Politics." *Journal of Democracy* 5, no. 2 (1994): 105-16.

Freinkman, Lev, and Plamen Yossifov. "Decentralization in Regional Fiscal Systems in Russia: Trends and Links to Economic Performance." Washington, D.C.: World Bank, 1999.

Friedgut, Theodore H. "Community Structure, Political Participation, Soviet Local Government: The Case of Kutaisi." Pp. 261-96 in *Soviet Politics and Society in the 1970s*, edited by Henry W. Morton and Rudolf L. Tokes. New York: Free Press, 1974.

———. *Political Participation in the USSR*. Princeton, N.J.: Princeton University Press, 1979.

Friedrich, Carl J. "Totalitarianism: Recent Trends." Pp. 16-27 in *Between Totalitarianism and Pluralism*, edited by Alexander Dallin. New York: Garland, 1992.

Frolic, B. Michael. "Decision Making in Soviet Cities." *American Political Science Review* 66, no. 1 (1972): 38-52.

Gabdrafikov, Il'dar. *Respublika Bashkortostan: Model' etnologicheskogo monitoringa*. Moscow: Rossiyskaya akademiya nauk, Institut etnologii i antropologii, 1998.

Gamson, William A. "The Social Psychology of Collective Action." Pp. 53-76 in *Frontiers in Social Movement Theory*, edited by Aldon D. Morris and Carol M. Mueller. New Haven, Conn.: Yale University Press, 1992.

———. *Talking Politics*. Cambridge: Cambridge University Press, 1992.

Gamson, William A., and David S. Meyer. "Framing Political Opportunity." Pp. 275-90 in *Comparative Perspectives on Social Movements: Political Opportunities, Mobilizing Structures, and Cultural Framings*, edited by Doug McAdam, John D. McCarthy, and Mayer N. Zald. Cambridge: Cambridge University Press, 1996.

Gamson, William A., and Andre Modigliani. "Media Discourse and Public Opinion on Nuclear Power: A Constructionist Approach." *American Journal of Sociology* 95, no. 1 (1989): 1-37.

Gazier, Anne. "Les Pouvoirs Locaux dans les Régions Russes du Centre-Terres Noires." *Les Cahiers du CERI* 5 (1993).

Gellner, Ernst. *Nations and Nationalism*. Ithaca, N.Y.: Cornell University Press, 1983.

Gel'man, Vladimir. Y. "Federal'naya politika: Reforma mestnoy vlasti v gorodakh Rossii." Paper presented at the Seminar on Russia's Regions, Centre d'Études et de Recherches Internationales, Sciences Po, Paris, 2000.

———. "Regional'naya vlast' v sovremennoy Rossii: Instituty, rejhimy, i praktiki." *Polis* 1 (1998): 87-105.

Gel'man, Vladimir Y., and Grigorii V. Golosov. "Regional Party System Formation in Russia: The Deviant Case of Sverdlovsk Oblast." *Journal of Communist Studies and Transition Politics* 14, no. 1 (1998): 31-53.

Gel'man, Vladimir Y., Sergei Ryzhenkov, Michael Brie, Boris Ovchinnikov, and Igor Semenov. *Making and Breaking Democratic Transitions: The Comparative Politics of Russia's Regions*. Lanham, Md.: Rowman & Littlefield, 2003.

Gel'man, Vladimir Y., and Inessa Tarusina. "Studies of Political Elites in Russia: Issues and Alternatives." *Communist and Post-Communist Studies* 33, no. 3 (2000): 311-29.

Giddens, Anthony, ed. *Emile Durkheim: Selected Writings*. Cambridge: Cambridge University Press, 1972.

Giuliano, Elise. "Who Determines the Self in the Politics of Self-Determination: Identity and Preference Formation in Tatarstan's Nationalist Mobilization." *Comparative Politics* 32, no. 3 (2000): 295-316.

Gleason, Gregory. *Federalism and Nationalism: The Struggle for Republican Rights in the USSR*. Boulder, Colo.: Westview, 1990.

———. "The 'National Factor' and the Logic of Sovietology." Pp. 1-29 in *The Post-Soviet Nations: Perspectives on the Demise of the USSR*, edited by Alexander Motyl. New York: Columbia University Press, 1992.

Goldsmith, Michael G., and Kenneth Newton. "Introduction." *European Journal of Political Research*, Special Issue, "Centralisation and Decentralisation: Changing Patterns of Intergovernmental Relations in Advanced Western Societies," 16, no. 4 (1988): 359-63.

Gorenburg, Dmitry. "Not with One Voice: An Explanation of Intragroup Variation in Nationalist Sentiment." *World Politics* 53, no. 1 (2000): 115-42.

Goryunov, P. A., N. A. Kulyasova, V. A. Malyshev, S. Yu. Nesterov, V. G. Sitnik, E. V. Shloma, and S. N. Shusharin. *Formirovanie organov mestnogo samoupravleniya v Rossiyskoy federatsii: Elektoral'naya statistika*. Moscow: Ves' mir, 1999.

Gostieva, L. K., and A. B. Dzadziev, eds. *Severnaya Osetiya: Etnopoliticheskie protsessy, 1990-1994: Ocherki, dokumenty, khronika*. Vol. 2. Moscow: Rossiyskaya akademiya nauk, Institut etnologii i antropologii, 1995.

Gostieva, L. K., A. B. Dzadziev, and A. A. Dzarasov. "Severnaya Osetiya: Ot vyborov do vyborov (1993-1995)." Pp. 90-157 in *Razvivayushchiysya elektorat Rossii*, edited by G. A. Komarova. Moscow: Rossiyskaya akademiya nauk, Institut etnologii i antropologii, 1996.

Government of India, Home Department. *Report of the States Reorganisation Commission, 1955*. New Delhi: Government of India Press, 1955.

Guboglo, Michael, ed. *Etnopoliticheskaya mozayka Bashkortostana*. Moscow: Rossiyskaya akademiya nauk, Institut etnologii i antropologii, 1992.

Gurr, Ted R. *Minorities at Risk: A Global View of Ethno-Political Conflicts*. Washington, D.C.: United States Institute of Peace, 1995.

Hahn, Jeffrey W. "Conclusions: Common Features of Post-Soviet Local Politics." Pp. 270-80 in *Local Power and Post-Soviet Politics*, edited by Theodore H. Friedgut and Jeffrey W. Hahn. London: Sharpe, 1994.

———. "The Development of Local Legislatures in Russia: The Case of Yaroslavl." Pp. 159-96 in *Democratisation in Russia: The Development of Legislative Institutions*, edited by Jeffrey W. Hahn. London: Sharpe, 1996.

———. "How Democratic Are Local Russian Deputies?" Pp. 62-85 in *In Search of Pluralism: Soviet and Post-Soviet Politics*, edited by Carol R. Saivetz and Anthony Jones. Boulder, Colo.: Westview, 1994.

———. "Local Politics and Political Power in Russia: The Case of Yaroslavl." *Soviet Economy* 7, no. 4 (1991): 322-41.

———. "Reforming Post-Soviet Russia: The Attitudes of Local Politicians." Pp. 208-38 in *Local Power and Post-Soviet Politics*, edited by Theodore Friedgut and Jeffrey W. Hahn. London: Sharpe, 1994.

———. *Soviet Grassroots: Citizen Participation in Local Soviet Government*. London: Tauris, 1988.

Hajdu, Zoltan. "Local Government Reform in Hungary." Pp. 208-24 in *Local Government in the New Europe*, edited by Robert J. Bennett. London: Belhaven, 1993.

Hale, Henry E. "Machine Politics and Institutionalized Electorates: A Comparative Analysis of Six Duma Elections in Bashkortostan." *Journal of Communist Studies and Transition Politics* 15, no. 4 (1999): 70-110.

Healey, Nigel M., Vladimir Leksin, and Alexandr Svetsov. "The Municipalization of Enterprise-Owned 'Social Assets' in Russia." *Post-Soviet Affairs* 15, no. 3 (1999): 262-80.

Heinemann-Grüder, Andreas. "Der asymmetrische Föderalismus Russlands und die Rolle der Regionen." Pp. 78-86 in *Russland unter neuer Führung: Politik, Wirtschaft und Gesellschaft am Beginn des 21. Jahrhunderts*, edited by Hans-Hermann Höhmann and Hans-Henning Schröder. Berlin: Bundeszentrale für politische Bildung, 2001.

Hill, Fiona. "'Russia's Tinderbox': Conflict in the North Caucasus and Its Implications for the Future of the Russian Federation." Cambridge, Mass.: Harvard University, John F. Kennedy School of Government, Strengthening Democratic Institutions Project, 1995.

Hirschman, Albert O. *Exit, Voice, and Loyalty: Responses to Decline in Firms, Organizations, and States*. Cambridge, Mass.: Harvard University Press, 1970.

Hoffer, Eric. *The True Believer: Thoughts on the Nature of Mass Movements*. New York: Harper & Row, 1951.

Hoffmann, Erik P. "The Dynamics of State-Society Relations in Post-Soviet Russia." Pp. 69-101 in *Can Democracy Take Root in Post-Soviet Russia?* edited by Harry Eckstein, Jr., Frederic J. Fleron, Erik P. Hoffmann, and William M. Reisinger. Lanham, Md.: Rowman & Littlefield, 1998.

Holmes, Stephen. "Gag Rules or the Politics of Omission." Pp. 19-58 in *Constitutionalism and Democracy*, edited by Jon Elster and Rune Slagstand. New York: Cambridge University Press, 1988.

Hooghe, Liesbet. *A Leap in the Dark: Nationalist Conflict and Federal Reform in Belgium*, Western Societies Program Occasional Papers, vol. 27. Ithaca, N.Y.: Cornell University Press, 1991.

Horowitz, Donald L. *Ethnic Groups in Conflict*. Berkeley: University of California Press, 1985.

———. "How to Begin Thinking Comparatively about Soviet Ethnic Problems." Pp. 9-22 in *Thinking Theoretically about Soviet Nationalities: History and Comparison in the Study of the USSR*, edited by Alexander J. Motyl. New York: Columbia University Press, 1992.

Hough, Jerry F. "Sociology, the State, and Language Politics." *Post-Soviet Affairs* 12, no. 2 (1996): 95-117.

———. *The Soviet Prefects: The Local Party Organs in Industrial Decision-Making*. Cambridge, Mass.: Harvard University Press, 1969.

Hough, Jerry F., and Merle Fainsod. *How the Soviet Union is Governed*. Cambridge, Mass.: Harvard University Press, 1979.

Hughes, James. "Sub-National Elites and Post-Communist Transformation in Russia: A Reply to Kryshtanovskaya and White." *Europe-Asia Studies* 49, no. 6 (1997): 1017-36.

Hunt, Lynn A. *Revolution and Urban Politics in Provincial France: Troyes and Reims, 1786-1790*. Stanford, Calif.: Stanford University Press, 1978.

Huntington, Samuel P. "Democracy for the Long Haul." *Journal of Democracy* 7, no. 2 (1996): 3-13.

Huskey, Eugene. "Political Leadership and the Center-Periphery Struggle: Putin's Administrative Reforms." Pp. 113-41 in *Gorbachev, Yeltsin, and Putin: Political Leadership in Russia's Transition*, edited by Archie Brown and Lilia Shevtsova. Washington, D.C.: Carnegie Endowment for International Peace, 2001.

Hutchcroft, Paul D. "Centralisation and Decentralisation in Administration and Politics: Assessing the Territorial Dimension of Authority and Power." *Governance* 14, no. 1 (2001): 23-53.

Huttenbach, Henry, ed. *Soviet Nationality Policies: Ruling Ethnic Groups in the USSR*. London: Mansell, 1990.

"The Ingush-Ossetian Conflict in the Prigorodnyi Region." New York: Human Rights Watch/Helsinki, 1996.

Institut ekonomiki goroda. *Munitsipal'noe ekonomicheskoe razvitie*. Moscow: Institut ekonomiki goroda, 1999.

Jacobs, Everett M., ed. *Soviet Local Politics and Government*. London: Allen & Unwin, 1983.

Jenkins, Craig J., and Craig M. Eckert. "Channeling Black Insurgency: Elite Patronage and Professional Social Movement Organization in the Development of the Black Movement." *American Sociological Review* 51 (1986): 812-29.

Kahn, Jeffrey. *Federalism, Democratization, and the Rule of Law in Russia*. Oxford: Oxford University Press, 2002.

———. "The Parade of Sovereignties: Establishing the Vocabulary of the New Russian Federalism." *Post-Soviet Affairs* 16, no. 1 (2000): 58-89.

Kaiser, Robert J. *The Geography of Nationalism in Russia and the USSR*. Princeton, N.J.: Princeton University Press, 1994.

Kara, Jan, and Jiri Blazek. "Czechoslovakia: Regional and Local Government." Pp. 246-58 in *Local Government in the New Europe*, edited by Robert J. Bennett. London: Belhaven, 1993.

Karpov, Yu. Yu. "K probleme ingushskoy avtonomii." *Sovetskaya etnografiya* (September-October 1990): 29-33.

Kassof, Allen. "The Administered Society: Totalitarianism without Terror." *World Politics* 16, no. 4 (1964): 558-75.

Kazantsev, B. N. "Severnyy Kavkaz: Sotsial'no-demograficheskie problemy gorodskogo naseleniya, pyatidesyatye-shestidesyatye gody." Pp. 219-35 in *Severnyy Kavkaz: Vybor puti natsional'nogo razvitiya*, edited by N. F. Bugay. Maykop, Russia: Meoty, 1994.

Khlynina, T. P. "Adygskie narody Kubanskoy oblasti: Problemy sovetizatsii (Nachalo 20-kh godov)." Pp. 100-12 in *Severnyy Kavkaz: Vybor puti natsional'nogo razvitiya*, edited by N. F. Bugay. Maykop, Russia: Meoty, 1994.

King, Charles. "Nations and Nationalism in British Political Studies." Pp. 313-43 in *The British Study of Politics in the Twentieth Century*, edited by Jack Hayward, Brian Barry, and Archie Brown. Oxford: Oxford University Press, 1999.

Kirkow, Peter. "Local Self-Government in Russia: Awakening from Slumber?" *Europe-Asia Studies* 49, no. 1 (1997): 43-58.

———. "Regional Warlordism in Russia: The Case of Primorskii Krai." *Europe-Asia Studies* 47, no. 6 (1995): 923-47.

Kirkwood, Michael, ed. *Language Planning in the Soviet Union*. London: Macmillan, 1989.

Kitschelt, Herbert. "Resource Mobilization Theory: A Critique." Pp. 323-47 in *Research on Social Movements: The State of the Art in Western Europe and the USA*, edited by Dieter Rucht. Boulder, Colo.: Westview, 1991.

Klandermans, Bert. "The Social Construction of Protest and Multiorganizational Fields." Pp. 77-103 in *Frontiers in Social Movement Theory*, edited by Aldon D. Morris and Carol McClurg Mueller. New Haven, Conn.: Yale University Press, 1992.

———. *The Social Psychology of Protest*. Cambridge, Mass.: Blackwell, 1997.

Kokiev, G. A. "Snosheniya Rossii s narodami severnogo Kavkaza." In *Iz istorii vzaimootnosheniy Dagestana s Rossiey i s narodami Kavkaza*. Makhachkala, Russia: Dagestanskiy filial Akademii nauk SSSR, 1982.

Kolstoe, Paul. *Russians in the Former Soviet Republics*. London: Hurst, 1995.

Koroteeva, Vika V. *Ekonomicheskie interesy i natsionalizm*. Moscow: Rossiyskiy gosudarstvennyy gumanitarnyy universitet, 2000.

Kothari, Rajni. *The State against Democracy: In Search of Humane Governance*. Delhi: Ajanta, 1989.

Krasnov, M. A. "Mestnoe samoupravlenie: Gosudarstvennoe ili obshchestvennoe?" *Sovetskoe gosudarstvo i pravo* 10 (1990): 81-9.

Kubicek, Paul. "Post-Communist Studies: Ten Years Later, Twenty Years Behind?" *Communist and Post-Communist Studies* 33 (2000): 295-309.

———. *Unbroken Ties: The State, Interest Associations, and Corporatism in Post-Soviet Ukraine*. Ann Arbor: University of Michigan Press, 1999.

———. "Variations on a Corporatist Theme: Interest Associations in Post-Soviet Ukraine and Russia." *Europe-Asia Studies* 48, no. 1 (1996): 27-46.

Kukolev, I. "Vybory v gorodke N." *Vlast'* 8 (1997): 27-33.

Kymlicka, Will. *Multicultural Citizenship: A Liberal Theory of Minority Rights*. Oxford: Clarendon, 1995.

Laitin, David D. *Identity in Formation: The Russian-Speaking Nationality in Estonia and Bashkortostan*, Studies in Public Policy, vol. 249. Glasgow: University of Strathclyde, 1995.

―――. *Identity in Formation: The Russian-Speaking Populations in the Near Abroad.* Ithaca, N.Y.: Cornell University Press, 1998.

―――. "Language and Nationalism in the Post-Soviet Republics." *Post-Soviet Affairs* 12, no. 1 (1996): 4-24.

Lallemand, Jean-Charles. "Gouvernance Introuvable à Briansk et à Smolensk." *La Revue Tocqueville/The Tocqueville Review* 19, no. 1 (1998): 75-102.

―――. "Politics for the Few: Elites in Bryansk and Smolensk." *Post-Soviet Affairs* 15, no. 4 (1999): 312-35.

Lankina, Tomila. "Local Government and Ethnic and Social Activism in Russia." Pp. 398-411 in *Contemporary Russian Politics: A Reader*, edited by Archie Brown. Oxford: Oxford University Press, 2001.

―――. "Local Self-Government or Government Gone Local? The Case of Adygeya." *Russian Regional Report* (electronic version) 4, no. 33 (1999).

―――. "Showcase of Manipulated Democracy: Shadow-Puppet Elections in Bashkortostan." *Transitions* 5, no. 8 (1998): 62-4.

Lapidus, Gail W. "Asymmetrical Federalism and State Breakdown in Russia." *Post-Soviet Affairs* 15, no. 1 (1999): 74-82.

Lapidus, Gail W., and Edward W. Walker. "Nationalism, Regionalism and Federalism: Center-Periphery Relations in Post-Communist Russia." Pp. 79-113 in *The New Russia: Troubled Transformation*, edited by Gail Lapidus. Boulder, Colo.: Westview, 1995.

Lapidus, Ira. *A History of Islamic Societies.* Cambridge: Cambridge University Press, 1993.

Le Bon, Gustave. *Psychologie des Foules.* Paris: Librairie Felix Alcan, 1912.

Le Huerou, Anne. "Elites in Omsk." *Post-Soviet Affairs* 15, no. 4 (1999): 362-86.

Lenin, Vladimir I. "The Tasks of the Proletariat in the Present Revolution." Pp. 21-9 in *V. I. Lenin, Collected Works*, vol. 24. 4th ed. Translated by Bernard Isaacs. Moscow: Progress, 1964.

Lijphart, Arend. *Democracy in Plural Societies: A Comparative Exploration.* New Haven, Conn.: Yale University Press, 1977.

―――. "The Puzzle of Indian Democracy: A Consociational Interpretation." *American Political Science Review* 90, no. 2 (1996): 258-68.

Linz, Juan J. "An Authoritarian Regime: Spain." Pp. 257-66 in *Mass Politics: Studies in Political Sociology.* New York: Free Press, 1970.

Linz, Juan J., and Alfred Stepan. *Problems of Democratic Transition and Consolidation: Southern Europe, South America, and Post-Communist Europe.* Baltimore, Md.: Johns Hopkins University Press, 1996.

Lipset, Seymour M. "The Social Requisites of Democracy Revisited." *American Sociological Review* 59, no. 1 (1994): 1-22.

Lustick, Ian. "Stability in Deeply Divided Societies: Consociationalism versus Control." *World Politics* 31, no. 3 (1979): 325-44.

Mabileau, Albert. "Local Government in Britain and Local Politics and Administration in France." Pp. 17-33 in *Local Politics and Participation in Britain and France*, edited by Albert Mabileau, George Moyser, Geraint Parry, and Patrick Quantin. Cambridge: Cambridge University Press, 1989.

Mabileau, Albert, George Moyser, Geraint Parry, and Patrick Quantin. "People and Local Politics: Themes and Concepts." Pp. 1-16 in *Local Politics and Participation in Britain and France*, edited by Albert Mabileau, George Moyser, Geraint Parry, and Patrick Quantin. Cambridge: Cambridge University Press, 1989.

March, James G., and Johan P. Olsen. *Rediscovering Institutions: The Organizational Basis of Politics*. New York: Free Press, 1989.

Marcou, Gérard. "New Tendencies of Local Government Development in Europe." Pp. 51-66 in *Local Government in the New Europe*, edited by Robert J. Bennett. London: Belhaven, 1993.

Marx, Karl. "The Civil War in France." Pp. 526-76 in *The Marx-Engels Reader*, edited by Robert C. Tucker. New York: Norton, 1972.

Matsuzato, Kimitaka. "From Communist Boss Politics to Post-Communist Caciquismo." *Communist and Post-Communist Studies* 34, no. 2 (2001): 175-201.

———. "Local Elites under Transition: County and City Politics in Russia 1985-1996." *Europe-Asia Studies* 51, no. 8 (1999): 1367-400.

———, ed. *Tret'e zveno gosudarstvennogo stroitel'stva Rossii:Ppodgotovka i realizatsiya federal'nogo zakona Ob obshchikh printsipakh organizatsii mestnogo samoupravleniya v Rossiyskoy federatsii*. Sapporo, Japan: Slavic Research Center, Hokkaido University, 1998.

McAdam, Doug. *Political Process and the Development of Black Insurgency, 1930-1970*. Chicago: University of Chicago Press, 1982.

———. "Tactical Innovation and the Pace of Insurgency." *American Sociological Review* 48 (1983): 735-54.

McAdam, Doug, John D. McCarthy, and Mayer N. Zald, eds. *Comparative Perspectives on Social Movements: Political Opportunities, Mobilizing Structures, and Cultural Framings*. Cambridge: Cambridge University Press, 1996.

McAuley, Mary. "Politics, Economics, and Elite Realignment in Russia: A Regional Perspective." *Soviet Economy* 8, no. 1 (1992): 46-88.

———. *Russia's Politics of Uncertainty*. Cambridge: Cambridge University Press, 1997.

McCarthy, John D., and Mayer N. Zald. "Resource Mobilization and Social Movements: A Partial Theory." *American Journal of Sociology* 82, no. 6 (1977): 1212-41.

McFaul, Michael, and Nikolay Petrov, eds. *Politicheskiy al'manakh Rossii 1997*. Vol. 2. Moscow: Moscow Carnegie Center, 1998.

McRae, Kenneth. "Canada: Reflections on Two Conflicts." Pp. 197-217 in *Conflict and Peacemaking in Multiethnic Societies*, edited by Joseph Montville. Lexington, Mass.: Lexington Books, 1990.

Meadcroft, John. "Political Recruitment and Local Representation: The Case of Liberal Democrat Councilors." *Local Government Studies* 27, no. 1 (2001): 19-36.

Melucci, Alberto. "The Symbolic Challenge of Contemporary Movements." *Social Research* 52, no. 4 (1985): 789-816.

Mendras, Marie. "How Regional Elites Preserve Their Power." *Post-Soviet Affairs* 15, no. 4 (1999): 295-311.

———. "L'État, L'Argent, La Clientèle." *La Revue Tocqueville/The Tocqueville Review* 1 (1998): 35-54.

Michels, Robert. *Political Parties: A Sociological Study of the Oligarchical Tendencies of Modern Democracy*. 2d ed. New York: Free Press, 1966.

Miles, Matthew B., and Michael A. Huberman. *Qualitative Data Analysis: An Expanded Sourcebook*. 2d ed. London: Sage, 1994.

Miller, John H. "Cadres Policy in Nationality Areas: Recruitment of CPSU First and Second Secretaries in Non-Russian Republics of the USSR." *Soviet Studies* 29, no. 1 (1977): 3-36.

Miller, Robert F. "Concluding Essay." Pp. 130-47 in *The Developments of Civil Society in Communist Systems*, edited by Robert F. Miller. Sydney: Allen & Unwin, 1992.

Mitrokhin, Sergei. "Realizatsiya munitsipal'nogo proekta v Rossii: Nekotorye aspekty federal'noy politiki." Pp. 26-43 in *Reforma mestnogo samoupravleniya v regional'nom izmerenii*, edited by Sergei Ryzhenkov and Nikolay Vinnik. Moscow: Moskovskiy obshchestvennyy nauchnyy fond, 1999.

———. "V Otsutstviye pozitsii Prezidenta." *Munitsipal'naya politika* 10-11, no. 26 (2000): 3-7.

Morris, Aldon D., and Carol M. Mueller, eds. *Frontiers in Social Movement Theory*. New Haven, Conn.: Yale University Press, 1992.

Moser, Robert. "Independents and Party Formation: Elite Partisanship as an Intervening Variable in Russian Politics." *Comparative Politics* 31, no. 2 (1999): 147-65.

Moyser, George, and Geraint Parry. "Councilors, Citizens and Agendas: Aspects of Local Decision-Making in Britain." Pp. 157-77 in *Local Politics and Participation in Britain and France*, edited by Albert Mabileau, George Moyser, Geraint Parry, and Patrick Quantin. Cambridge: Cambridge University Press, 1989.

Muzaev, Timur M. *Etnicheskiy separatizm v Rossii*. Moscow: Panorama, 1999.

Muzaev, Timur M., and Zurab Todua. *Novaya Checheno-Ingushetiya*. Moscow: Panorama, 1992.

Nagel, Beverly. "Gypsies in the United States and Great Britain: Ethnic Boundaries and Political Mobilization." Pp. 69-90 in *Competitive Ethnic Relations*, edited by Suzan Olzak and Joane Nagel. Orlando, Fla.: Academic Press, 1986.

Nagel, Joane, and Susan Olzak. "Ethnic Mobilization in New and Old States: An Extension of the Competition Model." *Social Problems* 30, no. 2 (1982): 127-43.

Newton, Kenneth. *Second City Politics: Democratic Processes and Decision-Making in Birmingham*. Oxford: Clarendon, 1976.

Nordlinger, Erik. *Conflict Regulation in Divided Societies*. Occasional Papers in International Affairs, vol. 29. Cambridge, Mass.: Harvard University Center for International Affairs, 1972.

North, Douglas. *Institutions, Institutional Changes, and Economic Performance*. Cambridge: Cambridge University Press, 1990.

Norton, Alan. "What East European Democracies Might Learn from the West." Pp. 264-80 in *Local Government in Eastern Europe: Establishing Democracy at the Grassroots*, edited by Andrew Coulson. Aldershot, England: Elgar, 1995.

Oberschall, Anthony. "Opportunities and Framing in the Eastern European Revolts of 1989." Pp. 93-121 in *Comparative Perspectives on Social Movements: Political Opportunities, Mobilizing Structures, and Cultural Framings*, edited by Doug McAdam, John D. McCarthy, and Mayer N. Zald. Cambridge: Cambridge University Press, 1996.

———. *Social Conflict and Social Movements*. Englewood Cliffs, N.J.: Prentice Hall, 1973.

Offe, Claus. "Designing Institutions in East European Transitions." Pp. 199-226 in *The Theory of Institutional Design*, edited by Robert E. Goodin. Cambridge: Cambridge University Press, 1996.

Offerdal, Audun, Dan Hanspach, Andrzej Kowalczyk, and Jiri Patocka. "Elites and Parties." Pp. 105-41 in *Local Democracy and the Processes of Transformation in East-Central Europe*, edited by Harald Baldersheim, Michal Illner, Audun Offerdal, Lawrence Rose, and Pawel Swianiewicz. Boulder, Colo.: Westview, 1996.

Oi, Jean C. *Rural China Takes Off: Institutional Foundations of Economic Reform*. Berkeley: University of California Press, 1999.

Oliver, James H. "Citizen Demands and the Soviet Political System." *American Political Science Review* 63, no. 2 (1968).

Olson, David M. "Democratic and Political Participation: The Experience of the Czech Republic." Pp. 40-65 in *The Consolidation of Democracy in East-Central Europe*, edited by Karen Dawisha and Bruce Parrott. Cambridge: Cambridge University Press, 1997.

Olson, Mancur. *The Logic of Collective Action*. Cambridge, Mass.: Harvard University Press, 1965.

Orlov, O. P. "Cherez dva goda posle voyny: Problema vynujhdennykh pereselentsev v zone osetino-ingushskogo konflikta." Moscow: Human Rights Center Memorial, 1994.

Osborne, Stephen P., and Aniko Kaposvari. "Nongovernmental Organizations, Local Government and the Development of Social Services: Managing Social Needs in Postcommunist Hungary." Budapest: Open Society Institute, 1998.

Ostrom, Elinor. *Governing the Commons: The Evolution of Institutions for Collective Action*. Cambridge: Cambridge University Press, 1990.

Ostrowski, Krzysztof, and Adam Przeworski. "Local Leadership in Poland." Pp. 33-65 in *Local Politics in Poland: Twenty Years of Research*, edited by Jerzy J. Wiatr. Warsaw: University of Warsaw Institute of Sociology, 1984.

Ovchinnikov, Boris. "Munitsipal'nye vybory: tendentsii i zakonomernosti." Pp. 107-33 in *Reforma mestnogo samoupravleniya v regional'nom izmerenii*, edited by Sergei Ryzhenkov and N. Vinnik. Moscow: Moskovskiy obshchestvennyy nauchnyy fond, 1999.

Parrott, Bruce. "Perspectives on Postcommunist Democratization." Pp. 1-39 in *The Consolidation of Democracy in East-Central Europe*, edited by Karen Dawisha and Bruce Parrott. Cambridge: Cambridge University Press, 1997.

Parsons, Talcott. "Some Sociological Aspects of the Fascist Movements." Pp. 82-97 in *Politics and Social Structure*. New York: Free Press, 1969.

Pchelintseva, N. D., and L. V. Samarina. *Sovremennaya etnopoliticheskaya i etnokul'turnaya situatsiya v Respublike Adygeya*. Issledovaniya po prikladnoy i neotlojhnoy etnologii, vol. 47. Moscow: Rossiyskaya akademiya nauk, Institut etnologii i antropologii, 1993.

Petro, Nicolai. *Jumpstarting Democracy: The Novgorod Model of Rapid Social Change*. Ithaca, N.Y.: Cornell University Press, in press.

———. "The Novgorod Region: A Russian Success Story." *Post-Soviet Affairs* 15, no. 3 (1999): 235-61.

Petrov, Nikolai. "Seven Faces of Putin's Russia: Federal Districts as the New Level of State-Territorial Composition." *Security Dialogue* 33, no. 1 (2002): 73-91.

Petrov, Nikolai, and Darrell Slider. "Putin and the Regions." Pp. 203-24 in *Putin's Russia: Past Imperfect, Future Uncertain*, edited by Dale R. Herspring. Lanham, Md.: Rowman & Littlefield, 2003.

Pipes, Richard. *The Formation of the Soviet Union*. Cambridge, Mass.: Harvard University Press, 1964.

Przeworski, Adam. *Democracy and the Market*. Cambridge: Cambridge University Press, 1991.

Przeworski, Adam, and Henry Teune. *The Logic of Comparative Social Inquiry*. 2d ed. Malabar, Fla.: Krieger, 1982.

Putnam, Robert. *Making Democracy Work: Civic Traditions in Modern Italy*. Princeton, N.J.: Princeton University Press, 1993.

Rakowska-Harmstrone, Teresa. "Minority Nationalism Today: An Overview." Pp. 235-64 in *The Last Empire: The Nationality and the Soviet Future*, edited by Robert Conquest. Stanford, Calif.: Hoover Institution Press, 1986.

Reddaway, Peter. "Will Putin Be Able to Consolidate Power?" *Post-Soviet Affairs* 17, no. 1 (2001): 23-44.

Remington, Thomas F. "Democratization and the New Political Order in Russia." Pp. 69-129 in *Democratization and Authoritarianism in Postcommunist Societies*, edited by Karen Dawisha and Bruce Parrott. Cambridge: Cambridge University Press, 1997.

Rhodes, R. A. W. *Control and Power in Central-Local Government Relations*. 2d ed. Aldershot, England: Ashgate, 1999.

Riasanovsky, Nicholas V. *A History of Russia*. 5th ed. Oxford: Oxford University Press, 1993.

Richter, James. "Evaluating Western Assistance to Russian Women's Organizations." Pp. 54-90 in *The Power and Limits of NGOs: A Critical Look at Building Democracy in Eastern Europe and Eurasia*, edited by Sarah E. Mendelson and John K, Glenn. New York: Columbia University Press, 2002.

Rigby, T. H. *Political Elites in the USSR: Central Leaders and Local Cadres from Lenin to Gorbachev*. Aldershot, England: Elgar, 1990.

———. "Politics in the Mono-Organizational Society." Pp. 163-212 in *Between Totalitarianism and Pluralism*, edited by Alexander Dallin. New York: Garland, 1992.

———. "The USSR: End of a Long, Dark Night?" Pp. 11-23 in *The Developments of Civil Society in Communist Systems*, edited by Robert J. Miller. Sydney: Allen & Unwin, 1992.

Rigby, T. H., and Bohdan Hyrasymiw. *Leadership Selection and Patron-Client Relations in the USSR and Yugoslavia*. London: Allen & Unwin, 1983.

Riker, William H. *Federalism: Origin, Operation, Significance*. Boston: Little, Brown, 1964.

Roeder, Philip. "Soviet Federalism and Ethnic Mobilization." *World Politics* 43, no. 2 (1991): 196-232.

Rokkan, Stein, and Derek Urwin. *Economy, Territory, Identity: Politics of West European Peripheries*. London: Sage, 1983.

Romanov, Pavel, and Irina Tartakovskaya. "Samara Oblast': A Governor and His Guberniya." *Communist Economies and Economic Transformation* 10, no. 3 (1998): 341-61.

Rose, Richard, and Doh Chull Shin. "Democratization Backwards: The Problem of Third Wave Democracies." *British Journal of Political Science* 31, no. 2 (2001): 331-54.

Ross, Cameron. *Federalism and Democratisation in Russia*. Manchester, England: Manchester University Press, 2002.

———. "Putin's Federal Reforms and the Consolidation of Federalism in Russia: One Step Forward, Two Steps Back!" *Communist and Post-Communist Studies* 36 (2003): 29-47.

Rustow, Dunkwart A. "Transitions to Democracy: Toward a Dynamic Model." *Comparative Politics* 2 (1970): 337-65.

Rutland, Peter. *The Politics of Economic Stagnation in the Soviet Union: The Role of Local Party Organs in Economic Management*. New York: Cambridge University Press, 1992.

Rywkin, Michael. *Moscow's Lost Empire*. Armonk, N.Y.: Sharpe, 1994.

Ryzhenkov, Sergei. "Regional'naya elita i mestnoe samoupravlenie: Aktory, pravila igry i logika reformy." Pp. 85-106 in *Reforma mestnogo samoupravleniya v regional'nom izmerenii*, edited by Sergei Ryzhenkov and N. Vinnik. Moscow: Moskovskiy obshchestvennyy nauchnyy fond, 1999.

Ryzhenkov, Sergei, and N. Vinnik, eds. *Reforma mestnogo samoupravleniya v regional'nom izmerenii*. Moscow: Moskovskiy obshchestvennyy nauchnyy fond, 1999.

Sakwa, Richard. *Russian Politics and Society*. London: Routledge, 1991.

Schattschneider, E. E. *The Semi-Sovereign People: A Realist's View of Democracy in America*. New York: Holt, Rinehart & Winston, 1960.

Schwartz, Lee. "Regional Population Redistribution and National Homelands in the USSR." Pp. 121-61 in *Soviet Nationalities Policies: Ruling Ethnic Groups in the USSR*, edited by Henry Huttenbach. London: Mansell, 1990.

Schwartz, Michael, and Shuva Paul. "Resource Mobilization vs. the Mobilization of People: Why Consensus Movements Cannot Be Instruments of Social Change." Pp. 205-23 in *Frontiers in Social Movement Theory*, edited by Aldon D. Morris and Carol M. Mueller. New Haven, Conn.: Yale University Press, 1992.

Selznick, Philip. *TVA and the Grass Roots: A Study in the Sociology of Formal Organization*. New York: Harper & Row, 1966.

Seton-Watson, Hugh. *The Russian Empire: 1801-1917*. Oxford: Clarendon, 1967.

Sharpe, L. J. "The Growth and Decentralisation of the Modern Democratic State." *European Journal of Political Research*, Special Issue: "Centralisation and Decentralisation: Changing Patterns of Intergovernmental Relations in Advanced Western Societies," 16, no. 4 (1988): 365-80.

Shlapentokh, Vladimir. "No One Needs Public Opinion Data in Post Communist Russia." *Communist and Post-Communist Studies* 32 (1999): 453-60.

Skalnik Leff, Carol. "Democratization and Disintegration in Multinational States: The Breakup of the Communist Federations." *World Politics* 51, no. 1 (1999): 205-35.

Skilling, H. Gordon. "Interest Groups and Communist Politics." Pp. 117-61 in *Between Totalitarianism and Pluralism*, edited by Alexander Dallin. New York: Garland, 1992.

———. "Interest Groups and Communist Politics Revisited." Pp. 117-61 in *Between Totalitarianism and Pluralism*, edited by Alexander Dallin. New York: Garland, 1992.

Skocpol, Theda. *States and Social Revolutions: A Comparative Analysis of France, Russia, and China*. Cambridge: Cambridge University Press, 1991.

Slider, Darrell. "Elections to Russia's Regional Assemblies." *Post-Soviet Affairs* 12, no. 3 (1996): 243-64.

Smelser, Neil J. *Theory of Collective Behaviour*. London: Routledge, 1962.

Smirnyagin, Leonid. "Mayors against Governors?" *Russian Regional Report* (electronic version) 4, no. 9 (1999).

Smith, Anthony D. "Ethnic Identity and Territorial Nationalism in Comparative Perspective." Pp. 45-65 in *Thinking Theoretically about Soviet Nationalities: History and Comparison in the Study of the USSR*, edited by Alexander J. Motyl. New York: Columbia University Press, 1992.

Smith, Graham, ed. *Federalism: The Multiethnic Challenge*. New York: Longman, 1995.

Smith, Graham, and Andrew Wilson. "Rethinking Russia's Post-Soviet Diaspora: The Potential for Political Mobilisation in Eastern Ukraine and North-East Estonia." *Europe-Asia Studies* 49, no. 5 (1997): 845-64.

Snow, David A., Jr., E. Burke Rochford, Steven K. Worden, and Robert D. Benford. "Frame Alignment Processes, Micromobilization, and Movement Participation." *American Sociological Review* 51 (August 1986): 464-81.

Snow, David A., Jr., Louis A. Zurcher, and Sheldon Ekland. "Social Networks and Social Movements: A Microstructural Approach to Differential Recruitment." *American Sociological Review* 45 (October 1980): 787-801.

Solnick, Steven. "Gubernatorial Elections in Russia, 1996-1997." *Post-Soviet Affairs* 14, no. 1 (1998): 48-80.

Sperling, Valerie. *Organizing Women in Contemporary Russia: Engendering Transition.* Cambridge: Cambridge University Press, 1999.

Startsev, Yaroslav. "Gubernatorial Politics in Sverdlovsk Oblast." *Post-Soviet Affairs* 15, no. 4 (1999): 336-61.

Steiner, Jurg. "Power-Sharing: Another Swiss 'Export Product'?" Pp. 107-14 in *Conflict and Peacemaking in Multiethnic Societies*, edited by Joseph Montville. Lexington, Mass.: Lexington Books, 1990.

Stepan, Alfred. "Russian Federalism in Comparative Perspective," *Post-Soviet Affairs* 16 (April 2000): 133-76.

———. *The State and Society: Peru in Comparative Perspective.* Princeton, N.J.: Princeton University Press, 1978.

Stoker, Gerry. "Introduction: Normative Theories of Local Government and Democracy." Pp. 1-27 in *Rethinking Local Democracy*, edited by Desmond King and Gerry Stoker. London: Macmillan, 1996.

Suny, Ronald Gregor. *The Revenge of the Past: Nationalism, Revolution, and the Collapse of the Soviet Union.* Stanford, Calif.: Stanford University Press, 1993.

Szuks, Stefan. *Democracy in the Head: A Comparative Analysis of Democratic Leadership Orientations among Local Elites in Three Phases of Democratisation.* Goteborg, Sweden: Center for Public Sector Research, Goteborg University, 1998.

Tarrow, Sidney. *Between Center and Periphery: Grassroots Politicians in Italy and France.* New Haven, Conn.: Yale University Press, 1977.

———. *Power in Movement: Social Movements, Collective Action and Politics.* Cambridge: Cambridge University Press, 1996.

Tilly, Charles. *From Mobilization to Revolution.* Reading, Mass.: Wesley, 1978.

Tishkov, Valery. *Ethnicity, Nationalism and Conflict in and after the Soviet Union: The Mind Aflame.* London: Sage, 1997.

———, ed. *Narody Rossii: Entsiklopediya.* Moscow: Nauchnoe izdatel'stvo Bol'shaya rossiyskaya entsiklopediya, 1994.

Tismaneanu, Vladimir. *Reinventing Politics: Eastern Europe from Stalin to Havel.* New York: Free Press, 1993.

Tocqueville, Alexis de. "Townships, Municipal Administration, State Government." In *Democracy in America*, edited by J. P. Mayer. London: Fontana, 1994.

Tokes, Rudolf L. "Hungary: Elites and the Use and Abuse of Democratic Institutions." Pp. 71-85 in *Elites after State Socialism: Theories and Analysis*, edited by John Higley and Georgy Lengyel. Lanham, Md.: Rowman & Littlefield, 2000.

———. *Hungary's Negotiated Revolution.* Cambridge: Cambridge University Press, 1996.

Treisman, Daniel S. *After the Deluge: Regional Crises and Political Consolidation in Russia.* Ann Arbor: University of Michigan Press, 1999.

———. "Russia's 'Ethnic Revival': The Separatist Activism of Regional Leaders in a Post-Communist Order." *World Politics* (1997): 212-49.

Trotsky, Leon. *1905.* Bungay, England: Chaucer, 1971.

Truman, David B. *The Governmental Process: Political Interests and Public Opinion.* 2d ed. New York: Knopf, 1971.

Tsitsin, P. G. *Problemy ustoichivogo sotsial'no-ekonomicheskogo razvitiya munitsi-pal'nykh obrazovaniy i puti ikh resheniya.* Moscow: Novyy vek, 2002.

Tsutsiev, A. A. *Osetino-Ingushskiy konflikt (1992- . . .): Ego predystoriya i faktory razvitiya.* Moscow: Rosspen, 1998.

Turner, Ralph H., and Lewis M. Killian. *Collective Behavior.* Englewood Cliffs, N.J.: Prentice Hall, 1957.

Turovskiy, R. F. "Otnosheniya 'tsentr-regiony' v 1997-1998 godakh: Mejhdu konfliktom i konsensusom." *Politiya* 1, no. 7 (1998): 5-32.

Urban, Michael E. *An Algebra of Soviet Power: Elite Circulation in the Belorussian Republic, 1966-86.* Cambridge: Cambridge University Press, 1989.

———. *More Power to the Soviets: The Democratic Revolution in the USSR.* Aldershot, England: Elgar, 1990.

Urban, Michael E., Vyacheslav Igrunov, and Sergei Mitrokhin. *The Rebirth of Politics in Russia.* Cambridge: Cambridge University Press, 1997.

Varshney, Ashutosh. *Democracy, Development, and the Countryside: Urban-Rural Struggles in India.* Cambridge: Cambridge University Press, 1995.

Vorob'ev, D. V., and D. V. Grushkin. *Ideya natsional'noy gosudarstvennosti i problemy etnicheskoy diskriminatsii v respublike Bashkortostan.* Moscow: Zven'ya, 1999.

Voslensky, Michael. *Nomenklatura: Anatomy of the Soviet Ruling Class.* Translated by Eric Mosbacher. London: Bodley Head, 1983.

Weiner, Myron, ed. *State Politics in India.* Princeton, N.J.: Princeton University Press, 1968.

Wesson, Robert G. "Volunteers and Soviets." *Soviet Studies* 15, no. 3 (1964): 230-49.

White, Stephen. "Pluralism, Civil Society, and Post-Soviet Politics." Pp. 5-26 in *In Search of Pluralism: Soviet and Post-Soviet Politics,* edited by Carol R. Saivetz and Anthony Jones. Boulder, Colo.: Westview, 1994.

Whitefield, Stephen. *Industrial Power and the Soviet State.* Oxford: Clarendon, 1993.

Wixman, Ron. "The Middle Volga: Ethnic Archipelago in a Russian Sea." Pp. 421-47 in *Nations and Politics in the Soviet Successor States,* edited by Ian Bremmer and Ray Taras. Cambridge: Cambridge University Press, 1993.

Wollmann, Hellmut. "Institution Building and Decentralization in Formerly Socialist Countries: The Cases of Poland, Hungary, and East Germany." *Government and Policy* 15 (1997): 463-80.

Young, John F. "Zakonodatel'stvo Rossii po mestnomu samoupravleniyu." Pp. 109-29 in *Tret'e zveno gosudarstvennogo stroitel'stva Rossii: Podgotovka i realizatsiya federal'nogo zakona Ob obshchikh printsipakh organizatsii mestnogo samouprav-leniya v Rossiyskoy Federatsii,* edited by Kimitaka Matsuzato. Sapporo, Japan: Slavic Research Center, Hokkaido University, 1998.

Zald, Mayer N., and Bert Useem. "Movement and Countermovement Interaction." Pp. 247-72 in *Social Movements in an Organizational Society,* edited by Mayer N. Zald and John D. McCarthy. New Brunswick, N.J.: Transaction Books, 1987.

Zaslavsky, Viktor. "Successes and Collapse: Traditional Soviet Nationalities Policy." Pp. 29-42 in *Nations and Politics in the Soviet Successor States,* edited by Ian Bremmer and Ray Taras. Cambridge: Cambridge University Press, 1993.

Zeigler, Harmon. *Pluralism, Corporatism, and Confucianism: Political Association and Conflict Regulation in the United States, Europe, and Taiwan.* Philadelphia: Temple University Press, 1988.

Zuykina, E. A. "K voprosu o russkikh v sisteme mejhnatsional'nykh otnosheniy na severnom Kavkaze." Pp. 127-39 in *Severnyy Kavkaz: Vybor puti natsional'nogo razvitiya,* edited by N. F. Bugay. Maykop, Russia: Meoty, 1994.

Zverev, Aleksey. "Etnicheskie konflikty na Kavkaze, 1988-1994." Pp. 10-76 in *Spornye granitsy na Kavkaze*, edited by Bruno Koppieters. Moscow: Ves' mir, 1996.

Index

About the Author

Tomila Lankina is a research fellow at the Institute for the Social Sciences of the Humboldt University in Berlin. She received her D.Phil. from the University of Oxford in England. Dr. Lankina is the author of several articles on local and regional politics in Russia and a coauthor of a forthcoming book on decentralization in Central and Eastern Europe (with Hellmut Wollmann and Anneke Hudalla). Her most recent work is a chapter on President Putin's reform of local government in a monograph edited by Peter Reddaway and Robert Orttung, *The Dynamics of Russian Politics: Putin's Reform of Federal-Regional Relations*, Volume 2 (Rowman & Littlefield, forthcoming in 2004).